D1713102

Managing a Small HRD Department

▲ ▲

CAROL P. McCOY

▲ ▲

Managing a Small HRD Department

▲ ▲

You Can Do More Than You Think

JOSSEY-BASS PUBLISHERS
San Francisco

Substantial discounts on bulk quantities of Jossey-Bass books
are available to corporations, professional associations, and other
organizations. For details and discount information, contact the
special sales department at Jossey-Bass Inc., Publishers.
(415) 433-1740; Fax (415) 433-0499.

For sales outside the United States, contact Maxwell Macmillan
International Publishing Group, 866 Third Avenue, New York,
New York 10022.

Manufactured in the United States of America

The paper used in this book is acid-free and meets the guidelines for
permanence and durability of the Committee on Production Guidelines
for Book Longevity of the Council on Library Resources.

Library of Congress Cataloging-in-Publication Data

McCoy, Carol P., date.
    Managing a small HRD department : you can do more than you think /
Carol P. McCoy. — 1st ed.
        p.   cm. — (The Jossey-Bass management series)
    Includes bibliographical references and index.
    ISBN 1-55542-529-1 (alk. paper)
    1. Employees—Training of.   2. Employee training personnel.
3. Employee training directors.   4. Personnel departments—
Management.   I. Title.   II. Series.
HF5546.5.T7M3695   1993
658.3—dc20   92-43607
                                                                    CIP

FIRST EDITION
PB Printing   10 9 8 7 6 5 4 3 2 1   *Code 9331*

THE JOSSEY-BASS MANAGEMENT SERIES

▲ ▲

Consulting Editors
HUMAN RESOURCES

Leonard Nadler
Zeace Nadler
College Park, Maryland

Contents

List of Tables

List of Exhibits

▲ ▲

List of Worksheets

▲ ▲

Preface

Increasing competition, cost consciousness, and a desire to serve customers better have persuaded many organizations to form small training or human resource development departments. According to Leonard and Zeace Nadler (1989, p. 6), human resource development involves training, educating, and developing employees. In this book, I will use the term *human resource development*, or *HRD*, to refer primarily to these learning activities. *Training* refers to planned learning that is focused on improving current job performance. *Education* refers to planned learning that is focused on preparing an individual for a future job. *Development* refers to learning that is broader than *education* and not specifically job related, that is, to learning that pertains to personal growth. All of these HRD learning activities may be directed at improving managerial, technical, or personal competence and thereby contribute to improving the performance of the organization.

AUDIENCE

This book is a tool kit for HRD and training managers, trainers, and administrative assistants in *small* HRD departments. It is also for human resource generalists with responsibility for training along with such other human resource functions as staffing, recruitment, compensation, and employee relations. The book will be especially helpful to the novice trainer and to the human resource manager who has had little formal training experience but has now assumed increased responsibilities for human resource development. It can help anyone who is considering moving to a small HRD department decide whether working in such a department is an appropriate choice. In addition, this book is for line managers who want to learn how to work effectively with a small HRD department so that human resource development makes a significant contribution to the organization's success.

By *small*, I mean a one-, two-, or three-person department, which usually consists of a training manager and a full- or part-time secretary, administrative assistant, or training specialist. Small companies may create a one-person training department when their business expands or changes significantly. Large diversified companies may form small training departments as part of the growing trend toward decentralizing lines of business and staff functions or as a result of downsizing a large HRD department into a smaller unit.

By *small*, I also refer to the size of the HRD budget. While large corporations may spend more than $60 million annually on training, small training departments usually have budgets ranging from $50,000 to $500,000. Many have less than $100,000 to spend on training annually. Nevertheless, this small shop is expected to provide adequate training support to the organization.

PURPOSE

The principles presented here apply to any small HRD department. Whether you work in a small organization or in a small, decentralized department in a large corporation, you face unique challenges. Managing a small HRD department requires a special perspective and special competencies. With only limited resources, it is particularly important to focus your efforts on business priorities. You need to build your credibility with senior management and within the organization. You must also develop and implement a resource strategy that provides HRD support without the benefit of a large staff. And you must be skillful in marketing your HRD programs and services so that employees will know clearly what you can and cannot do. If you are creating a department from scratch, you face additional pressures because some people may want you to meet their HRD needs before you have had adequate time to plan your strategy.

Whether you are starting up or taking over an HRD function, there is much planning to be done: you have to determine the company's business priorities and HRD needs, create a mission and formulate goals, project a budget, develop programs, find instructors, develop a marketing strategy, and set up procedures. When you are in the throes of managing, it is sometimes difficult to identify priorities, develop a sound strategy, or implement a plan. How will you know which strategies work best and what pitfalls to avoid? How can you adapt the strategies used by large training departments for use on a smaller scale? Finding the answers to these and other questions is crucial. Luckily, you do not have to do it all on your own.

Managing a Small HRD Department will help you set up and manage a small HRD department, build credibility, and make the most of your resources. In reading the book, you will benefit from the experiences of other managers. You will find out what a small HRD department can contribute to the success of an organization and the strategies that will help ensure your training department's effectiveness. Here you will find tools and checklists that will enable you to run a small, efficient, business-focused HRD department that directly contributes to accomplishment of business goals. It will help you do the following:

1. Address critical business issues and avoid common pitfalls involved in creating and managing a small training department

2. Create a realistic plan that supports your company's business goals and enhances your credibility within the organization

3. Forecast, negotiate, and manage a training budget

4. Effectively marshal resources to design and deliver HRD programs

5. Market human resource development to build company involvement in the function

6. Identify the skills and qualities essential to being an effective training manager or assistant

7. Plan appropriate developmental activities for the training staff

8. Evaluate the effectiveness of your HRD function

This book draws on the author's experiences in creating and managing a two-person HRD department in a new business unit at a large bank and in directing a small corporate HRD department at an insurance company. Included are the results of the author's research about other managers of small training departments in a wide range of fields, including financial services, health care, city government, pharmaceuticals, the restaurant business, the fur industry, and publishing. The results of the research and the author's experiences suggest several basic success strategies for running small training departments effectively:

- Build a partnership with the organization by assessing what its business priorities are and how a training department can contribute to meeting them, and agree on mutual expectations to gain management's sponsorship and support of human resource development

- Create a vision and a realistic plan based on sound needs analysis, to ensure that your programs will address business-focused HRD needs and help enhance your credibility

- Be creative in finding internal and external resources to design and deliver programs and services so that HRD has an impact far beyond the direct staff power of your department

- Market human resource development so that employees understand how your department supports the company and how they are expected to participate in HRD activities to ensure that the organization gets the most out of any HRD effort

- Manage time wisely so that you stick to priorities and avoid getting bogged down in insignificant activities or projects

- Manage the budget carefully by knowing what HRD costs and what the return on investment in HRD will be

- Develop your staff and network so that you and your staff will grow professionally, remain energized, and stay on top of changes in the organization, the business world, and the professional community

- Track your effectiveness and make adjustments to keep pace with changing demands of the organization and make sure that your programs are meeting its needs

These success strategies are closely interrelated: your results in one area tend to influence your effectiveness in others. *Managing a Small HRD Department* will contribute to your understanding of how other training managers have used these strategies and how you can apply them in your own training department.

OVERVIEW OF CONTENTS

Part One deals with the challenges and opportunities of managing a small HRD department and with planning your strategy. It will help you create your mission and plan so that you gain management sponsorship and set the stage for success.

Chapter One gives you a sense of the workings of small HRD departments — what companies expect from them and what they can contribute to a company's success. Several cases illustrate both the excitement and the difficulty of managing a small HRD department. Reading this chapter will provide you with a better understanding of what successful managers of small HRD departments do to build their credibility.

Chapter Two discusses how to build a partnership with senior management. It explains how to assess the organization's business priorities and HRD needs so that you can formulate a mission and gain senior management's commitment to human resource development.

Chapter Three explains how to create and develop a business-focused HRD plan. It will help you set realistic goals and say no to inappropriate requests for training. Because the first program or activity you offer is crucial in either establishing or destroying your reputation, this chapter offers guidelines for selecting a successful first program to get you off to the right start and begin to build your credibility.

Having created a plan, you need to decide how you are going to deliver your HRD programs and services so that they best meet the business needs of your organization. Chapter Four presents the advantages and disadvantages of various delivery methods, so that you can make educated decisions about whether to offer classroom training, individual study programs, or other delivery vehicles. Once you have selected your method of delivery, you must decide whether to get resources to develop and teach your programs from inside or outside the company. This chapter will help you decide whether to buy an off-the-shelf HRD program from a vendor, use a program offered by a college or university, hire a consultant to design a customized program, or develop the program yourself, using resources within the organization.

Once you have set your goals and chosen a delivery strategy, you need to project and negotiate a budget that is sufficient to accommodate your plan. Because new HRD managers frequently are not aware of the costs of HRD, Chapter Five deals with the budget implications of different resource strategies and reviews the elements of a sound HRD budget. It will help you determine the costs of different HRD strategies, select the best option for your organization, and prepare to negotiate your budget with senior management.

Part Two deals with issues involved in implementing your plan. Effectively marshaling resources may be the most difficult challenge in a small HRD department because you must implement your plan with few or no staff resources. As manager of a small department, you must understand how to find and work effectively with both internal and external resources to develop and deliver HRD programs.

Chapter Six will help you manage program development so that you build up the credibility of the HRD function and create a sense of partnership with the organization. The chapter describes the program development process and the HRD manager's role in it. It shows how to develop and implement HRD programs by building a resource network and learning to work effectively with internal subject-matter experts as well as external consultants.

Chapter Seven will help you effectively market HRD programs and services to other managers and employees within the organization. Once they understand what human resource development can contribute to the organization's business, they can gain greater benefit from your programs and services.

Running a small HRD department involves managing a great number of logistical tasks with very few resources. If you become bogged down in details, you can lose track of what is happening within the organization. Chapter Eight discusses the roles of the HRD manager and administrative assistant in the delivery and administration of HRD programs and services. This chapter advocates sensible division of tasks: if your assistant can handle administration effectively, you will be free to focus on other priorities.

Chapter Nine discusses the benefits of tracking the effectiveness of your programs and suggests how you can do this. By tracking program effectiveness, you can determine whether your department is accomplishing its mission and make necessary improvements. The chapter will also assist you in finding ways to reinforce the positive effects of your programs and increase the chances that employees will actually apply the new behaviors they have learned in your programs to their work situations.

Part Three summarizes ongoing management issues in a small department. It deals with managing a budget, developing your own and your staff's skills, and preparing for the future.

Chapter Ten discusses the management of a training budget. The chapter gives advice on monitoring expenses. You need to know that money is being well spent and that there is an adequate return on investment in training. Even if you do not have control of the budget, understanding how to manage a training budget will help you in efforts to gain control of the budget in the future and to secure adequate funding for your department.

Chapter Eleven provides ideas to help you and your assistant develop professionally. Staying connected to the organization and networking within the professional community are highlighted as ways of developing skills, finding resources, and avoiding burnout, a constant danger in a small department.

Chapter Twelve describes key organizational trends that have a potential impact on small HRD departments, such as trends toward empowerment, decentralization, and the use of technology. It also summarizes strategies discussed earlier for managing a successful small HRD department and suggests an action plan for future success.

The Resources section includes a detailed action plan and other worksheets to help you plan, produce, deliver, and evaluate your training activities in a systematic way. You may reproduce these worksheets and use them to manage your department more effectively.

ACKNOWLEDGMENTS

In June of 1989, at the Financial Services Conference of the American Society for Training and Development, I presented my thoughts and views on creating and running a small training department in a talk entitled "You

Can Do More Than You Think." The size of the standing-room-only audience made it clear that I was not alone in my interest in this topic. Following the talk, many of us in the room decided to form a training network to help break the isolation and begin to share ideas about what had worked well for us. My research began with the formation of that group and expanded as my network of managers of small HRD departments grew.

When Leonard and Zeace Nadler approached me about writing a book on managing a small HRD department, I was delighted. I knew that the topic had been neglected within the professional literature, because I had wished in vain for such a book when I was managing an HRD department in the International Consumer Banking Division at Chase Manhattan. No doubt the gap existed because managers of small HRD departments rarely have extra time to write books about what they do. My heartfelt appreciation goes out to the Nadlers for their help, encouragement, and support on this project.

Special thanks go to the HRD managers who contributed to my research: Carolyn Balling, John Barb, Ann Barkey, Christine Birnbaum, Lynn Brailsford, Robert Browning, Ronald Carter, Anita Cox, Ann Daniells, Carol Ryan Ertz, Harris Ginsberg, Sheila Hewitt, Anita Hope, Mary Huffman, Robert Jendusa, Jr., Ellen Kamp, Susan Kotler, Michael Kusinitz, Amy Lampert, David Lindelof, Crystine Mancini, Kathryn O'Neill, Mark Pine, Joanne Rogovin, Mitchell Rosen, Ricardo Shaw, Debra Shine, Janet Sliasky, Iris Staubus, Melinda Taylor, and others.

I would also like to thank my colleagues Diane Guernsey and Marlene Silva and my sisters, Kathryn Joy and Jane McCoy, who gave me continual encouragement and helpful suggestions on how to improve the manuscript. In addition, I would like to express my gratitude to Janet Nelson of Chase Manhattan Bank and Karen Lukas of UNUM Life Insurance Company of America for their patience and their support of this project. Finally, I would like to thank Sarah Polster and the editorial staff of Jossey-Bass for all their help in making the book a reality.

Falmouth, Maine   Carol P. McCoy
February 1993

▲ ▲

The Author

Carol P. McCoy is director of corporate training and development for UNUM Life Insurance Company of America. She received her B.A. degree (1970) from Connecticut College in psychology, and her M.S. (1974) and Ph.D. (1980) degrees from Rutgers University, also in psychology, with a concentration on social-personality theory.

Before joining UNUM, McCoy worked in various areas of human resource development for Chase Manhattan Bank from 1980 until 1991. She began her career at Chase as a training designer and instructor in a large corporate training department. In 1985, she created and managed a small HRD department in Chase's International Consumer Banking Division. In a one- or sometimes two-person department, she oversaw management training for managers in fifteen countries. Before starting her career in the financial services industry, she taught psychology at Livingston College and Rutgers University and was chairperson of a one-person social science department at Misericordia Hospital School of Nursing, in the Bronx, New York. McCoy currently resides in Falmouth, Maine, where she enjoys a change of lifestyle from the Upper West Side of Manhattan. She is an avid baseball fan and has an extensive baseball card collection going back to the early 1950s.

Managing a Small HRD Department

▲▲▲▲▲▲▲▲▲▲▲▲▲▲▲▲▲▲▲▲▲

*Setting
the
Stage
for
Success*

Small Department, Big Impact: Establishing Credibility

*I*t is easy for the manager of a small HRD department to feel unable to influence the success of the organization in a meaningful way. Building the credibility of a one- or two-person department is a major challenge, but it can be done. A small budget and minimal staff do not have to limit the department's impact. Many small HRD departments have a significant effect on their organizations by using resources wisely and sticking to priorities. A key to success is creating a partnership with critical people in your organization and finding ways to show them that human resource development makes a valuable contribution. This chapter looks at both the opportunities and challenges of managing a small HRD department and examines strategies that experienced managers of such departments have used to achieve success.

OPPORTUNITIES OF MANAGING A SMALL HRD DEPARTMENT

Why would anyone want to manage a small HRD department? Debra Shine, a self-taught individual, joined a bank right after she graduated from high school. For twelve years she worked for the bank as a teller, customer service representative, and operations manager, managing more than three hundred people. Ultimately, Debra became the bank holding company's director of product and sales training in a one-person department whose mission was to see that employees in more than five hundred offices had product knowledge and sales skills. What would she gain from this assignment? In her words:

> Never underestimate what can be done through creative use of resources and other people within the organization. You can do a lot without money or staff. You cannot wallow in your lack of resources. You need to redirect your energy: there is no limit to what a person can do. Being a one-person department affords you the opportunity to develop your own individual skills to a great degree. I learned how to do the most with the least amount of resources, how to be proactive instead of reactive. There was no fat there. I had to utilize my own abilities and find creative ways to use other people and resources to get the job done. I learned time management and met really tight deadlines. I have never learned more from any other assignment [Debra Shine, interview with the author, June 20, 1990].

Unlike the managers of larger departments, which often are responsible for a variety of tangential activities, you are likely to work mainly on extremely important projects, and what you do will probably have a considerable impact on the success of your organization. In the words of another manager of a small HRD department, "You can only afford to work on business priorities. You cannot afford to have any hobbies."

Perhaps the greatest reward in managing a small department lies in having the opportunity to create exactly what you think the organization needs. In many cases, senior managers have told their HRD managers: "You do what you think is best—you're the expert." For those of you expecting to be told what to do by senior management, this level of freedom may be somewhat anxiety provoking. Ultimately, however, it enables you to realize your vision of what human resource development should be.

One reason you can accomplish so much is that in most small HRD departments the manager works very closely with the organization and its senior managers. This tends to be true whether the department is the only HRD department in a small company or part of a decentralized line of business. In such a department you can usually take action fairly quickly because decision making is generally much simpler in smaller organizations. You don't have to go through several levels of management to get approval for your plans, and you are often able to meet extremely tight deadlines because you have the active support of senior management in finding resources necessary to design and implement HRD instructional programs.

Along with affording you the opportunity to help a company accomplish its mission and to enact your own vision of human resource development, managing a small HRD department provides an excellent opportunity for personal development. No matter what your level of skill is initially, you will be able to develop broad-based HRD skills because you are likely to become involved in a wide range of activities, from strategic planning to marketing, designing, teaching, and evaluating HRD programs. The job also provides a chance for you to improve your skills in a more general way. Successfully managing such a department inevitably improves your ability to lead and influence others, to take risks, to handle pressure, to plan your time wisely, and to be flexible in your approach to problems and challenges. Managing a small HRD department provides an opportunity for personal growth because it is a constant challenge.

CHALLENGES OF MANAGING A SMALL HRD DEPARTMENT

What makes the HRD manager's role so challenging? A major challenge is maintaining your level of energy in the face of the demands of the job. Those who succeed are those who become very creative at finding ways to solve problems and keep themselves energized. For many HRD managers, it is difficult to move from a large department to a small one that does not have HRD professionals to assist with the design and implementation of programs and interventions. Your role as manager—especially your skill in locating and managing indirect resources—is crucial to the success of a small HRD function. Managing a small department is more difficult if the company fails to provide you with much support or guidance when you have to create an HRD function. And many people are in one-person shops because they are setting up a new function in the organization.

Founders of small HRD departments often must go through a process of trial and error to learn which strategies work and which do not. Furthermore, creating and managing this kind of department usually represent an increase in the nature and scope of one's responsibilities. Most managers have not created or managed a small HRD department before.

They come from a wide variety of backgrounds. They may be training specialists (designers/instructors) in a large corporate HRD department or an educational institution. They may be successful employees or line managers who have had no HRD experience but are suddenly expected to know how to set up an HRD function, or they may have HRD management experience but are used to having a large staff to help them.

A common scenario involves moving from a training specialist position in a large corporate HRD staff to managing a one- or two-person de-centralized department. This transition is challenging partly because of the change in role. If you are a training specialist, you have a narrow focus: you design and teach training programs. If you are in a corporate department, you are probably managed by experts and surrounded by people who believe in human resource development. You may have the luxury of ample time and numerous colleagues to help create programs. You usually do not have to worry about budgets or setting up new administrative procedures. How does the situation change when you begin to manage a two-person HRD department in a line of business?

As the creator or manager of a small HRD department, you determine the direction and mission of human resource development. You manage and negotiate a budget. You establish the credibility of the function and are responsible for managing program development and implementation without any trainers on your staff. As manager, you must market HRD. To do this effectively, you have to educate people about it and may even have to refute common myths, such as the idea that human resource development can improve all performance problems or make up for a lack of good management practices. If the organization has never before had a systematic HRD program, the demands on your time are tremendous. Although naive clients may expect instant training, you will need time to develop programs, find instructors, and set up administrative procedures.

It is easy to lose your focus and stumble into common pitfalls, such as being pressured into acting before you have had time to gain an understanding of the organization and its HRD needs. Another common mistake, especially among new managers, is to propose unrealistic plans, take on too much, or try to solve nontraining problems with training solutions. If you have come from a large HRD department with high standards of professionalism, you may feel you must do everything according to those same high standards rather than doing what is expedient and will work in the current situation.

As the pressure to produce increases, there is a danger that you may rely too much on your training skills, try to do too much yourself, and thereby become isolated from the organization and the HRD professional community. This can result in your becoming cut off from organizational issues and priorities, being unaware of people who could help develop or deliver HRD programs or unaware of programs available in the industry, and missing out on potential sources of support. Perhaps the greatest danger of all is losing optimism and believing that you can do nothing because you have no training resources to support you. To better understand small HRD departments, let's look at some examples.

SUCCESS STORIES

Managing a small HRD department provides a tremendous opportunity to create a vision, to experiment, and to learn. What comes through when talking with successful managers of small HRD departments is their enthusiasm, pride, creativity, and involvement. The managers whose stories are featured throughout this book have used many different approaches in building HRD's credibility within their organizations. Let us take a look at some of their stories to understand the challenges they have faced and the strategies they have used to meet those challenges.

Creating a Small HRD Department in a Commercial Bank

Several years ago, a global financial services corporation had a large corporate training department and a large credit training department as well as a few small, decentralized HRD departments in some well-established business units. Based on market opportunity and on its strong worldwide reputation and global network, the company decided to form a new international consumer banking division. Managers of this rapidly growing business unit needed broad technical knowledge and management skill to compete successfully against powerful local and foreign competitors. This small — but critical — population of international consumer employees had very specific developmental needs that were not going to be met by the corporate training department. To support the HRD needs of the new division, the organization hired a dedicated HRD manager who had only one direct resource — a secretary / administrative assistant — to help oversee human resource development for managers in fifteen countries. I was that manager.

After five years as a training specialist, designing and instructing training programs in corporate HRD, I leapt at the chance to develop and manage a curriculum, deal with an international population, and become more closely involved in a business. I was optimistic at first but quickly became aware of the differences between my old and new roles. These differences caused me some anxiety and confusion about what to do and how to do it. Despite the existence of other HRD departments in the corporation, as the manager of a small HRD department in a new division, I was isolated from my colleagues and basically on my own in learning how to create and manage an effective HRD effort. As is often the case, I learned a great deal about pitfalls by falling into them. I felt pressured to produce a plan without having an opportunity to conduct a business-focused HRD needs analysis, and as a consequence I created an unrealistic plan and was then saddled with the responsibility of implementing it. In the beginning I tried to do too much myself without drawing on the large base of resources that existed throughout the corporation. Moreover, I fell into perhaps the most dangerous trap of all: I became isolated from the organization in my efforts to produce training program after training program.

Eventually, I discovered a better way. I found a wealth of resources as I began to work much more closely with managers from my own business unit and throughout the rest of the organization. In creating future plans, I carefully determined priorities and made sure they had the backing of senior management. I spent much more time communicating about and marketing human resource development than producing training materials. Ultimately, I built a resource network and offered a management curriculum that included a range of programs teaching management skills, risk management, sales management, and operations management. In my three years on the job my emotions ranged from early optimism to discouragement at the realities and difficulties of my job to confidence and pride in what I could accomplish. From my research I found that my experience was not unique. Let's look at some other companies and the challenges the managers of their small HRD departments have faced.

Gaining Results Quickly in a Fur Company
Through Key Partnerships

Ann Barkey (interviewed by the author on Jan. 30, 1990) was hired as training director of a growing fur company because the chairman recognized a need to train the staff regarding products, sales, and customer care. In the three years of Ann's tenure, the firm became a public company and grew from 100 employees in three stores to more than 450 employees in sixteen stores; its sales increased from $20 million to $100 million. When Ann was hired, the chairman asked her to "create the training department. Just figure out how to do it." She worked alone in this endeavor until she was given a part-time assistant two and a half years later.

Ann's first challenge was to produce a one-week training program to refresh people's knowledge of products and selling skills, which she did within her first five weeks on the job. This was a significant challenge because she did not know anything about the company or the fur business. She was able to accomplish her goal because she had the total support of senior managers who helped her form partnerships with people throughout the company. She used her creativity in finding ways to get reluctant employees to participate in the program. Having established her credibility with a successful first program, Ann eventually offered a wide range of management, technical, and selling skills programs. As a result of Ann's efforts, training that had been in "the oral tradition" was formalized and professionalized to support the growing organization.

Working with Senior Managers to Implement HRD
in a Regional Hospital

Mike Kusinitz is manager of training and development in a 450-bed regional hospital with three thousand employees and $185 million in income. Mike was hired to provide training, management development, and organizational development. His primary focus is on three hundred managers, although he also serves other employees on occasion. Technical training is provided by another department. At first Mike had only a half-time secretary to help him, but after two years he received a training specialist.

Mike's responsibility is to translate the organization's mission into reality — to get the management philosophy out to the management team, to see that unit objectives are tied to the mission, to ensure that people have management skills to carry out the mission, and to provide coaching and counseling to management. After interviewing the senior managers, Mike discovered that the hospital was not ready for training: it needed a communication process before programs could be put into place. Mike worked with senior managers to provide the Management Interaction Program for the entire management team. He helped the CEO introduce key corporate concepts and gather managers' ideas on how to increase empowerment, accountability, and risk taking. Now he offers a core curriculum of short, practical programs such as Essentials of Management, the Power of Recognition, and Persuasive Communication. In Mike's opinion the most critical issue for the manager of a small HRD department is to understand the power base and politics of the organization. In his words, "You need to step back and look at how you can tie in with senior management's philosophy and support it" (interview with the author, Feb. 6, 1990).

Creative Use of Resources to Provide
Business-Relevant Programs in a Brokerage House

Joanne Rogovin (interview with the author, Feb. 7, 1990) served as training manager at Kidder Peabody, a major investment bank and brokerage firm with five thousand employees. The firm suffered several serious blows in the late eighties, including acquisition by another company, an insider-trading scandal, and the stock market crash of 1987. In this turbulent environment, the parent company decided that Kidder Peabody needed someone to work with managers to develop a management perspective. Joanne was hired by the managing director of human resources to conduct executive and management development, succession planning, organization development, and team building. She handled this responsibility with a senior training consultant whom she hired to replace a junior training assistant. Another department handled sales training in the company's branches.

During her first few months on the job Joanne focused her attention on learning the company's business priorities by interviewing the managing directors of each business and asking them to describe what they did, what stumbling blocks they faced, and how each business fit into the total organization. She realized that something had to be done to bridge gaps in communication at the senior management level. Joanne's initial training program grew out of a legal settlement in which the firm agreed to conduct compliance and ethics training. By involving a great number of experts throughout the company in developing materials and providing such training, Joanne created a partnership with the organization and built her credibility as a helpful resource. She conducted instructor training and put together a "foolproof" manual for line trainers, who have since trained a total of four thousand professionals in ethics and compliance. Instead of complaining that their time is wasted in training, branch managers wrote her fan mail claiming that the program made them look good. During her tenure, Joanne developed other effective programs by involving employees in their development and delivery and by keeping people informed of the progress of key HRD projects.

Building Credibility by Becoming Involved and Responding to Urgent Needs in a Public Works Department

Anita Cox was hired as the training manager for the Public Works Department of a large city government as a result of growing negative publicity and productivity problems within the department. The director of public works had hired Anita, an employment specialist in another division of the government, to develop a supervisory training program to improve productivity and service. She began with only a part-time secretary and received a full-time trainer after a year and a half. Her biggest challenge was establishing her credibility in a male-dominated field.

Anita began her needs analysis by talking with the assistant directors and discovered that not everyone was in support of her position. One assistant director came into her office and told her: "I don't know who you are or how you got here, but you're young, female, and not an engineer. You'll never make it here." She realized that she needed to begin work in an area where someone was receptive to her or the training would be sabotaged. She chose the Street Maintenance and Bridge Division. Anita gained a knowledge of the division's work by immersing herself in its day-to-day activities. She rode around with the supervisors in their cars and asked what was difficult about their jobs and what would make their jobs easier. She even went down into trenching holes to observe men working on sewer lines in order to understand how the crew operated.

Within the first six months, Anita met a crucial need by developing a handbook of policies and procedures and a flexible supervisory skills program. When word spread outside the department that something good was happening in public works, departmental relations within the total city system improved. The HRD department was given some credit for the improved performance, and over time the HRD staff gained fourteen trainers. In Anita's opinion the department flourished because "We understood the jobs, we were responsive, and we were innovative in how we implemented programs. We met employee needs by training on the 'graveyard shift.' There was a lot of experiential learning and not a lot of lecture" (interview with the author, Feb. 6, 1990).

Understanding Priorities and Creating Involvement in HRD at a Large Newspaper

Bob Jendusa, a personnel specialist with a large northern newspaper, was hired as training director to initiate the training function of a major southern newspaper. The paper had two hundred supervisors, who had little idea of what good management entailed. Bob was convinced that there was a strong commitment to training because he would report directly to the president rather than to the head of personnel. After one year on the job, Bob was given a part-time secretary, and after three years he received a full-time trainer. For a period of five years Bob's training department set high standards for training in newspaper publishing and the department flourished. Unfortunately, when the publisher changed and the local economy bottomed out, the department was cut back, and Bob's other personnel responsibilities increased to such an extent that he had little time to focus on human resource development. The downturn of the department was the result of a worsening economic and management situation.

When management was favorable to human resource development, Bob did a number of things that helped build his credibility. He conducted an extensive needs analysis by sending every supervisor a questionnaire and then interviewing department heads to find out which were priority training problems and which were "organizational constraints." On the basis of his analysis, he offered programs in customer service, supervisory skills, and time and territory management. Bob felt that his biggest challenge was becoming accepted and gaining the trust of the employees. He did this by building a partnership and getting managers involved in the courses. When people asked Bob, "What are you going to do for me?" he would say, "This is what we are going to do together." He talked with top managers about what was required for success, how they needed to present courses to their employees and reinforce what was learned on the job. Bob was especially proud of the broad acceptance of training in the newsroom. In his words: "We had strong support from the managing editor, who attended our programs and urged his people to attend them. It was a hard audience to crack, and they were waiting to go to training. We were effective because we had credibility. If we said we could do something, we did it. We never made a commitment unless we felt we could do it" (Robert Jendusa JR, interview with the author, Feb. 14, 1990). As an example of the latter, when a manager asked Bob to create a program to teach people to communicate upward, he told him that was not a training issue.

SUMMARY: STRATEGIES FOR SUCCESSFULLY MANAGING A SMALL HRD DEPARTMENT

What can we learn from what has worked well in managing small HRD departments? My research and experience suggest that the following basic strategies are involved in managing an effective small HRD department.

■ *Working in partnership with the organization to understand its HRD needs and priorities.* As the manager, you need to set a direction for human resource development that supports your company while making sure people have realistic expectations of what your function can contribute. Successful HRD managers work in partnership with senior management to assess their company's business priorities and HRD needs and thus gain management's sponsorship and support of appropriate HRD programs.

■ *Creating a vision and a realistic plan.* A vision and a plan that focus on the business of the organization and address its priorities go a long way toward establishing your credibility. In a small department it is easy to over- or underestimate what you can do. It is critical that your plan be based on a sound needs analysis. The plan must also focus on priorities and provide appropriate solutions to problems. Choosing your first program is particularly important because getting off to the right start is crucial to establishing your credibility.

■ *Being creative in finding resources and delivering HRD.* Developing a sound resource strategy and building a solid resource network may be the number one challenge of small HRD departments. The successful manager knows how to build an internal network and to work successfully with consultants so that human resource development has an impact far beyond the number of members of his or her department.

■ *Attracting customers by communicating what HRD can do for the organization.* Communicating the mission of your department, how it supports the company, and how employees and managers are expected to participate in HRD ac- tivities is a critical strategy for your success. Ongoing communication helps build your partnership with the organization and ensures that it and its employ- ees get the most out of any HRD effort.

■ *Managing time wisely.* In a small department, it is essential to stick to priorities and avoid getting bogged down in insignificant activities or projects. In a one- or two-person department, it is a constant challenge to manage the logistical details of providing human resource development. Because of the many demands for your time, you must also learn what is essential and what is less important.

■ *Managing the budget carefully.* Since small HRD departments frequently have small budgets, it is important to know what human resource development costs and how to spend the available money where it will do the most good. Even in cases where the manager does not have direct control over the budget, knowing the costs and the return on investment of HRD can help you make the most of resources and eventually gain more control over the budget.

■ *Developing your staff and networking.* Because of the amount of work involved in managing a small department, becoming isolated and ignoring your own developmental needs are major pitfalls. Making sure that you and your staff develop professionally and stay connected to the firm, the business commu- nity, and professional organizations is important for your personal and profes- sional well-being. Continuing to develop and network with others helps you keep up-to-date in the field and locate resources, HRD programs, and other sources of support that can energize you and increase your effectiveness.

■ *Tracking your effectiveness and making adjustments.* Successful managers monitor measures of their department's effectiveness and know how to dem- onstrate the value of human resource development to management. They are flexible in adjusting what they do in order to keep pace with the changing demands of the organization.

These success strategies are closely interrelated; how well you do with one tends to influence your effectiveness with the others. For example, working in partnership with the organization and establishing realistic expectations among management and staff make it easier to establish a viable plan, develop sponsorship, and build your credibility. It is very difficult to gain the sponsorship of senior management without establishing your credibility as someone who knows the company and how your function can contribute to its success. At the same time, credibility and management sponsorship are critical to your being able to marshal resources, both human and financial. And the kinds of resources that you use in human resource development can make or break your credibility.

The foundation of any successful HRD department rests on your knowledge of the organization. Establishing a partnership with your company by assessing its business priorities and HRD needs is crucial to planning your HRD mission and strategy. Chapter Two deals with this topic.

Assessing Your Company's Business Priorities and HRD Needs

By assessing the company's business priorities and HRD needs, the HRD manager begins to build a partnership with the organization that ultimately results in the delivery of a business-focused HRD plan. Establishing such a partnership is an increasingly important theme in HRD development and what managing a small HRD department is all about. Sheila Hewitt, the former manager of a two-person HRD department in a pharmaceutical company, describes partnership this way: "For us, a working partnership means being clear about the goal, and communicating openly and honestly at different stages of the design process. It also means that we and management are equally committed to the program and make time to gather information, discuss design, and test critical parts. We use focus groups, interviews, and surveys to obtain data. Most of all, we trust and respect each other, and together we create a practical and useful program" (interview with the author, March 2, 1990).

For HRD to have an impact on your company, you need to understand your customers: external customers, who use your company's goods and services, and internal customers, who use your HRD programs and services. You must know the dynamics of your organization, that is, what it must do to succeed. You also need to know your target audience within the company, your potential sponsors, the prevailing attitudes toward human resource development, and the people who can help or hinder you. To assist your company, your HRD plan must be based on a sound understanding of the company's business priorities and how HRD can provide employees with the knowledge and skills needed to accomplish those objectives. You learn how human resource development can contribute by conducting a needs assessment.

What do we mean by the term *needs assessment*? Basically, a need is a gap between what *is* and what *should be* in terms of employees' knowledge and skills; assessment involves determining the specific things people need to learn and how human resource development may help them do this. Your needs assessment can focus on an individual, a work group, a department, a region, or the entire organization. Needs can be assessed informally and intuitively or through more formal and complex procedures. No matter how you determine needs, you, as the HRD manager, must decide whether the benefits of any HRD activity outweigh its costs. In a one- or two-person department it is especially important that your activities focus on business priorities; your needs analysis is the key to making smart choices about what to do. Your assesssment of the company's business priorities and HRD needs should answer the following questions:

- What are the company's most important business issues and objectives?

- Which populations are essential to the organization's success?

- What knowledge, skills, attributes, and values will employees need in order for the organization to succeed in the coming year and over the next decade?

- In what areas do employees have the skills and knowledge required, and where are there gaps?

- What populations within the organization most need HRD support, and what are their most urgent developmental needs?

- In light of the above, what are three to five areas in which you can have the most impact?

BENEFITS OF ASSESSING BUSINESS PRIORITIES AND HRD NEEDS

An assessment of your company's business priorities and HRD needs is vital when you are new to an organization or an industry. It helps you learn the jargon, the culture, how things are done. Your assessment can help you formulate a strategy, build sponsorship, identify resources, gain visibility, and evaluate the effectiveness of your efforts. In some cases, especially when you are establishing an HRD department or when there has been no human resource development in the company for a long time, you may feel pressured to create a plan before conducting a thorough HRD needs analysis. You may think, "Why take the time to assess HRD needs when I have so few resources?" Your programs and services are much more likely to meet real business objectives if you have made a needs assessment. In the words of Susan Warshauer (1988, p. 15), a well-done needs assessment "can generate excitement, creativity, energy, and commitment."

Formulating Your HRD Strategy

Assessing your company's priorities and HRD needs enables you to focus on specific problem areas and critical issues within the organization rather than taking a random approach. It can help you decide which types of programs to offer, which employees to concentrate on, how to reach them, and the best way to teach them. Speaking directly with people in the course of identifying HRD needs not only helps you develop a sound vision but can also clarify your real target audience. For example, when I started my job in international consumer banking, I felt pressured to create a plan based on a consultant's vague analysis, which defined my role rather narrowly: I was to be a training coordinator who would oversee the training of a very small population—consumer managers in different countries. In talking with these managers, I began to build important relationships. I learned that other levels of employees also needed training, and I succeeded in convincing senior management to broaden my responsibilities to include a larger population.

Your needs assessment can help identify sources of support and resistance to human resource development so that you can begin working with receptive people and gradually overcome the resistance. When Anita Cox (referred to in Chapter One) began assessing the HRD needs of a local city government, she was told by an assistant director that she would never succeed because of her youth and inexperience. However, in the course of her assessment she met with a more receptive department head with whom she began working, and ultimately she was able to develop a reputation as a valuable asset to the organization.

Obtaining Managers' and Participants' Commitment to HRD

When managers understand the need for human resource development and how it will contribute to the organization's success, they are much more likely to pay for programs, send their people for training, and provide a work environment that reinforces those people's newly gained skills. Furthermore, people are more motivated to attend HRD programs when they understand their purpose and have been involved in the effort from the beginning. A needs assessment can also increase potential participants' commitment to your HRD programs.

Making the Best Use of HRD Resources

With limited resources in a small HRD department, you will need to make choices about what HRD can and should do and where to focus your efforts. You can do this more effectively when you have discovered what it is that senior management values and when you have examined problem areas and assessed the appropriateness of human resource development as a solution. Although you must be responsive to senior management's needs, you must also make sure that your responses are aimed at problems that can be improved by training, education, or development.

Executives in small companies who have not had much experience with HRD sometimes have unrealistic expectations of HRD as a cure-all. Frequently, too, management is unclear about a problem's exact nature or causes and automatically assumes that HRD will provide the best solution whether it actually can or cannot. Nevertheless, some managers of small HRD departments believe that they can never say no to senior management. In reality, however, senior managers often appreciate being shown ways to improve organizational effectiveness or avoid wasted HRD efforts.

Some skills and knowledge required for success can be taught through HRD programs, but others cannot. For example, when I began my assignment in the International Consumer Banking Division at Chase Manhattan, some senior managers assumed that I could develop a program that could teach the consumer banking managers of various countries everything they needed to know to succeed. In reality, several of the managers lacked the essential skills, knowledge, or personality qualities needed to run a business in a highly competitive marketplace successfully. A few weeks of training could not teach them sound business judgment or leadership ability. This problem could have been better solved by replacing those managers with others who possessed the appropriate qualifications. On the other hand, some of the better qualified managers who participated in our HRD programs were able to learn and apply such skills as selling, risk management, and change management.

Identifying Potential Resources Who Can Help

As head of a small HRD department, you will have to rely on others to help deliver human resource development. Involving managers and employees in a needs assessment can generate enthusiasm for a project and enable you to learn about people's skills and expertise, which may be useful in designing programs or teaching. In the course of the assessment process you may also gain ideas for constructing role plays, case studies, or simulations so that they will address real situations to which employees can relate.

Gaining Visibility in the Organization

A common pitfall of small HRD departments is isolation. This is usually the result of spending too much time designing, teaching, and administering programs and not enough time getting to know the company and the people within it. If you do not know the people and they do not know who you are and what you do, it is difficult to have an impact on the organization—no matter how good your HRD programs are. A needs assessment gives you the opportunity to talk to people about your area of expertise and can help you build relationships with the organization's key players.

Obtaining Data to Evaluate the Effectiveness of HRD

You can make a much more valid evaluation of any program's effectiveness if you have information on performance problems *before* carrying out any HRD intervention. These data provide you with a basis on which to demonstrate improvement afterward. For example, if you know the error rate in some process before you train people to perform procedures correctly, you can measure the change in error rate after the training and show solid business results. Quantifying the impact of human resource development can be particularly helpful when you need to justify expenses.

PHASES OF THE ASSESSMENT PROCESS

What is the best way for a small department to discover the company's HRD needs? The same way a larger organization would—you begin by learning about the company's business priorities, about senior management's goals and values, and about how HRD can contribute to their achievement. Needs assessment is an ongoing process, not a one-time event. Smith, Delahaye, and Gates (1990) describe this proces as having three phases: surveillance, investigation, and analysis.

Surveillance is a continuing process. It involves knowing about current trends and future directions within the organization. You need to stay involved and keep yourself informed by making sure that crucial organizational documents and reports are circulated to you and by keeping in touch with key people.

While surveillance provides you with the big picture, *investigation* helps you understand the trends and problems and gives you a sound basis for deciding whether or not HRD can help solve the latter. You investigate when you receive a request for human resource development or suspect that a potential or actual performance problem may derive from employees' lack of knowledge or ability. A variety of needs assessment methods are available to assist you in such investigation.

Finally, in the *analysis* phase, you study the information that you have uncovered in your investigation and summarize the conclusions that you have reached. In essence, analysis involves doing some sort of cost-benefit comparison so that you can decide whether or not human resource development would be appropriate and worthwhile.

METHODS FOR ASSESSING HRD NEEDS

As already noted, many techniques for learning about HRD needs are available to small departments. The *ASTD Trainer's Toolkit: Needs Assessment Instruments* (Allen, 1990) is an excellent source for these. Knowing the advantages and disadvantages of various methods and the criteria that are important to your organization can help you select the best approach for your situation. Among those that can work well in a small HRD department are organizational documents and reports, questionnaires for managers and employees, interviews with managers and employees (individually or in groups), advisory groups, and observation of work situations. For a summary of the major advantages and disadvantages of each, see Table 2.1. Now let's look more closely at each method.

Organizational Documents

Becoming familiar with written documents such as the company's annual report, strategic plan, business plan, and mission statement can provide information about

- The organization's business, goods, and services

- The organization's key objectives and strategies

- Competitors and how well the organization is doing in comparison with them

- Factors that influence how well the organization does

- How much change and what types of change the organization is experiencing

- The organization's core values and whether they are upheld values or values in name only

As Smith, Delahaye, and Gates (1990) point out, there are many readily available sources of data regarding possible HRD needs. Many reports focus on organizational performance and provide information that is meaningful to management—absenteeism, turnover, customer service, service quality, productivity, profitability, and so on. This type of quantifiable data can be obtained quickly and inexpensively and may provide powerful clues to HRD needs. Possible sources of organizational data and what they suggest include the following:

- *Written organizational goals and objectives* show where training emphasis should be placed and can serve as normative standards by which to evaluate training.

- *Manpower inventories* can indicate HRD needs created by retirement, aging, or turnover and can provide a data base regarding the possible scope of training needs.

Table 2.1. Major Advantages and Disadvantages of Needs Assessment Methods.

Method	Advantages	Disadvantages
Organizational documents	Provide relevant, quantifiable data Inexpensive Fast May build management involvement	Do not build employee involvement Not necessarily focused on HRD May not identify causes May not provide visibility
Questionnaires/surveys	Can reach many people in a short time Build involvement Relatively inexpensive Yield relevant, quantifiable data that are easy to summarize Allow for anonymity, which may encourage more honest responses	Require time and skill to develop May generate low response rates or inaccurate responses Provide no opportunity to clarify questions May restrict freedom of response May lead to unrealistic expectations about HRD
Group interviews with employees and managers (focus groups)	Build involvement and support Provide relevant data Provide you with visibility May elicit important topics you had not expected Permit on-the-spot sharing and synthesis of different views	Moderately time-consuming (but less so than individual interviews) Moderately expensive Difficult to conduct May be difficult to analyze and quantify data
Individual interviews with employees and managers	Build involvement and support Allow for clarification Provide relevant data Easier to conduct than group interviews May uncover information that would not be brought up in a group	Expensive in terms of time and travel costs Require strong interviewing skills May be difficult to analyze and quantify results May make interviewees self-conscious
Advisory committees	Build management involvement and sponsorship Provide visibility Inexpensive Allow synthesis of opinions of key decision makers Can help identify resources	Time-consuming and difficult to manage logistically Fail to build lower-level employee involvement Poor source of quantifiable data May lead to groupthink or turf wars
Observation of work situations	Builds employee involvement Provides excellent information when coaching an individual Builds your credibility Generates relevant, quantifiable data	Requires a highly skilled observer Does not involve management Time-consuming May change performance or be perceived as spying May be logistically difficult to implement

■ *Organizational climate indexes* such as labor-management data, grievances, turnover, productivity, absenteeism, and attitude surveys may suggest problems that have HRD components.

■ *Analyses of efficiency indexes* such as costs of labor, materials, and distribution; product quality; downtime; late deliveries; repairs, and so on can indicate gaps in performance and be useful in a cost-benefit analysis of HRD.

■ *Job descriptions and performance appraisals* outline typical duties and responsibilities and may help in defining performance discrepancies.

■ *Reports on exit interviews* may indicate problem areas, especially with regard to supervisory training needs.

■ *Announcements about changes in equipment*, such as the introduction of new computer systems, may indicate the existence of a training need.

On the other hand, organizational reports used by themselves have several disadvantages. They do not build the involvement of sponsors, managers, or employees; they do not allow for any visibility or interaction on your part; and they may not indicate specific causes of or solutions to problems. You will want to supplement this method of gathering information with methods of building involvement and allowing for the investigation of problems.

Questionnaires/Surveys

Questionnaires and surveys can be sent to potential users of HRD programs and to various levels of management. In constructing questionnaires or surveys, consider using a mix of closed- and open-ended questions. Closed-ended questions make it easier for you to tabulate data. For example, you can have people check off skills for which they believe training is needed or use a scale to rate their satisfaction with various programs. Having respondents rank programs according to their usefulness can help you determine priorities when your budget is limited. Open-ended questions, on the other hand, allow people more freedom of response and may provide you with more information than closed-ended questions do.

Questionnaires have numerous advantages. They allow you to reach a large number of people in a relatively short period of time and in a cost-effective manner. They build involvement of the people surveyed, although not the degree of involvement that the two-way communication of an interview stimulates. However, if people feel that their responses are anonymous, they may be more honest on a questionnaire than they would be in an interview.

Questionnaires also have several disadvantages. As already noted, they only allow one-way communication: you cannot ask clarifying questions. If questions are poorly worded, it is difficult for people to provide clear, definitive answers. Asking clear questions one at a time and avoiding leading questions and jargon can help reduce fuzzy or misguided responses. Questionnaires also allow less freedom of response than interviews do, although including some open-ended questions on the former can help mitigate this shortcoming.

A majority of people do not return surveys. Nevertheless, while a 30 percent response rate is not unusual, a response rate of 80 percent is possible under the right circumstances (Robinson and Robinson, 1989). Response rates can be improved by making a survey interesting, non-threatening, and easy to complete. Well-written cover letters and incentives to complete surveys (such as a free lunch or a discount on a training program) can also increase the chances that people will return completed ones.

Questionnaires or surveys can also raise false expectations. People may request training that is inconsistent with the corporate strategy and be disappointed when programs they have asked for are not offered or skills they have acquired are not needed on the job. For example, one company's managers requested and attended computer training, but the company had no plans to provide the managers with personal computers. Another danger is that people may misdiagnose their needs. For example, in another company, supervisors requested a workshop to deal more effectively with problem subordinates. Although a coaching skills workshop was offered and was well attended, it did nothing to address the problem because what the supervisors really needed was more knowledge of the company's union contract and the role played by the union representative (Graham and Mihal, 1990, p. 220).

Surveys that ask individuals to assess their own learning needs are valuable because they create involvement and encourage people to take responsibility for development. You may use self-assessment surveys with managers or with nonmanagement employees. However, it is also important to remember that people may not accurately understand their own needs or may identify marginal or unrealistic needs that are not organizational priorities.

Graham and Mihal (1990, p. 221) suggest a process to ensure that self-assessments are relevant, realistic, and related to strategic corporate goals. First, have people create a comprehensive list of potential development needs. Then ask them to create a wish list of tasks they "would like to perform more effectively, . . . areas of expertise they would like to know more about," and "skills and traits they would like to strengthen." Having people ask for training they *want* rather than *need* helps bring to the surface needs they recognize but are reluctant to admit to. Next, have the respondents prioritize their needs as they relate to organizational priorities by identifying up to five *performance improvement targets* — tasks that could contribute most to improved organizational performance — and the associated *knowledge and skills improvement targets* — areas of expertise and skills that could help accomplish their performance improvement targets. Finally, have supervisors validate their subordinates' self-assessments. This motivates people to give their full attention to the self-assessment process; it also allows supervisors to check for misperceptions regarding strengths and weaknesses and to learn about their subordinates' developmental concerns so that they can be more supportive.

Interviews

Interviews involve talking to people about their values and their perceptions of problems and solutions. Interviews can involve managers and/or non-managerial employees or others, be conducted on the phone or in person, be relatively structured or unstructured, and be conducted with one other person or with a group of people. Let's take a brief look at each alternative.

It is helpful to obtain information from both managers and non-managers because the two groups frequently view problems from different perspectives. In general, and especially if you are new to the organization, you may want to conduct interviews in person, since you can observe verbal and nonverbal responses and build a greater rapport with interviewees. If you already know many people in the organization or if people's offices are spread out geographically and your deadline is tight, you may want to conduct some interviews over the phone. It is always wise to plan your interview questions in advance even though you may ask a number of unplanned questions as well. Whereas initial interviews tend to be relatively freewheeling because you want to uncover potential problems and issues, follow-up interviews, in which you want to probe for specific information, tend to be more structured.

Finally, individual interviews allow you to probe more deeply and can sometimes elicit more controversial information than group interviews do. On the other hand, group interviews that focus on a specific topic— sometimes called focus groups—can allow you to synthesize different points of view, promote general understanding and agreement of needs and priorities, and build support for HRD. Group interviews are superior to individual interviews when many employees have information about a problem and when they feel that they will not get in trouble for revealing information (Gilley and Eggland, 1987, p. 205).

Interviews have numerous advantages as an assessment method. They encourage the involvement of both potential sponsors and participants, allow freedom of response, and encourage the sharing of ideas when people are not certain of their answers. In addition, interviews provide for "process, as well as content information," permit two-way communication, and allow HRD managers to "observe how managers and subordinates communicate and how they react verbally and nonverbally to change and development issues" (Kaman, 1990, p. 244). Two-way communication allows you to clarify the meaning of questions and to build your credibility as an HRD expert who can give advice, information, and useful feedback and "influence employees to think about their futures, their roles in the organization, and their training and development needs" (Kaman, 1990, p. 244).

Interviews also have disadvantages: they are time-consuming, require special skills, and produce data that may be difficult to quantify. Interviews work best when you carefully plan your questions, provide a comfortable environment by encouraging people to talk about positive experiences before asking difficult questions, and ask probing and clarifying questions to ensure you understand what is being said both verbally and nonverbally. It is also important to give some thought to how you can record information without distracting the interviewees, inhibiting honesty, and influencing responses in the direction you want. Taking notes may be less expensive and less inhibiting than using a tape recorder.

Advisory Committees

Advisory committees may be composed of a variety of interested people throughout the organization, such as senior managers, other managers and supervisors, nonmanagerial employees, and representatives of human re-sources (generalists or trainers from various divisions). Advisory commit-tees can help you brainstorm about problems and issues and help provide the energy and sense of joint ownership needed to solve HRD problems. If people on the advisory committee have credibility and expertise, this can be an excellent way to begin to form a partnership with the organization. Members of the committee can be an invaluable source of suggestions about how to proceed and the resources to use in human resource development.

On the other hand, difficulties in scheduling committee meetings, especially if senior people are involved, can slow your progress. Moreover, members may be subject to groupthink, in which case individuals will hesitate to express opinions that differ from the majority, and junior members may feel inhibited by the presence of senior representatives on the committee. Even worse, if strong political conflicts exist within the organi-zation, advisory committees can become arenas for turf wars, in which some people oppose others merely for the sake of opposition. You will need to consider carefully whether advisory committees will work well in your organization, and, if so, who should serve on them.

Observation of Work Situations

It is helpful for you to see for yourself what is actually happening within the organization. Observation is particularly important when you are new to an industry or organization. It helps you learn company operating pro-cedures, cultural norms, and jargon, as well as gain visibility with its employees. Being able to describe work situations and performance prob-lems first-hand can go a long way toward building your credibility with senior management and employees. When Harris Ginsberg (interviewed by the author on Oct. 5, 1990) joined a consumer goods company as a one-person training department, he realized that he needed to get a better feel for the company. He visited its soap production plant and rode to the top of a huge tower that had a slippery catwalk and spewed soap flakes into the air and into the nostrils of anyone inside the plant. The experience was well worth the trouble because it helped Harris obtain first-hand knowledge of work problems and begin to build his reputation as someone who was willing to be involved and learn the business.

Mary Huffman (interviewed by the author on Aug. 21, 1990) was training and development manager for a major newspaper where many employees had been with the organization for more than thirty years. Because these employees had so much experience with the company, Mary decided to take a low-key approach to needs analysis. In one situation the manager of the department in charge of reserving advertisements asked for Mary's help because he was dissatisfied with the way his people handled phone calls. The manager, assuming that communication skills were the problem, asked for a training program to increase his employee's confidence in responding to customer's questions. Wanting to explore the situation further, Mary asked whether she could observe what people did on the job. Because so many people had been with the company for decades, she tactfully asked the phone representatives to "teach me what you do."

From her observations, Mary realized that the employees actually handled most calls very effectively. They lacked confidence only when they did not know answers because they did not have critical information about advertising promotions or strategy. The real need was to improve departmental communication. Mary held a series of informal idea exchanges. During these exchanges people suggested that they needed more information about the whole process in order to serve customers. They needed information, not skills training. Once key information about advertising strategy and promotions was circulated to the telephone representatives, they were able to answer customers' questions more confidently and to offer constructive suggestions to resolve problems.

More formal and complex observational techniques, such as job or task analyses, require a great deal of time and skill. Zemke and Kramlinger (1989) provide excellent guidance on performing such analyses. If you want to conduct a job analysis and have the funds, consider hiring an outside consultant to assist you. Often, however, simple observational techniques will be sufficient for you to gain an understanding of work situations and potential HRD problems.

GUIDELINES FOR CONDUCTING A NEEDS ASSESSMENT AND REPORTING THE RESULTS

It is helpful to take the following items into consideration when you select your approach to needs assessment: degree of management involvement, degree of participant involvement, cost, time needed for implementation, degree of relevant and quantifiable data, ease of implementation, the culture of the organization, and senior management's preferences regarding data collection methods (Newstrom and Lilyquist, 1990). Also to help you select the most appropriate approach, Stephen Steadham (1980) suggests asking yourself the following questions:

- *What resources do I need and have available to conduct the needs assessment?* (Consider costs of processing surveys, indirect costs of using staff to conduct interviews, people available outside the HRD department to help you conduct interviews, and so forth.)

- *What budget is available to implement new programs?* (There is no sense in collecting reams of data in an expensive process if you have an extremely limited budget with which to develop programs.)

- *How much time do I have to develop and implement the data collection process before I have to take action?*

- *Whom do I want to involve in data collection?* Why should I include or exclude certain people?

- *How healthy is my organization?* How confidential should the data be? (If there are massive communication blocks, it is best to avoid group discussion.)

- *Do my sponsors/decision makers prefer one method over another?*

- *To what extent are the needs already known?* Do I want to focus on needs that potential program participants are aware of rather than those that others observe or presume participants have or should have?

- *What are the plans for using the needs assessment results?* (It is extremely important that something constructive happen as a result of your needs assessment, especially if you choose a time-consuming, expensive, or highly visible process.)

In addition to using your own criteria, there are at least a half-dozen general principles that can help you determine your needs assessment strategy.

1. *Use more than one needs assessment method.* There is no one best way to determine what goes on in organizations. Using several methods can

help you validate your data and offset the weaknesses of any one. Organizational documents and questionnaires, for example, may provide important clues to performance problems, but they usually do not pinpoint causes or suggest solutions; you can investigate these with other methods that encourage the involvement of managers and employees. Table 2.1 summarizes the major advantages and disadvantages of various methods you can use to assess HRD needs. Different methods sometimes yield different conclusions because of the limits of any given method. (Differing conclusions can also be the result of the unique perspective of the subjects you select, however. For example, employees are likely to list different needs or wants than their managers do.) People may be more candid on questionnaires than they would be in interviews, particularly in group interviews, where groupthink can be a danger. Using several methods can help overcome these discrepancies. On the other hand, one method—say, interviews—may suggest problems you will want to explore further with another method, such as a survey.

2. *Use methods that involve senior managers.* Involvement creates a sense of ownership among company members and provides you with an opportunity to meet people in the organization. Someone must pay for human resource development, and managers who do not understand how it will benefit the organization will be reluctant to spend money on HRD efforts. When you involve senior managers in your needs analysis—by interviewing them or including them on an advisory committee or review board, for example—they are more likely to understand their needs, why and how HRD can help, and what would happen if no HRD activities took place. When this "joint ownership" of problems is established, managers are not likely to cut the HRD budget or refrain from sending employees to training programs.

3. *Use methods that foster the involvement of potential allies and clients and even of those who are resistant to HRD.* As a one- or two-person HRD department, you will need to call on many people to help you design and deliver your products as well as to support their effectiveness once newly trained employees are back on the job. Getting a broad spectrum of people involved at the needs analysis stage fosters enthusiasm early on and helps you build your resource network. Even those who openly criticize HRD can have valuable ideas about how to improve its effectiveness (Warshauer, 1988).

Let's look at a brief example of how I used an advisory group in an insurance company to determine training needs and elicit involvement. I asked human resource representatives from the major business units to nominate experienced, well-respected supervisors and managers who understood the company's need to increase its leadership skills and would be willing to help develop a leadership training program. In an all-day meeting, this informal advisory group helped me clarify the need for leadership training and design a two-day workshop. The advisory group validated and refined the learning objectives I proposed, suggested learning activities that would work well given organizational norms, and advised me to keep the program to a maximum of two days because of work pressures. Then members of the group helped me test the workshop's effectiveness by participating in a pilot program several months later. One member even helped to co-teach the pilot program.

4. *Ask all available personnel to help.* You may be able to call on people in other parts of the organization for assistance. Susan Warshauer (1988) describes how the HRD manager of a two-person training department in a chain of retail stores asked the human resource generalists to help by conducting interviews with employees in the stores. The generalists normally went to the stores only to deal with crises and problems. Using the generalists in this way enabled the HRD manager and the training assistant to conduct research in collaboration with management and to complete the assessment within a reasonable time.

5. *Include the "right people" in your needs assessment.* The question of who to include and who not to include in the information-gathering portion of your assessment can have political ramifications. As already explained, you will certainly want to know senior management's perception of problems and priorities as well as its attitude toward human resource development before you proceed with your needs assessment. As a rule, start your assessment at the highest level in the organization and work your way down (Zemke and Kramlinger, 1989). It is wise to include anyone who has control over the budget or effectiveness of HRD and is likely to resent being excluded (Warshauer, 1988). Among other possible people to include are managers, experts, potential or former program participants, employees who work for participants, customers, human resource generalists, and members of job-related work groups (Warshauer, 1988). Be sure to include people who are in touch with the real problems of the organization. (Senior

managers may be unaware of the needs of middle managers or front-line employees who do the "real work" of the company.)

Because of limited time and resources, however, you often cannot question all employees. Robinson and Robinson (1989) suggest that you sample at least twelve people in each major category to determine trends. As a general rule, you only need interview or survey four people in the same type of job at any particular level to obtain useful information.

6. *Carefully document and publicize your findings and recommendations in order to build awareness of HRD needs.* In many ways your needs assessment is often your first "product." A well-written, carefully documented needs analysis can enlighten a company as to what its employees need to know or do in order to succeed, as to how HRD can help both employees and managers develop needed competencies, and as to what is required in order for HRD to be successful. Furthermore, the manner in which you present your findings, in both written form and orally, can help build your credibility as an expert who understands the company and how human resource development can improve it.

Although there are many ways that you can present your findings, be sure to create a professional-looking document that highlights your main conclusions. Worksheet 2 in the Resources section of this book can help you prepare your report. Consider including the following information:

- *Business rationale for the needs assessment.* Do not assume that everyone agrees with you that conducting an assessment was necessary. Take care to explain the current business situation that led you to investigate HRD needs and your reasons for conducting the analysis.

- *Brief description of your approach to the needs assessment.* What methods did you use and why? Who was included in the data-gathering process? From what data sources and people did you elicit information?

- *Summary of your major findings and conclusions for key target groups.* What are your major conclusions regarding the key groups for whom you expect to provide HRD programs and services? What are their most urgent needs to develop knowledge and skill in order to perform their current jobs? What skills and knowledge must they learn in order to be prepared for future jobs? How do you know that they do not already have these skills and knowledge? Be sure to provide summary data that clearly support your conclusions, such as numbers that show the extent of the problem. You may also wish to include remarks made by key people who advocate the need for HRD.

■ *Your recommendations.* What do you propose to do on the basis of your findings? If your assessment does not lead to a relevant response, it is useless. Try to make your recommendations address the most urgent business needs in the most cost-effective way.

■ *Cost-benefit information.* It is helpful to show that the benefits of your proposed HRD recommendations outweigh the costs and provide a better return on the investment than some other solution would. You can also compare the costs/benefits of implementing your recommendations with the costs/benefits of not doing so. Senior management is much more likely to endorse your recommendations if you have carefully considered the costs of human resource development.

■ *Implementation.* What actions will be necessary to close the gap in skill and knowledge? What are the next steps and tentative deadlines for carrying out those actions?

What information you share with different people and how you present your conclusions have significant political implications. For example, sharing information about a department or function with the manager *before* it is shared with nonmanagerial employees helps avoid embarrassing the manager. Also, managers may wish to influence whether and how findings of the assessment are presented to their employees to avoid the risk of raising false expectations.

. . . .

SUCCESS STORIES

Let's look at how some successful HRD managers have handled the challenge of assessing a company's business priorities and HRD needs and forming a partnership with its senior management.

Building a Partnership with Future Resources in an Investment Firm

Joanne Rogovin, whom we met in the first chapter, served as training manager of Kidder Peabody, a leading investment firm. She was hired following a period of turmoil to help build a management perspective. The previous training manager had done virtually no work above the supervisory level. Not surprisingly, Kidder's managing directors saw themselves not as managers but as supertraders. The mandate from Joanne's boss was "Do what you think is best—you're the expert." How did she determine what to do? In her words, she took advantage of the opportunity to play "new kid on the block" by interviewing the managing directors and asking them about their businesses and the stumbling-blocks they faced. During this time Joanne built relationships with managers whom she later used as experts to assist in the design and instruction of training programs that were produced with the help of outside consultants. Joanne set herself up not as the expert but as a facilitator and consultant. Through the extensive use of line managers, she established a climate where the managers "owned" the training. Sharing ownership is what partnership is all about.

Creating Widespread Involvement in Assessing HRD Needs in a Regional Hospital

Understanding an organization's business priorities and mission and working as part of a team play an important role in building a partnership with the organization. Mike Kusinitz, who was also introduced in Chapter One, was hired as manager of training and development for a large regional hospital that had gone without management training for quite awhile. With only a part-time secretary as his support staff, Mike was responsible for providing human resource development to approximately three hundred managers. How did he determine what needed to be done? During the first month, he interviewed senior management—the senior physicians/chairpersons of ten departments, as well as supervisors in key areas—to gain an understanding of the hospital's priorities and mission and to determine how decisions were made and what skills people had or needed to develop. He observed that managers saw the organization as a not-for-profit hospital even though the CEO wanted people to treat it as a for-profit operation.

Mike realized that more than training would be necessary to support the CEO's goals of enabling doctors to be responsible for management and budgets, pushing decision making down to lower levels, providing recognition to employees, and improving communication.

After one month of interviewing, Mike wrote a report stating that before there could be any training in support of the organization's mission, the CEO needed to communicate his vision to the employees. Mike worked closely with the CEO on a two-hour management interaction program, in which the CEO introduced the key corporate concepts to the management team. Following a film on excellence in business, Mike led a discussion on what managers liked or disliked about the corporate concepts, why they were not following them, and what managers needed to do or have in order to implement them. On the basis of this discussion, Mike helped develop a number of formal and informal human resource programs that improved communication, employee recognition, and skills by bringing together people from all levels of the organization. He recognized the need to develop human resource programs that went beyond the usual scope of HRD before he could effectively implement more traditional HRD programs. Mike's story illustrates how even when your primary responsibility is HRD, you need to work with senior management and others to find out how human resources can best support management's philosophy.

Meeting Business Needs at a Pharmaceutical Company

Sheila Hewitt, whom we met earlier in this chapter, was an HRD manager for the international pharmaceuticals division of Schering Plough International. Under the direction of her manager, David Roy, Sheila provided management training and organizational development to eight thousand employees in more than forty countries. The division had aggressive sales goals and underwent a change from a slow, risk-averse approach to a faster-paced, higher-risk one. Sheila conducted her initial needs analysis by looking at performance appraisals and development plans, interviewing personnel in different parts of the world, and examining various management inventories. She worked closely with the president of Schering International, who was instrumental in the change in approach. Through an informal process, Sheila and the human resource team discovered that senior managers were not always reinforcing the president's key values. She helped solidify the management team by working with outside consultants to design a three-day leadership program and team-building session for the senior managers. This program was extended over the following two years in a series of ongoing workshops.

Sheila and her former manager are extremely business-focused. Their programs are based on business needs and coordinated with business functions. For example, when the company was developing a business strategy, it became clear that the managers in one geographic area needed to learn about strategic thinking. Sheila hired a consultant to develop a strategic thinking and implementation program that centered on an actual business case and was customized to Schering's business-planning process. Initially offered in one geographical area, the program was so successful that it was then offered to managers in other parts of the world as well.

Discovering HRD Needs at an Industrial Manufacturing Company

Tennant, a leading manufacturer of nonresidential floor maintenance equipment and related products, is known for its quality, service, and commitment to employee involvement and training. At Tennant, different training managers are in charge of quality service, sales, technical, and employee training. Iris Staubus (interviewed by the author on June 26, 1990) manages a one-person employee training department that serves 950 employees in the Minneapolis area. At management's request, Iris spent her first nine months on the job determining how well the existing training programs were meeting the company's needs.

First, she led focus groups to uncover the prevailing concerns. Then, working with the research department, Iris developed separate questionnaires for employees and managers. She asked employees to indicate whether current training programs served their needs, which additional training courses would be important, and what the employees' preferences were for delivery of training. One-third of all employees returned the survey; they expressed an interest in more than two hundred topics. This diversity of needs led Iris to subscribe to an outside service that helped her identify external training opportunities in the Minneapolis area.

The managers' survey asked managers to rate themselves on their need to develop in sixteen skill areas and to indicate their preferences for delivery of training. Half of all managers returned the survey. Their self-assessments led to the beginning of a management development program focusing first on areas where the strongest needs were indicated.

Iris used other channels in her needs assessment as well. She asked other companies about their approaches to training and also examined internal training data to detect trends—for example, one-on-one communication skills training had been emphasized in the early 1980s but had been neglected later in the decade. As part of a communications study, Iris chaired a committee to investigate communications training for managers and supervisors by looking at focus-group transcripts. Comments to the effect that meetings were not conducted efficiently and that agendas were not followed indicated that managers needed to improve their communication skills.

Finally, Iris presented her findings and recommendations to management, who agreed with her main findings and also suggested that Tennant model itself on the best companies and measure its training effectiveness more formally. As a result of her analysis. Iris developed a three-year training plan that was shared with managers and nonmanagers. Twice a year she produces a calendar that lists a curriculum of more than fifty courses and sends it to all employees. Training at Tennant is viewed as a process that is integral to the company rather than as a series of programs offered piecemeal.

SUMMARY: STRATEGIES FOR ASSESSING YOUR COMPANY'S BUSINESS PRIORITIES AND HRD NEEDS

1. Remember that your needs assessment is the key to your success. Time spent on a well-planned assessment pays off in the quality of your programs and in the effectiveness of your approach. Your needs assessment helps you to establish your credibility, gather information needed to develop your strategy and programs, generate enthusiasm for and "ownership" of human resource development, and build a partnership with the business.

2. Take advantage of the numerous needs assessment methods available to you: organizational documents, surveys and questionnaires, interviews (with groups or individuals), advisory committees, and observation of work situations. Using a combination of approaches gives you multiple perspectives and more valid information than using a single one.

3. Consider these guidelines in conducting a needs analysis:

    ■   Use assessment methods that enable you to obtain the involvement of senior managers and employees.

    ■   Include interactive methods that provide you with visibility and richer information and begin to build key relationships.

    ■   Ask all available personnel to help.

    ■   Include the right people in your needs assessment.

4. In your report of your assessment, document your findings. Also be sure to include the business rationale for the assessment, a summary of your approach to the assessment, major findings on gaps in skill and knowledge for each key population, your recommendations for action, cost-benefit information regarding your recommendations, and proposed next steps.

Creating a Business-Focused HRD Plan

*I*n a small HRD department you must strive to be responsive to the business needs of your company and to deliver what you promise. One of your biggest challenges is setting priorities and clarifying how your HRD department can best help your company. Line managers who have problems within their departments may bombard you with all sorts of requests for training, especially if there has never been a training department before. Wanting to be responsive, you may say yes to every request and find that you are involved in low-impact activities or that you have made commitments you cannot fulfill.

According to Joanne Rogovin, former training manager at Kidder Peabody: "It's important to find out where the real value-added is versus what kills time and has no payoff. It is easy to be seduced by interesting projects that lack impact. You may be tempted to say yes to everything, but this can lead you down some blind alleys" (interview with the author, Feb. 7, 1990). For example, a managing director whose department had mushroomed from 4 to 250 people in one year told Joanne he needed help with improving his staff members' time management because people were "spinning their wheels." After some investigation, Joanne realized that inefficient time management was not the core problem; the problem was that people were uncertain of the department's direction and mission and of their roles within it. Joanne was able to help the director see that he needed to articulate and clarify his business mission. His staff needed to work as a group to set goals, determine roles, and set measures and schedules *before* time management training could have an impact.

The road to success lies in forming a partnership in which you and the key business managers can jointly agree on what the priority HRD needs are and what is required for you to meet these needs successfully. In the book *Training for Impact*, Dana and James Robinson (1989) describe the importance of collaborating with management to determine the most critical business issues and how HRD can contribute to the success of the organization by preparing employees to achieve its objectives. As discussed in Chapter Two, your needs assessment can be a major tool in building management commitment and ownership of the HRD process. If you work with management to identify clearly how human resource development can help solve business problems and contribute to the bottom line, it is easier to build support for strategic HRD programs. Instead of functioning as a one- or two-person HRD department, a business-focused HRD manager can often gain the cooperation of people throughout the organization who can help identify training needs and design, develop, and even teach programs.

• •

FORMULATING YOUR DEPARTMENT'S MISSION

A mission that is shared with and agreed to by management helps focus your efforts and keeps you from being pulled in different directions. You will want to formulate a mission for your HRD department that is based on your assessment of business issues, needs, and objectives in the coming year and in the more distant future. Your mission statement should broadly describe how your function will contribute to the organization. It should clarify the types of programs and services you plan to offer, and to which people you propose to offer them, and how you intend to collaborate with the organization. This statement should focus on populations most essential to the success of the company and address their most urgent developmental needs.

You will want to specify what your initial direction will be and how it will need to change in order to support the company over the long term. For example, the manager of a new HRD department in a small savings bank was initially responsible for computer-conversion training. Once the conversion was accomplished, the manager was able to expand her mission to include much needed training in interpersonal and management skills.

Because you cannot address every developmental need of the organization, it is necessary to determine where you can have the most impact. Your needs assessment should help you to decide where to focus your efforts — on the management population and the skills they need to direct the company or on the workers and the technical skills they need to perform their jobs. You might, for example, need to concentrate on one or more of the following types of HRD programs: management/supervisory training, new-employee orientation, or technical/data processing training.

Your mission should support the business trend of your company. Is the company going through a period of expansion, or is it cutting back? If it is expanding by acquiring other companies or hiring many people, your number one priority may be to provide an orientation program. New employees will need a quick way to gain an understanding of the organization's mission, goals, strategies, norms, and operating procedures. Providing employee orientation not only helps you meet a vital need of the organization, but it also helps you learn the business and build relationships with employees at a time when they are most impressionable.

In establishing your mission, first determine which *functional groups* — sales, service, manufacturing, quality control, or finance — are most vital to your organization's business strategy.

Next, decide what *organizational level(s)* you should concentrate on: managers, front-line supervisors, or workers. Focus your HRD programs and communication on the level(s) most crucial to the business of the organization and most in need of HRD. For example, you may need to concentrate primarily on managerial training if your organization is growing so rapidly that inexperienced employees have been promoted into managerial positions without having had time to learn management skills through experience or training. If your company is undergoing significant strategic change, you should concentrate on managers who are instrumental in bringing about the change. On the other hand, if your company is introducing new work procedures, concentrate on the employees who are using the new procedures.

Third, identify the *types of HRD programs and services* that are most essential to your priority customers. If your organization has highly ambitious leadership goals and is experiencing rapid growth, you may want to concentrate on training programs that teach leadership skills to executives and managers. On the other hand, if you are in a financial services organization in a weak economy and your company is faced with burgeoning loan losses, you may need to offer training that enables risk managers to identify risky loans and to manage the loan portfolio more effectively. If your company's major objective is reducing expenses and increasing productivity, your number one priority may be working with production managers to develop training programs that teach people the skills and procedures needed to achieve expense and productivity goals.

Consider the importance of technology in your organization. Is your company dependent on technology for success or introducing new technology throughout the organization? If technology is key to your company's business, you may need to concentrate on technology training to ensure that all employees know how to make the most of your organization's technological capabilities. Large companies usually have separate technology and management training departments, but in a small company you may need to offer both technology and management training. If your mission includes providing technology training, there are special resource implications for your department. People will need to practice working with various computer programs if they are to gain skill in using them. The technology training manager needs to have access to on- or off-site computer-training facilities.

Once you have completed your needs assessment, you can use Worksheet 3 in the Resources section to help you create your own mission. For sample mission statements, see Exhibits 3.1 and 3.2. The *ASTD Trainer's Toolkit: Mission Statements for HRD* (Olivetti, 1990) is also a useful reference that includes sample HRD mission statements and helpful ideas on how to write a mission statement.

The mission statement shown in Exhibit 3.1 (on page 44) is intended to illustrate the types of information that can be included in the mission statement of a small HRD department. International Consumer Banking (ICB) Management Development consisted of a training manager and an administrative assistant and was responsible for overseeing management training in approximately fifteen countries. ICB local staffs were relatively small and were managed by an ICB country manager. Countries were grouped into three large geographic areas, which were managed by three area consumer executives (ACEs). Some countries had an ICB-dedicated human resource manager, but only three countries had large enough businesses to justify an ICB-dedicated training manager. Exhibit 3.1 presents a modified version of ICB Management Development's mission statement, which includes information about the curriculum and how to participate in it.

Exhibit 3.1. Sample Mission Statement:
International Consumer Banking Management Development.

Mission. The mission of ICB Management Development is to provide quality training and development to develop required skills and knowledge of key international consumer managers in priority countries in support of the business objectives.

Populations Served. The target population for training is the country consumer banking manager, direct reports of the country consumer manager, and other key consumer managers, as well as ICB support staff.

Strategies. We will use the following strategies to support the mission:

- Conduct training needs analyses and plan developmental activities for key positions
- Develop and deliver customized international consumer-dedicated training programs
- Coordinate participation in relevant, high-quality training programs sponsored by other Chase Manhattan divisions and select vendors
- Conduct train-the-trainer programs for ICB managers who will instruct Chase and vendor programs locally
- Support area consumer executives and ICB country managers in development planning and identification of appropriate developmental experiences
- Evaluate and track participation in training (quality of training, numbers of people trained, cost of training and its impact)

Training and Development Curriculum. The ICB training curriculum provides a systematic process for the development of required skills among ICB managers. The curriculum is a broad-based modular system that can be tailored to individual needs. For each module there is a core program providing knowledge considered essential for designated ICB managers. The following eight modules have been identified as necessary for ICB managers:

1. Business Planning and Control
2. Managing Organizational Change
3. Marketing Management
4. Branch Management
5. Consumer Products and Services
6. Human Resource Management
7. Risk Management
8. Operations and Systems Management

For several modules there are elective programs appropriate for managers on a selected basis. Refer to the program catalogue for a description of the program objectives, target audiences, and prerequisite courses. ICB country managers should meet with their area consumer executives to determine the most appropriate training for themselves and their key managers on the basis of developmental needs. In general, core courses should be taken in the order listed since program content builds on knowledge learned in previous modules. The ICB training manager will work closely with the consumer area executives to identify candidates for specific training programs.

UNUM Life Insurance Company of America is the leading disability insurance company in the United States. UNUM has approximately fifty-five hundred employees worldwide, thirty-five hundred of whom are located in Portland, Maine, its home base. Training at UNUM is partly centralized in a corporate HRD department and partly decentralized in various business divisions. The mission statement shown in Exhibit 3.2 (on page 46) represents part of the corporate HRD department's charter, which is intended to help clarify the purpose of the department for internal customers.

· ·

GUIDELINES FOR DEVELOPING YOUR PLAN

Once you have determined your HRD department's mission, created a mission statement, and gained the support of key stakeholders, you will want to develop a plan that spells out what you intend to accomplish over the coming year. HRD departments that have a mission and a plan that are tied to the organization's goals will be much more likely to have an impact on the organization than departments that act only in response to requests for human resource development. Let's review some guidelines for creating a successful plan.

Focus on Business Priorities and Key Populations

It is important that you and senior management have a common understanding of what your business-focused objectives are for the coming year. Consider the condition of the business—is it growing, stabilizing, or shrinking? On the basis of your answer to this question, focus your programs on building sales, providing leadership, containing costs, improving quality, managing change, and so on. Determine where your company is most vulnerable and provide appropriate support. Once you are relatively certain that you have pinpointed the right things to do, you need to formulate a reasonable implementation plan.

Set Realistic Objectives

Take into account your resource and budgetary constraints and the business environment. A common mistake is to think that you can do every-

Exhibit 3.2. Sample Mission Statement: UNUM Training and Development Charter.

Mission

- Provide employees with a common foundation and framework needed to operate effectively in today's business environment
- Design and implement training programs that teach critical competencies needed to meet business challenges
- Support the divisions in the delivery of corporate training programs within the business units and functions where applicable

Leadership Role

- Provide a framework for training to ensure linkages between training for all levels and to ensure that all employees have critical competencies to meet business challenges
- Ensure that training and development are aligned with business needs by

  Assessing training needs against business goals and strategies
  Providing quality assessment of programs
  Measuring the impact of training on business results

- Provide education and guidance to UNUM managers and employees on how to move UNUM forward in becoming a "learning organization"
- Encourage collaboration and synergy in development and delivery of training across business units and functions throughout UNUM

Primary Accountabilities

- Develop training programs that teach managers generic competencies that cut across business units and functions
- Provide guidance to managers and division directors regarding appropriate training and development interventions for managers and individual contributors
- For Portland-located employees, provide access to training programs that teach competencies needed to live out the vision and values, and marketing strategy; develop or identify training programs and learning experiences that teach employees crucial, generic competencies required by the corporation as a whole
- For employees located outside of Portland, look for creative ways to export relevant parts of the curriculum through technology and decentralized resources
- Provide train-the-trainer support to help prepare decentralized trainers and managers to deliver training programs

thing and to try to satisfy everyone. Attempting to meet unrealistic goals jeopardizes your work, your credibility, and your health. When I began my assignment in the International Consumer Banking Division at Chase, I developed a clear mission: to develop and oversee the implementation of a management curriculum for our key managers overseas. Senior management was very enthusiastic about the proposed curriculum. Unfortunately, in my eagerness to accomplish my mission I proposed an unrealistic implementation plan that was endorsed by my manager, who was not an experienced HRD professional. Later I realized that the deadlines I had proposed would seriously jeopardize program quality, but I knew I could change my original schedule only if business conditions dictated such a change. Fortunately, just when I thought I was going to turn into a "training factory," conditions did change, allowing me to shift to a more reasonable schedule. It was a hard lesson, and one I will never forget.

In putting together a schedule, consider the time required to determine specific needs for programs, develop materials, select and prepare instructors, and arrange for training facilities. You will also need to allow enough time to announce programs, identify participants, follow up on registration, and send out confirmation notices and preprogram assignments. If you are in a one- or two-person department, you are likely to be involved in all of these activities.

In creating your plan, you must also consider your development strategy: whether to buy off-the-shelf programs or develop your own. It takes time to develop good programs. If you have a small budget, you may not be able to use outside consultants to design programs or to teach them. Even if you do use outside consultants to develop programs, you must set aside enough time to conduct a needs analysis and to manage program development. Decide how often you expect to offer programs. If you are developing programs that will be repeated several times, you will need time to pilot the program and develop a leader's guide.

The instructors you use will affect the time needed to implement programs. Decide whether you will use outside consultants, line managers, or employees as instructors or whether you or another trainer will be doing the teaching. If you are the sole instructor, that will limit the number of programs you can offer, as well as the scope of your contribution. On the other hand, if you use line managers as instructors, you will need time to conduct instructor training. We will explore delivery strategies in more detail in Chapter Four.

Project the Resources Necessary to Accomplish Your Objectives

Managing others' expectations is very important in building your credibility. Managers are often not aware of what is required to produce and implement successful HRD programs. Bob Jendusa, the former HRD manager of a southern newspaper mentioned earlier, puts it this way: "You need to realize you can't fix a year-old problem with a one-day program. You cannot fix a $100,000 problem with a $10 training program. It can be real frustrating because managers want you to. You have to be careful about setting expectations" (interview with the author, Feb. 14, 1990).

Managers frequently understand neither the nature of the real problems nor the amount of time, money, work, and collaboration required in a successful HRD effort. You will need to advise management of the requirements of different HRD strategies. If deadlines are tight, you may need to pull in outside resources that cost more money. In most cases and especially if both deadlines and budget are tight, you will probably need to request the cooperation of many people in order to produce an effective program. In addition, you may have to explain the other types of activities necessary for large-scale change. For example, the training manager of a midwestern bank was asked to single-handedly turn the company into a sales-driven organization solely through the use of sales training programs carried out over a twelve-month period, and without considering the need to provide for ways to reward and track sales. She had to explain to management that in creating a "sales culture," tracking the activities of the sales force and rewarding members for sales are as important as teaching them selling skills.

Build in Flexibility to Make Changes as Conditions Change

Sometimes new training needs arise along with business or organizational change such as the introduction of new products or technology, changes in market conditions, or unexpected turnover. You will want to make your plan a "living" document that changes as business priorities change. It is useful to brainstorm possible business changes and "what if" strategies to deal with various scenarios. For example, organizations sometimes cut back their HRD budgets midway through the year on the basis of the organization's performance. It is helpful to consider in advance how you would operate if your budget were reduced. If you are serving a geographically dispersed population, you should consider the implications of alternate delivery strategies and delivery sites.

YOUR FIRST PROGRAM: STARTING OUT ON THE RIGHT FOOT

Your first program is crucial to your credibility. One training manager for an international bank gives this advice: "People may perceive a lack of commitment to training when the training department is small. You can overcome this perception with some visible 'wins' so that people see the results. Start small and focus on managers who support training. Get a 'win' before you institutionalize something and roll it out to others."

Criteria for a Successful First Program

A successful first program must meet the following criteria: have management sponsorship, address a genuine business-focused need, have business-wide impact, meet important deadlines, provide appropriate alternatives to training, when necessary, and have a receptive target audience. Worksheet 4 in Resources can help you to make a wise selection. Let's briefly review each of these criteria.

Obtaining Management Sponsorship. It is best to begin with a program endorsed by senior management. As Robinson and Robinson (1989) point out, for HRD to have an impact on the organization, there must be both quality training in which requisite skills are learned and a work environment that encourages the use of these skills on the job. As HRD manager, you are responsible for the quality of the learning experience; the business manager is responsible for the quality of the work environment. For the business manager to want to provide a work environment that supports training, he or she has to believe in the value of the program. The answers to the following questions can help you assess management's level of sponsorship:

- How important is the enactment of the program to senior management?

- Will anyone in management care if the program is not enacted?

- What level of management commitment is required for the program to succeed?

- What is senior management willing to do to support the program?

Senior managers will look to you for information about what type of support is needed from them. Support can take many forms. For example, you can ask senior managers to provide money for program development, identify internal resources (subject-matter experts) who can help develop the program and possibly serve as instructors, sign a memo announcing the importance of the program, recommend potential candidates to attend the program, be a speaker at the program, review the evaluation of the program, and support needed program revisions. Most importantly, senior managers can hold managers accountable for a work environment that supports the implementation of skills and knowledge taught in the program.

Addressing a True Business-Focused Need.   Choose a program that helps solve a business problem or takes advantage of a future business opportunity. Make sure that key clients perceive that the program meets a real need, not merely addresses a need that only you have identified.

Determining Potential Impact on the Business.   Focus on a topic and population that are key to the organization's success. Consider whether there is some legal, regulatory, or external pressure to offer a particular program at a certain time. For example, many companies began to offer sexual harassment prevention training as a result of the heightened awareness of sexual harassment following the Senate confirmation hearings on Clarence Thomas's nomination to the Supreme Court in the fall of 1991. In another example, Joanne Rogovin's selection of an ethics course as her first program was prompted by a Securities and Exchange Commission ruling against her company.

Meeting an Important Deadline.   Choose a program that can be developed or purchased in time to meet the organization's needs. In some cases you may already have designed a program or been certified to teach a program in a previous job or company. Can you use this expertise to meet a need early on? Some programs require a long period of time to develop. You do not want to jeopardize quality in order to meet an unrealistic deadline. On the other hand, when senior management is fully supportive, you can often achieve a great deal in a short period of time. As noted earlier, Ann Barkey, former HRD manager for Fred the Furrier, started a one-person department and was able to produce a successful one-week program a month after joining the company even though she was new to the fur industry. She made it clear to senior management that many employees would have to help identify content and participate in instruction during the seminar. With management's support, she built a partnership with the sales team and was able to meet the deadline.

Ensuring that Training Is the Appropriate Solution.   In some cases your needs analysis may reveal that other activities must take place before a training program can be effective. For example, recall from Chapter One Mike Kusinitz, the manager of a one-person HRD department in a regional hospital. The hospital's CEO wanted his managers' skills developed, but he needed to clarify his vision and values before management training could have an impact. Mike's first activity was to initiate a series of meetings where he assisted the CEO in persuading his managers to share his vision and in gaining people's commitment to fulfilling that vision. With the groundwork laid, Mike could then begin to offer more traditional training programs in management skills.

Managers can usually tell that a problem exists, but sometimes they view training as an appropriate solution when it is not. For example, in managing a small HRD department for a newspaper, Bob Jendusa (referred to earlier) conducted a thorough needs analysis. One department manager was having trouble with recruitment and wanted Bob to conduct training to improve his staff's skills in conducting recruitment interviews. Bob discovered that the employees knew how to conduct interviews but were exhausted from working sixty-hour weeks with no days off and had no time to interview people. The problem could not be solved by skills training; the department needed to hire more staff so that members could complete their work and be allowed time off.

Selecting a Receptive Target Audience.   It is vital that you gain good publicity from a successful first program. To do this, you will want to begin with a receptive audience who will help you build a reputation as a useful resource. In Bob Jendusa's words: "Don't beat your head against a wall. Go to a department where you have cooperation. Work where you've had successes. The word will spread around that what you do works" (interview with the author, Feb. 14, 1990). Even if your target audience is not initially receptive to training, you can present training as a way of solving a business problem or helping to make people's lives easier so that people can see its value.

SUCCESS STORIES

Let's look at how some HRD managers of small departments made their first programs a success.

Launching a Training Program in an Insurance Company

Even though you may be told what it is that management would like you to accomplish, it is important that you clarify your mission by learning as much as you can about the organization and its needs. Carolyn Balling (interview with author, June 20, 1990) directed a three-person HRD department in a small life insurance company that sold insurance policies primarily through the mail. When Carolyn started, the company had had virtually no training programs in more than a year, when the company was divested from its parent organization. She was hired to "get training started again and to put supervisory and management training in place" and to meet needs identified by a comprehensive firmwide training-needs analysis conducted in the previous year.

Carolyn decided to update the analysis and to learn about the company by talking to all the vice presidents to determine what their issues were and "what would make their lives easier." She also sent a survey to supervisors, managers, and directors, asking about the training they had had in the past and what they saw as the biggest issues facing them, their peers, and the people above and below them. She found that the needs for supervisory and management training and for orientation, insurance, and communications training had not changed much in a year. She reported the data to management during lunch meetings and to focus groups at different levels. This allowed her to flesh out some issues and confirm that the data were accurate. The process gave her the opportunity to explain her role, to orient herself to the company's goals, to gain support, and to identify potential best customers.

On the basis of her needs assessment, Carolyn gained management's agreement about what the priorities were and then took action. She was able to develop an orientation program, select a packaged program for management and supervisory training, provide consulting on how to improve communications, and improve the cost-effectiveness of technical training on life insurance. Carolyn offers this advice to small HRD departments: "Pick your spots. Figure out what your role should be and help the company to use you that way. Balance operational and strategic issues. Keep the company focused on how to use you—to determine needs, provide solutions and help manage change" (interview with the author, June 20, 1990).

Establishing HRD Credibility in an Insurance Company

Ellen Kamp (interview with the author, March 13, 1991) was hired by Corroon and Black (now known as Willis Corroon), America's fifth largest insurance broker, to set up a corporate training and development department at a time when little formal training existed and training was seen as a line responsibility. Ellen, who had experience with starting up training departments in the insurance industry, was attracted to the company because of the vision of its CEO, Dick Miller, who wanted to develop talent from within and to create the best development program in the industry. Acting as a one-person department during her first year at Corroon, Ellen was convinced of Miller's commitment to development and his desire to build a solid function even though Ellen's predecessor had left after only a few months. With a chuckle Ellen recounts her first day at work. On her desk was a memo from the CEO, requesting her plan for the year by the end of the week. Clearly that was not enough time to conduct a thorough needs assessment, yet Ellen knew she needed to produce a plan.

She also knew she could not conduct a survey because the previous training manager had spent all his time working on a survey—raising expectations and then doing nothing. She realized that the CEO wanted and expected her to do workshops. In Ellen's words: "You have to give them what they want, and then figure out what they need." She proposed offering "safe topics" that were real needs: management skills, presentation skills, writing skills, and sales skills. In her plan, she gave herself six months before offering the first course. During that time Ellen worked on preparing for delivery of the courses and on getting to know the company. She also worked on solving the company's need for a coherent education reimbursement policy because Corroon's subsidiaries had more than forty different policies. She was able to use her proposed policy and her training plan as a way of talking to the senior managers and regional directors at key meetings and discussing with them what human resource development could do for the organization.

Ellen took a risk and published a professional-looking brochure that resembled an annual report and described the courses she would offer. The booklet was of the highest quality to show that "the department was here to stay." By purchasing courses and tailoring them herself, Ellen was able to meet her deadline and to spend her time teaching rather than developing programs. Being in the classroom helped Ellen gain visibility, learn about real issues in the company, and demonstrate how training could teach valuable skills.

Ellen believes that it is too easy for a small HRD department to be reactive: "You need to have a vision and share it with others so that they buy it." Ellen's vision "is to have management understand how professional development is integrated into the success of their business goals—to have them understand that we provide the tools to help make their goals happen." Ellen knows that being successful early on is a key to building credibility. "In choosing where to begin, start where you are going to have success. You don't have to be everywhere in a company. Work in a division where you can have an impact, and figure out a way to add value. I'm a firm believer that success breeds success." Ellen did such an excellent job of establishing her credibility that by year's end all the training staff within Corroon Black reported to her.

Improving the Hiring Process in a Restaurant Chain

Ann Barkey (whose experience in a fur company you read about earlier) was also director of personnel and training for a national restaurant chain that had sixty-eight restaurants and three thousand employees in eight states divided into several regions. One of Ann's mandates was to start a training function because the company president believed that training was needed to improve service. The company had several regional directors who oversaw management of restaurants in their regions but who had limited authority. One pressing problem that affected service was employee turnover, which was almost 100 percent. The chain's highly inefficient hiring process severely restricted what Ann and the regional directors could do. As the personnel and training director, Ann hired the restaurant managers for all sixty-eight units. These managers in turn hired local people to work in their restaurants, but the regional directors had no hiring responsibilities.

Ann decided that her first training program should teach regional directors how to interview and hire people. She viewed the regional directors as "disempowered people who were supposed to manage but who did not feel part of the process. They had no ownership." Ann wanted them to be able to hire restaurant managers. She convinced the regional directors that this program would save them money since she would not have to fly all over the country to conduct the interviews and that the plan would save time because there was a need to replace people immediately.

As Ann describes it, she chose this program "out of instinct—I said to myself, 'I have to do something. What will give me the most ability to do my own job?' The situation was difficult because it involved training four people to do something that they thought they could already do but that they really did not know how to do most effectively." Since Ann was dealing with people who were convinced that they were already experts in the material she was teaching, she decided to teach them in individual half-day tutorial sessions.

As a result of the program and at Ann's insistence, the regional directors were given more authority to hire restaurant managers. The program had a significant effect. According to Ann, "regional directors felt: 'I hired this guy; I'm going to get him to succeed.' The group was inspired to be the best. There was a commitment to spread the word to their stores" (interview with the author, Jan. 30, 1990).

Retraining Tellers in a Regional Bank

Carrying out one's first significant program or project well can help tremendously in building credibility. A successful first program or project can actually result in a trainer's earning the position of HRD manager. Mary, a fictitious name for a real person, worked for a regional bank. She was originally hired as a teller to roam from branch to branch to provide refresher training for other tellers. On the basis of her initial work, rewriting the teller training manual, Mary was asked to join the training department as a trainer reporting to the training coordinator.

In the early 1980s the bank was having financial difficulties; the new head of retail banking recognized that a massive training effort would be required if people were to do things differently. It was clear that people did not understand their job responsibilities, and there was no consistency in the implementation policies. Mary convinced the new senior manager to let her carry out her program—a project that involved retraining all of the bank's five hundred tellers within six months. Lacking a budget, Mary designed and implemented a teller skills workshop that covered everything from customer service to fraud, systems, transaction processing, and products. To accomplish her objectives, she used the services of a former teller supervisor and three other technical experts whom the company put "on loan" to her. Because of her success, her staff was increased to four after one year.

The retraining project was Mary's first opportunity to coordinate efforts through other departments. It was a challenge to secure the cooperation of all the people needed for the project, but she succeeded by making these people see how valuable they were to the process. The retraining dramatically improved employees' comfort in applying policies and carrying out procedures. As a result, human resource practices were implemented more consistently, and there were fewer financial losses. In addition, employees who did not know answers could now look to trainers for solutions.

Retraining the branch employees was the turning point in Mary's career and led to her promotion to training manager. She believes that the key to success is having "people at the top believe that you can make a difference" and being responsive to their needs. Senior managers "may not clearly articulate the need, but they can recognize whether there is one. Figure out how to deliver the solution. Be there when you're needed."

Changing Managerial Behavior in a Consumer Goods Company

Harris Ginsberg (interviewed by the author on Oct. 5, 1990) was hired as training manager for a major U.S. firm that produces personal and home-care products. In his newly created position, he reported to the assistant director for training and development, who focused on career development, performance appraisal systems, and succession planning. Harris's mandate was to deliver training in oral and written communications, leadership, and management to seven hundred managers, professionals, and high-potential employees who worked at headquarters and in several manufacturing plants. His first major challenge was to learn the politics of the company and the nature of the business because he was new to the industry. He spent his first month talking to key vice presidents and visiting the plants to observe operations, learn the jargon, and find out what was important to people. He and his manager determined the crucial skill areas on which to focus by reviewing the CEO's vision statement and the qualities and activities necessary to the company's success.

Managerial skills appeared to be one pressing problem. Performance appraisals and exit interviews showed that some managers were either overmanaging their staffs or being underinvolved with them. This led to frustration, turnover, and a climate that did not foster cooperation. Other department managers failed to share important information among themselves, which led to costly errors with customers. For example, the sales people made promises that manufacturing could not deliver on. Harris was able to act quickly. He was already certified to conduct an excellent management skills program developed by a reputable consulting firm. Within his first two months on the job, Harris began to roll out the program to core managers, who showed strong support for the training. This ultimately helped to bring communication issues into the open, which improved communications between people in different departments.

Building Credibility Through an Orientation Program for Hospital Employees

Carol Ryan Ertz was hired as a training coordinator for a five-hundred-bed Catholic hospital whose mission was to serve the poor and the needy. Carol was responsible for all nonclinical training, including management skills training, communication skills training, and new-hire orientation for more than two thousand employees, with a special emphasis on supervisors and front-line managers. Nurses and doctors were responsible for the clinical training. Carol's biggest initial challenge was to build the credibility of the one-person training department that had been unstaffed for half a year and previously staffed by a trainer who had neglected to foster relationships with key hospital managers. Carol turned around the department's reputation by taking an important but floundering project and building it into a successful program that other organizations looked to as a model of excellence. How did Carol accomplish this?

Prior to her coming on board, the hospital's vice president of human resources had formed an advisory group that established the need for an orientation program for newly hired employees and provided input as to what the program should contain. The advisory group was consequently disappointed by the slow progress of the program's development. Carol took a sketchy outline for the orientation program and a misguided video script and designed a program that responded to the advisory group's concerns, solved several problems facing the nurse educators, and met a crucial need of the organization.

What made the program so successful? In Carol's words:

> It represented a big change from the previous half-day orientation that was given only once a month and was superficial in terms of content. People often waited for a month before attending the old orientation. Now orientation was held biweekly, and people could not start their jobs until they attended the one-and-a-half-day general hospital orientation. We had senior management represented at every program. The interactive program design encouraged people to explore the meaning of the hospital's values of charity, hospitality, excellence, respect, and integrity. Two videos depicted the hospital's mission, values, and history. And we covered safety training so that people met mandatory "in-service" requirements before starting work. They left the orientation feeling really psyched up and looking forward to contributing to the organization [interview with the author, July 20, 1992].

Carol helped to create a positive attitude by presenting an overview of the program's rationale, content, and benefits to the senior management group and to the head nurses. The orientation had several benefits: it reduced the time people needed to become productive contributors; it brought new employees up to certification standards on safety training; it built an understanding of the organization; and it created a sense of ownership and team spirit. Carol won the support of key influencers—the advisory committee and head nurses—and most important, she won the trust of all the new employees that she oriented. The new employees whom Carol had oriented ultimately became the biggest advocates of training during the four years that Carol worked for the hospital.

· ·

SUMMARY: STRATEGIES FOR CREATING A BUSINESS-FOCUSED HRD PLAN

1. Create a business-focused mission in collaboration with senior management and communicate it widely throughout the organization. Your mission should

describe your target audience, the nature of your products, and how you intend to work in collaboration with the organization.

2. Develop a business-focused, realistic plan to help keep yourself on track.

    ■ Focus on business priorities and key populations. Offer programs that support critical business initiatives and build skills for employees who are involved in carrying out those initiatives.

    ■ Set realistic objectives, taking into consideration your resources and budgetary constraints. (It is better to accomplish one or two important objectives than many insignificant ones.)

    ■ Clearly indicate the amount of people, dollars, and time you will need to accomplish your objectives.

    ■ Build in flexibility so you can make plan changes as business conditions change.

3. Deliver a first program that meets an important business need in a timely way. Successful first programs tend to have many of the following characteristics:

    ■ They have the active endorsement of management.

    ■ They meet an important business need, which is perceived as such by the organization.

    ■ They have the potential to affect the organization positively by focusing on a topic and population that are key to their success.

    ■ They meet a crucial deadline.

    ■ They help solve a business problem or set the stage for an appropriate solution.

    ■ They focus on a receptive target audience.

    ■ They give you visibility and emphasize your value to the organization.

▲ ▲ ▲ ▲ ▲ ▲ ▲ ▲ ▲ ▲ ▲ ▲ ▲ ▲ ▲ ▲ ▲ ▲ *Chapter* **4**

Developing a Cost-Effective Delivery Strategy

O nce you have determined your goals for the year, you need to develop a cost-effective strategy to achieve them. To do this you need to know the advantages and disadvantages of the various approaches to delivering human resource development, such as classroom training, self-study, coaching, and so forth. Should you hire a consultant, use a university-based program, or develop a program using internal resources, and what will each of these alternatives costs? This chapter explores ways to deliver HRD when resources are limited.

WHAT TO CONSIDER IN PLANNING YOUR DELIVERY STRATEGY

In determining how to carry out your business-focused HRD plan, you need to consider several factors: your mission and objectives, budget, time constraints, target audience, your department's and your organization's HRD capabilities, and your company's technological sophistication. Let's look briefly at each of these factors.

Your Mission and Objectives

Are you planning to concentrate on training programs designed to develop knowledge and skills needed to perform one's current job more effectively or on programs designed to prepare people for future jobs? On-the-job training and coaching, for example, are most useful in teaching skills for the current job, whereas workshops can be used to teach skills for either a current or a future job. Will you focus on the managerial skills of managers and supervisors or on the technical skills of nonsupervisory employees? Management training and technical training require different approaches. Managerial skills are generally learned most effectively in workshops, in which there is an opportunity to interact with other people and to receive feedback from them. Technical skills and knowledge, on the other hand, can often be learned through self-study methods and then be reinforced through job aids and opportunities to practice under supervision. Furthermore, technical skills may often be learned through computer-based training (CBT).

Your Budget

Do you have enough money in your budget to hire consultants to assist you with the design and instruction of workshops or with the development of audiovisual or computer-based programs? Even if you have no preassigned budget, prepare to make a persuasive argument to obtain the funding you need to develop or implement your HRD plan. Programs developed and instructed by internal resources may cost less in terms of direct dollars expended, but they may cost more in terms of loss of productivity as a result of time off the job. We will explore budgetary issues in greater depth in Chapter Five.

Your Time Constraints

Do you have the luxury of enough time to develop programs or must you implement them right away? Buying a program is faster than developing one yourself. If you do decide to develop your own program, you should be aware that audiovisual and computer-based programs generally require more time to develop than classroom training.

Your Target Audience's Needs

Consider how easy it will be for your target audience to come to one location at the same time for any type of training. Are employees situated in one or two primary locations, or are they geographically dispersed? Do employees work on a standard shift, or do they work on a variety of shifts? In cases where it is difficult or expensive for employees to come together for training, you will want to consider how you can best deliver on-site training on the employees' time. Computer-based or audiovisually (AV) based training may be best in such circumstances. If you do not have the budget to develop CBT or AV training, consider teaching the material one-on-one or teaching someone to deliver the training locally. If your organization has a central location with a large population and several dispersed field offices, it may be best to train others or hire external consultants to help train field employees.

You will want to consider other characteristics of your target audience as well. How sophisticated are they? If they are not adequately literate, self-study methods that involve reading would not be appropriate. Consider how you expect them to behave in a group setting. Would you expect personality clashes or power struggles that might interfere with learning in a classroom setting? Are they aware that they need training, or do they believe that they are already sufficiently skilled? For employees who are unaware of their need to improve and who are likely to be overly competitive in a group setting, personal coaching may be the best approach.

Sometimes training is not the right solution for the moment. It is important that a team or work unit be ready for human resource development before you intervene to give them skills training or help them work together more effectively. For example, one training manager leapt at the opportunity to conduct a team-building intervention without considering the staffing and performance issues that had to be addressed first. Consider what types of HRD activities people expect. Have they had prior experiences with HRD methods that make them receptive or resistant to specific methods? Typically, when most employees think of human resource development, they think of workshops. It may be necessary for you to offer workshops before introducing other types of activities. In some organizations a foundation for HRD needs to be laid. Remember Mike Kusinitz's case, in which the CEO of a hospital needed to communicate his vision and values to managers before management training programs could effectively teach them the skills needed to realize the CEO's vision.

Your Department's and Your Organization's HRD Capabilities

Consider the size and skills of your department and other possible resources. Do you have someone else to assist you with designing, instructing, and administering programs? Be sure to find out whether there are other departments within the company that can share their training programs or trainers with you. Is there any organizational precedent for using line managers or regular employees to develop or teach HRD programs? At Tennant, Iris Staubus was able to offer a large number of programs because of the widespread employee involvement in HRD. The Customer Service Department of UNUM Life Insurance Company of America was undergoing a major change from a traditional management structure to self-directed work teams and had an urgent need for training in communications skills and change awareness. The corporate training function did not have the resources to train the five hundred customer service employees itself but was able to train employees within customer services to teach these programs so that other employees could be trained in communications skills and change awareness in time to support the redesign effort.

Your Organization's Technological Sophistication

How high-tech is your company? If part of the organization's mission is to be on the leading edge of technology, you may be expected to provide sophisticated audiovisual or computer-based programs. If the organization does not have the capability to develop technologically based programs internally, be ready to present persuasive arguments for spending the money needed to hire a consultant to develop such programs. Companies who have never developed CBT or AV programs are frequently unaware of the amount of money, time, work, cooperation, and testing required to make such programs a success. See Hart (1987) and Kearsley (1983, 1984) for additional information on CBT.

. . . .

EVALUATING YOUR DELIVERY OPTIONS

Although many people think of human resource development as something that occurs in the classroom, there are actually several ways you can teach people the knowledge and skills they need to perform their current jobs more effectively or to prepare for greater responsibility in the future. Among your options are the following:

- Classroom training and workshops
- Coaching (counseling)

- On-the-job training

- Job rotations

- Self-study manuals

- Audiovisual training

- Computer-based training

- Job aids

Table 4.1 provides a summary of the major advantages and disadvantages of each of these approaches. For more detailed information on choosing HRD delivery options, see Heinich and Molenda, 1985; Kearsley, 1984; and Gordon, Zemke, and Jones, 1988. Now let's examine each of the options listed above.

Classroom Training and Workshops

Classroom training and workshops with instructors are excellent methods of teaching complex information that requires frequent updating. They allow you to use a wide range of instructional activities and media, such as lecture, discussion, case studies, role plays, and videotapes, and enable you to reach a large number of people at one time. Using senior-level speakers with high credibility can reinforce the message that the topic is important.

As an interactive method, classroom training and workshops have several advantages over noninteractive methods. You can tailor material to the audience by expanding upon, deleting, or customizing topics and activities to meet a specific group's needs. Participants can ask questions when they don't understand the material and can learn from an instructor who provides insights gained by observing role plays and exercises. In workshops, participants can also learn a great deal from each other. This interaction is essential in skill-building exercises, such as role plays, that require partners. Workshops allow team building in which participants can learn how to work with others in their department, in other functions, in other parts of the organization, or in different geographic locations.

Classroom training and workshops also have their disadvantages. You must either hire an instructor, teach the program yourself, or find other internal resources to do so. When you are teaching, you may have little time

Table 4.1. Advantages and Disadvantages of HRD Delivery Options.

Option	Advantages	Disadvantages
Classroom training and workshops	Excellent way to transmit complex and changing information Easy to update and customize Allow use of wide range of instructional activities and media Can reach many people at once Allow for interactive learning and practice in building interpersonal skills Help build a team	Teaching allows time for little else May require expensive consultants May not work well if group members have different needs Impractical if group members cannot get together at one time Registration process may be cumbersome and cancellations may disrupt program effectiveness
Coaching	Highly personalized, adaptable approach to skill building Allows for practice and frequent feedback Can be highly motivating because of personal attention Useful with those likely to be inhibited in a classroom	Time-consuming Requires sensitivity and skill in teaching and giving constructive feedback Can reach only one or two people at a time Learning limited by experience and skill of coach
On-the-job training	Allows for immediate application of skills and concepts to realities of current job Usually the responsibility of employees' manager or supervisor, not the training manager As training manager, you can improve effectiveness of trainers by designing content, exercises, and visual aids	Employee providing the training may not be an effective teacher or "model" of behavior Job pressures and distractions may interfere with learning May not be appropriate for teaching complex material or risky job behaviors where mistakes would be costly
Job rotations	Useful in training people to substitute for absent employees Build a broad perspective, broad-based skills, and a companywide network of people Promote organizational loyalty and interdepartmental communication Allow for learning from many people in real work situations Practice and real-world application help build skills	Require considerable interdepartmental cooperation and time to set up Managers may be reluctant to teach someone who won't ultimately work in their department People may not be given meaningful work assignments Managers may try to stop good trainees from rotating to other departments
Self-study manuals	Allow trainees to work alone at any location at their own pace Good for trainees who are overly competitive or have varying levels of skill or knowledge Good for providing a common foundation Many good generic manuals available	Trainees may lose interest and not finish manuals No opportunity for clarification Require trainees who can learn by reading Time-consuming to develop and may be difficult to update Limited applicability in teaching interpersonal skills

Table 4.1. Advantages and Disadvantages of HRD Delivery Options, Cont'd.

Option	Advantages	Disadvantages
Audiovisual training	Communicates the same message consistently over time Reaches large audience quickly Good for remote locations (audiotapes can be used in car or at home) May avoid instructor expense Audiovisuals enhance impact of message Good for providing models of effective behavior	Requires equipment Difficult and expensive to update Passive mode of learning (unless interactive video is used), works best when combined with other training methods No opportunity for clarification Production requires technical expertise, equipment, and money
Computer-based training	Efficient learning method Sustains learner's interest better than self-study manuals alone Especially effective when included in interactive video Good for teaching computer skills and technical information that does not change quickly Can sometimes replace a live instructor and save money Good self-assessment programs available	Very expensive, time-consuming, and difficult to develop Requires expertise and testing to debug programs Difficult and expensive to update Requires computer equipment Not very effective in building interpersonal skills Can rarely completely replace a live instructor
Job aids	Communicate a consistent message in an easy reference format Good for identifying correct procedures or clarifying complex information through graphics Relatively inexpensive and easy to update Help reinforce what was learned by other methods Can reach many people at dispersed locations	Limited applicability in teaching interpersonal skills Require technical expertise to develop Require literate trainees who can learn by reading Not effective as a stand-alone method; work best when combined with other methods When ineffective, can confuse people

for anything else. People who work on different shifts or are geographically dispersed may not be able to get together in one location at the same time. Travel can be time-consuming and prohibitively expensive. Classroom training requires some kind of registration process, which can be cumbersome. If participants cancel at the last minute, you may still incur fees from consultants and your course or workshop may be less effective.

Coaching (Counseling)

Coaching, or counseling, involves working individually with people to improve their performance. This usually entails observing a person perform the skill in question, providing the person with feedback, then giving him or her opportunities to refine the skill. The coaching may be done by you or by someone who works closely with the individual. Coaching is a powerful approach to skill building because it is highly personalized: people are most likely to learn when they are given an opportunity to practice a new skill and are given constructive comments about what they do well and about areas in which they need to improve.

Coaching is also useful in dealing with senior-level managers or others who are likely to be inhibited or uncomfortable in a classroom or group setting. Coaching senior-level managers on such matters as making effective presentations can be an excellent way to demonstrate your value to the company and build relationships within it. Remember the case of Ann Barkey's work for a national restaurant chain. She used personal coaching to teach interviewing skills to the regional managers, who were unaware that they needed to improve and unlikely to learn in a setting of their peers. As a result of the coaching, the regional managers became more skilled at hiring and were given more authority in that area. This helped to improve the regional managers' commitment to helping their people succeed on the job and also earned Ann the regional managers' support in other HRD efforts.

While coaching is one of the most effective methods of developing skills, it is extremely time-consuming and requires sensitivity and skill. It is effective in producing large-scale behavior change only if you can teach managers and supervisors to be competent coaches for their employees. You may want to provide workshops to enable supervisors to improve their coaching skills.

On-the-Job Training

In many cases employees can learn the skills they need while they are on the job provided that they are given adequate explanations of what to do, an opportunity to practice under supervision, and feedback about what they are doing correctly and what they need to do differently. It is generally not the role of the HRD department to teach new employees how to perform their jobs. This is usually the manager or supervisor's responsibility. You may, however, be asked to help a manager structure the way that employees learn to do their jobs — a tremendous opportunity for you.

Consulting with managers on how to improve on-the-job training can be an excellent way to learn about the business, to build credibility, and to form key relationships with line managers. Many competent managers are not particularly good teachers: they frequently give long-winded explanations without providing appropriate contexts, use unfamiliar jargon without defining basic terminology, present too much information to be absorbed at one setting, and fail to provide the employee an opportunity to practice. As an HRD consultant, you can help to structure information in a more logical way, develop visual aids that can help employees learn new material, develop a glossary of jargon and terms and acronyms used in the organization, and design exercises that allow employees to practice their newly acquired skills.

Job Rotations

In job rotations individuals work on a specific job for a period of time and then move to another job or jobs in a different area within the company. This can be a useful method of cross-training through which employees learn to perform more than one job so that they can back one another up in case of absence or emergency. Job rotations are particularly useful in management development programs in which trainees need to obtain a broader perspective than they would working at a single entry-level job. Job rotations in entry-level programs are helpful in developing broad-based skill and in promoting loyalty to the company. They help employees improve communication between departments, and they build a network of people throughout the company.

On the other hand, entry-level job rotation programs are time-consuming and require a great deal of interdepartmental cooperation. Some managers have difficulty understanding why they should spend time helping develop someone who will ultimately work for another person or department. Moreover, there is a danger that managers will not give rotating trainees meaningful work to do since they know the trainees will be there for a limited period of time. A manager who likes working with a trainee on a rotation may interfere with the trainee's continuing rotations to try to keep the trainee in his or her department. For entry-level job-rotation programs to be effective, you need to be involved to ensure that managers are providing meaningful work and supporting the goals of the program.

Self-Study Manuals

When it is difficult, expensive, or impractical for employees to come together in a classroom setting, you will want to consider using a self-study approach. Self-study programs can be written manuals or audiovisual or computer-based programs. We will look at each of these separately, although they have some common elements. Self-study approaches have several advantages: they allow employees to work alone, at their own pace, in their own environment. If trainees have varying levels of knowledge and skill or are likely to become highly competitive in a classroom setting, it is best to provide them with a self-study program that allows them to work on their own.

Self-study programs can help new employees orient themselves within the company if the number of people who have been hired is insufficient to justify an orientation class. Self-study approaches can also be used to provide an introduction to a topic that can then be expanded upon by other means. In some cases, off-the-shelf programs relating to your specific industry may be available. For example, among others, there are self-study programs on banking, real estate, insurance, and health care. You may be able to develop self-study manuals yourself provided that you have sufficient writing skills and knowledge of how adults learn.

While self-study manuals have all the advantages noted above, they have disadvantages too. They are time-consuming to develop, difficult to update, and require that their audience be sufficiently literate to learn by reading. Manuals also provide no opportunity to ask questions, and users may lose interest and not complete a manual. Finally, self-study manuals have only limited applicability in teaching interpersonal skills. See Budd (1987) for a helpful resource regarding various self-instructional methods.

Audiovisual Training

There are numerous advantages to using audiovisual aids to deliver HRD. You can communicate the same message consistently and professionally many times. If an AV program can be used on a stand-alone basis, you avoid the expense and trouble of hiring or arranging for a live instructor. If AV equipment is available, you can reach people who would have difficulty attending a workshop. People can listen to audiotapes in their homes or automobiles. Professionally done, an audiovisual aid can enhance the impact of a message. Ultimately, audiovisual training allows you to reach a much larger audience, more quickly, than you could reach with classroom training. If you want everyone in your organization to hear the same message, audiovisuals can be extremely helpful. For example, videos are available on topics such as prevention of sexual harassment and how to deal with a diverse work force.

Videotapes can also be invaluable in teaching skills by providing models of the correct behavior or procedure that you would like people to follow. Audiotapes are excellent tools for teaching audio-based subjects, such as professional telephone skills to customer service and sales representatives. Furthermore, audiovisuals can be used to enhance the effectiveness of other training methods. For example, some video training programs combine videotaped lectures with written workbook exercises.

There are several disadvantages to using audiovisuals. Producing quality videotapes and slides is expensive and requires technical expertise and specialized equipment. Videotapes are not appropriate for teaching information that changes frequently and requires constant updating. As a passive mode of learning, video is less effective than more interactive training methods. You can overcome this disadvantage by combining videotapes with exercises in both the classroom and self-study settings and by using interactive programs that combine video with CBT. For further information on audiovisual training, see Kearsley (1984), Heinich and Molenda (1985), and Wallington (1987).

Computer-Based Training

CBT is a very efficient learning methodology that is appropriate for teaching stable subject matter. CBT involves programming self-study material into a computer so that learners can actively direct the course and pacing of the training, depending on their individual interests and grasp of the material. If learners have trouble answering questions at various checkpoints in the program, they can review material on the computer until they can correctly answer the questions. CBT generally sustains the learner's interest better than self-study manuals. This is especially true of interactive video, which combines computer- and video-based training technologies. If CBT can be used on a stand-alone basis, you avoid the expense and trouble of arranging for an instructor. As with AV training, computer-based training allows you to reach people on-site and on their own time; this may eliminate the expense and difficulty of traveling to a workshop or classroom.

CBT is especially useful for teaching computer skills and other technical information. Some excellent generic CBT programs are now on the market, including various word processing and spreadsheet programs such as Lotus 1-2-3 and Microsoft Excel. Management training computer programs on topics such as assessing one's management style are also available. Internally produced CBT can be a useful way of imparting product knowledge.

Of all the options for delivering human resource development, CBT is the most expensive, time-consuming, and difficult to develop internally. A great deal of technical expertise and much testing are required to debug programs. Furthermore, CBT programs are even more expensive to update than other types of HRD delivery. CBT also requires that you have access to the necessary computer equipment. Although a goal may be to reduce the need for an instructor, it is difficult to produce CBT that completely replaces that need. Several major banks have spent years trying to refine interactive video as a means of teller training, but generally they must still supplement CBT with live instruction. For some helpful pointers on designing interactive training programs, see Hart (1987), Kearsley (1983), Siemasko (1988), and Smith (1988).

Job Aids

Job aids are step-by-step task summaries and written training materials that describe the procedures and practices needed to perform a job. They can be produced fairly cheaply, are easy to revise, and often reduce the amount of training time required. A major benefit is that they can greatly enhance a trainee's memory of knowledge or skills taught in a training program. According to Joe Harless (1985), without job aids, most trainees forget much of what they learn shortly after training. Job aids are especially effective when you need to reach many people who work at remote locations. In some cases, they may be able to substitute for training. Nasman (1988) describes a situation in which a bank was faced with the dilemma of training branch employees to fill out student loan applications correctly — an infrequent but complex procedure. Job aids, which break down complex tasks into simpler ones, were a perfect solution to the problem. They made it easier to explain the loan application process to new people and served as a useful reference when employees needed to complete applications correctly.

Job aids are most effective when combined with other methods because they provide no opportunity to ask questions, interact with others, or receive feedback. In some cases job aids may involve technology, such as a computer system that stores information about products or procedures. UNUM Life Insurance Company of America, for example, has its management practices guide on-line for ready access and updating.

Let's look at an example of effective use of written and computerized job aids. Tom managed a one-person training department for a call-in product information center of a bank. The center was open twenty-four hours a day, seven days a week. Product information specialists needed to be able to respond quickly to customers' questions about a wide variety of financial services provided by several different departments. Tom provided a month of classroom training to give the information specialists an introduction to financial services, product knowledge, and customer service skills. He also used two different types of job aids to help specialists remember the vast amount of information they needed. Product information stored in a computer system provided a summary of product features, benefits, pricing, and answers to typical customer questions. In addition, Tom worked with a consultant to develop a brief written product chart to serve as a quick reference to all the bank's products. This job aid was also used by customer service representatives in other departments who did not have access to the information center's computer system.

In summary, job aids can reduce the amount of training time required, improve the amount of knowledge retained after training, and in some cases entirely replace training. See "How to Produce Great Job Aids" (McCampbell, 1989) for some helpful tips on producing effective job aids.

SELECTING A PROGRAM DEVELOPMENT STRATEGY

When it comes to obtaining programs, you have several options:

- Design programs yourself.

- Work with other resources within the company to design programs.

- Buy off-the-shelf programs.

- Hire consultants to design or customize programs.

- Use programs offered by colleges or universities.

- Use some combination of the above.

Designing Programs Yourself

Designing programs yourself has numerous advantages. If you have a small budget and cannot afford outside consultants, this option enables you to achieve a high-quality program. You have control over the program materials: you can customize them for your organization, update them when changes occur, and reproduce them with variations, all at minor expense. For programs that you plan to instruct yourself, being involved in the program design enables you to cut corners with the leader's guide and decreases the time you will need to prepare for teaching. Designing programs can also be an excellent opportunity to build relationships with employees and to learn about how your organization operates.

There are disadvantages to designing all of your programs yourself, however. If you lack expertise in the subject, your programs may be limited in depth. If production capability in your department is limited, the quality of your program materials may be low or your ability to meet a crucial deadline may be compromised. Furthermore, if you spend all your time designing programs and editing materials, you risk becoming isolated from the business and cut off from other people in it. You must balance program design with other, more visible activities.

Working with Other Resources Within the Company to Design Programs

Developing programs in conjunction with line managers throughout the company can be a tremendously satisfying experience. It is critical that you draw on subject-matter experts when you do not have the expertise yourself. Using line managers to help with design is an excellent way both to ensure that the program is relevant to the organization and to build joint ownership of the program. People are much more likely to publicize and endorse programs, send attendees, and reinforce skills taught in programs that they have had a hand in developing.

Some caveats about using internal resources to assist with developing your programs: spend time educating employees about the program development process, be open to incorporating the ideas of others, and make sure that people are recognized or rewarded for their contributions. We'll look more closely at how to build an internal resource network in Chapter Six.

Buying Off-the-Shelf Programs

Buying an off-the-shelf or "canned" program can provide you with a polished product within a short time. Consultants often have the expertise and technological capability to produce more sophisticated materials than you can produce internally. Off-the-shelf programs can work well if you are trying to meet a generic HRD need that is basically the same in different companies, such as management or communication skills. When you use a generic program, you can often make it much more effective by doing some minor customizing, such as providing examples, case studies, role plays and exercises that are relevant and realistic for your particular organization. You can also make an off-the-shelf program relevant to your company if you or someone else within the company teaches the program.

The major disadvantages in using off-the-shelf programs are the cost of purchasing the materials, the possibility that the program will be inappropriate for your organization because of its content or style, and potential limitations on how you can implement or modify the program. Such generic programs may be inappropriate because of the sensitive nature of material taught, such as company policies and procedures. Because of licensing agreements, producers of these programs generally restrict reproduction or customization of their materials. See Table 4.2 to help you decide whether or not to buy an off-the-shelf program.

Hiring Consultants to Customize Programs

Provided that you have the budget, you may want to consider hiring consultants to provide you with programs tailored to meet your and your organization's specific needs. Consultants can often produce customized programs that are more professional than those you can produce internally.

Table 4.2. Advantages and Potential Disadvantages of Off-the-Shelf Programs.

Advantages	*Potential disadvantages*
Excellent for meeting needs for generic skills and knowledge	Inappropriate for organization-specific or very sensitive knowlege
Can save development money and may be cheaper in long run	Possible bias against "canned" programs (can be overcome by buying best products, doing some customization, previewing with influential people)
Save development time	
Free you to work on other programs that require internal development	
May be of higher quality than you could produce internally	You may not have the budget to hire a consultant
Simple way to conduct a pilot program	Existence may be unknown (can be overcome by checking out training periodicals, conferences, trade shows, colleagues for programs in specific areas)
	Takes time to select best vendor

They can probably also produce good programs more quickly than you can. Or they may be able to modify one of their standard programs to fit your company's needs by modifying its language, exercises, and role plays rather than having to create the materials from scratch.

When using consultants, you need to be careful to maintain control of the project and to receive a fair deal for your investment. And you will still need to set aside enough time to analyze needs and to manage program development. For programs that will be repeated, you will need time to pilot the programs and to develop leader's guides.

You may be able to structure a contract for customized programs that allow you to reproduce and adapt materials as you need to. Some consultants, however, still charge licensing fees for customized programs and refuse to allow reproduction of or changes in their materials. Make sure that you negotiate the contract carefully and stay on top of the project. Chapter Six presents some in-depth guidelines for selecting and managing consultants.

Using Programs Provided by Associations or Colleges

In many cases, excellent HRD programs are available through colleges, universities, or industry associations. For example, a wide variety of programs are offered through the American Management Association, the American Marketing Association, the American Institute of Banking, and so forth. Outside sources can be especially helpful if you need to provide HRD on a wide range of topics. Remember the case of Iris Staubus (in Chapter Two). Iris worked for Tennant, and when employees expressed an interest in 247 different topics, she began subscribing to an outside service. The service helped her identify external training opportunities in the Minneapolis area.

External programs are also useful when dealing with senior-level managers who need to develop a broader perspective by interacting with their peers in other companies or industries. A large variety of executive education programs are available through such institutions as the Menninger Institute, Harvard University, Columbia University, the Center for Creative Leadership, Michigan State University, and so forth. Bricker's *International Directory*, published annually, can be a helpful resource in selecting outside programs. Executives view such programs not only as opportunities to acquire skills that will help make them better leaders and executives but also as well-deserved rewards because the programs are often held in attractive locations.

You need to weigh the pros and cons of an in-house versus a public-seminar approach. Public seminars have advantages and disadvantages. Participants may be less likely to attend public seminars, and they may also incur heavier travel and lodging expenses and miss the opportunity of interacting with their peers within the organization in public seminars. On the other hand, participants in public seminars may be more open and may gain a broader perspective as the result of interacting with people outside their organization. Publicizing outside seminars rather than offering them in-house may save considerable administration time and money if programs are not fully attended. Providing timely information on high-quality external HRD programs can be as valuable to some customers as sponsoring these programs yourself. You can encourage attendance at public seminars in the area by providing people with enough information on the benefits and logistics of programs in advance so that they can plan to attend them.

WHO SHOULD TEACH YOUR PROGRAMS?

For programs that require an instructor, you may have several options: you can teach the program yourself, hire a consultant, find another trainer within the company, use line managers or employees to teach programs, or use some combination of the foregoing. Which approach is right for your organization? Consider the following when you select instructors:

■ *Resources available to you inside and outside the company.* Find out whether there are other human resources or training professionals within your organization or parent company who might be able to help you. Is there a precedent for using line managers or employees to teach programs? Are external consultants or college instructors available to teach some programs?

■ *Expertise instructors need to be effective in teaching the program.* How important to successful instruction of the program are presentation skills, group facilitation skills, and technical knowledge? Employees may be willing to overlook the weak presentation skills of a highly reputable technical expert. In cases where you believe that the dynamics of the group may be difficult to manage, you will want to use an instructor with strong presentation and facilitation skills. Be aware that being able to give a formal presentation does not require the same kind of skill as facilitating a challenging group and ensuring that learning occurs from complex training exercises.

■ *Credibility of the instructor with the target audience.* Professional trainers will usually have credibility in teaching managerial and communication skills; experienced technical experts are likely to have more credibility in teaching advanced technical skills.

■ *Your time frame for implementing the program.* The instructors you plan to use will affect the time needed to implement programs. Outside consultants, line managers, employees, and professional trainers will probably require different levels of training to become successful instructors. Line managers may require a more elaborate leader's guide and train-the-trainer session than would a professional trainer or consultant.

■ *Your budget, if any, for hiring instructors.* Can you share expenses for the program with other departments in your organization?

■ *Need for your involvement.* Is this a crucial enough topic or audience to warrant your active involvement in the classroom? As discussed below, instructing programs can be a way to enhance your visibility and credibility within the organization.

Instructing Programs Yourself

Being present at classroom training affords the HRD manager several advantages. You can learn about key issues facing people, work on establishing a network of internal people who can help you with HRD, and gain visibility as a helpful resource. You may want to present programs that will be offered only once provided that you have the expertise and credibility. In such cases, you will not need to develop a detailed leader's guide. As a skilled trainer, you can easily teach from a well-constructed participant's manual that you have designed yourself.

Ellen Kamp (first introduced in Chapter Three) believes that there is a great deal of value in doing some classroom training yourself, especially at the beginning of your assignment. She feels that being in the classroom was extremely valuable to her: it allowed her to deal with the people who ran the company and to build her credibility because she was seen as a "hands-on" person. She learned about the company and determined its key issues, meanwhile gaining visibility, and became a valued employee because other employees learned a lot from her classes.

On the other hand, there are disadvantages to instructing all your programs yourself. You will be limited in how many programs you can offer and in the scope of your contribution. You may not have the credibility and effectiveness that an expert would. Moreover, people may come to perceive you as an instructor rather than as a strategist.

Line Managers as Trainers

Line managers can be especially effective in conducting training when the instructor must have specific technological expertise and the credibility that comes from having actually done the job. Even if you are the primary instructor, line managers can add a great deal of value as guest speakers in segments of a program. Companies vary widely in the practice of using line managers. Some companies encourage their employees to support HRD within departments and interdepartmentally; others are unfamiliar with or resistant to having employees help design or teach HRD programs. If you use line managers as instructors, you will need time to conduct instructor training.

Debra Shine, an experienced training manager whom we met in Chapter One, believes that there is no limit to what you can do as a one-person department if you make wise use of other people in your organization. In Debra's words: "Never underestimate what can be done through creative use of resources and other people within the organization. I used to feel sorry for myself and say, 'I don't have any staff,' when I had six hundred people at my disposal. That they did not report directly to me was actually irrelevant if I could get them motivated and interested and could take the time to develop a rapport with other department managers and field people" (interview with the author, June 20, 1990).

Ronita Johnson, who oversees equal employment and affirmative action for Pacific Gas and Electric, was given the mandate from senior management to teach twenty-seven thousand employees about diversity within a few years (Johnson and O'Mara, 1992). Clearly she was not able to do all the teaching herself, and hiring a consultant to teach all the programs would have been prohibitively expensive. Ronita conducted an intense search to find a consultant who would help her train line managers and other employees who were passionately interested in diversity to become diversity trainers. She chose Julie O'Mara as her lead consultant. Ronita and Julie identified four competencies critical to a successful diversity awareness facilitator: self-knowledge, leadership, subject-matter understanding and expertise, and facilitation skills. Because of the emotionally demanding nature of the training, potential instructors went through an intense screening and training certification process to ensure that credible, motivated, well-prepared, and effective individuals would teach the workshops.

Johnson and O'Mara (1992) describe the train-the-trainer and certification process that has been used to teach more than one hundred Pacific Gas and Electric employees to lead diversity awareness workshops within their divisions. While there is some risk in using line employees rather than professional diversity consultants as trainers, holding line employees responsible for implementing training in their own divisions has several advantages. It greatly increases the speed with which training can be accomplished, and more importantly, it builds a vested interest in having the training succeed and increases the perception that the company is truly committed to making diversity a success.

Using a Combination of Approaches

Given a need to balance budget, time, and organizational needs, you may find that a combination of approaches to development and instruction works best. I used a variety of approaches to HRD development and delivery in the International Consumer Banking Division at Chase Manhattan. Despite the division's widely dispersed population, I chose workshops as my primary delivery vehicle because building a team across functions and countries was important to the success of the organization. I designed my first program on business planning with a consultant who helped to write a Chase-specific business case and with a local university professor who helped to conduct the workshop. I used Chase guest speakers to provide a company perspective on the business case. The next program, on managing change, was offered back-to-back with the first workshop in order to hold travel costs to a minimum. I purchased this program from an outside vendor and presented it in collaboration with another Chase trainer, who worked in a different department. Presenting the program enabled me to get to know the key business players and issues in a more direct way and to establish my credibility as an HRD professional.

Because of the need for speed in development and for marketing expertise, I used an outside consultant to develop and instruct a workshop on marketing management. Recognizing that this course did not sufficiently focus on our company's needs, I changed to a more customized approach. I worked closely with several other Chase divisions to develop programs on managing branches, home mortgages, and credit cards. These programs all made extensive use of line subject-matter experts as developers and instructors. I did this because being able to answer questions and provide real examples of business situations was more important than being able to facilitate group exercises. In addition, it was crucial for trainees to form relationships with experienced business managers who could provide them with ideas and resources and help them solve problems as business grew.

For generic needs, I used some ready-made programs. For our basic management skills program, I offered Chase's management skills workshop, with myself and members of our corporate training department as instructors. I also bought some generic selling and sales management programs from outside consultants and arranged to certify local Chase instructors so that we could provide the programs locally. To teach risk management, I used a two-pronged approach. For our credit analysts, I purchased a written self-study program on consumer lending that could be shipped overseas and tailored by local experts. For our credit managers, I contracted with a consultant to lead a portfolio management workshop that used a sophisticated computer-based simulation because I lacked the budget, expertise, and technical capability to produce such a program internally. This mix of generic and customized programs worked well as I tried to balance training needs, budget guidelines, and deadlines.

SUMMARY: DEVELOPING A COST-EFFECTIVE DELIVERY STRATEGY

1. Consider these factors in planning your delivery strategy:

   ■ Your mission and key objectives

   ■ Your budget

   ■ Time pressure to develop and implement HRD programs

   ■ The needs of your target audience

   ■ Your organization's experience with and readiness for human resource development

   ■ Your department's and organization's capabilities regarding HRD program development

   ■ The technological sophistication of your organization

2. A number of delivery options are open to you: classroom training, coaching, on-the-job training, job rotations, self-study manuals, audiovisual training, computer-based training, and job aids.

3. Select the best program development strategy for your situation:

   ■ Design programs yourself.

   ■ Design programs using internal resources.

   ■ Purchase off-the-shelf programs.

   ■ Use consultants to design customized programs.

   ■ Use a combination of the above.

4. Carefully consider the following when selecting instructors for training programs:

- Resources available inside and outside the company

- Expertise needed (including facilitation skills and subject-matter expertise)

- Credibility with the target audience

- Time frame for implementing the program (and time needed to prepare people to instruct the program)

- Budget (for hiring consultants)

- Appropriateness of your involvement as program instructor or in some other role given the subject and audience

Building and Negotiating a Budget

A challenge for many HRD managers is projecting and negotiating a budget. If the department is just getting started or if there has been a time gap between HRD managers, one of your first tasks may be to propose a budget. What if you have not had time to sufficiently analyze your department's needs? Remember the case of Ellen Kamp, who began her job as a one-person HRD department and was given one week to formulate and present her HRD plan and budget to senior management. What if you have never managed an HRD budget before? How can you determine the amount of money that you need to have a positive impact on the organization?

HOW MUCH MONEY SHOULD YOU SPEND?

Sometimes when initiating an HRD function, you may have the advantage of being able to request the amount of money you think you will need. To determine a reasonable estimate, you might compare your company with others in your industry. A 1986 American Society for Training and Development consortium study, for example, indicated that the average annual training cost per employee is $283. You can calculate this figure by dividing total training expenses by the total number of employees in your organization. Some companies measure HRD costs as a percentage of salary costs.

Organizations typically "allocate between 1.5 and 2.5 percent of their total employee salary cost to training and development" (Laird, 1985, p. 226).

Some situations require more funding. For start-up operations, the figure should be on the higher side. Organizations usually need more money for human resource development when they are opening a new plant or introducing a new product or service. If management development has been neglected for a long time and there is a need to train replacements when older managers retire, you may need to budget five to six times the normal amount. Specialized organizations, such as high-tech firms or research and development departments, may need three to four times more than other organizations (Laird, 1985). One study indicated that the training budget in high-tech companies could range as high as 7 percent of salary costs (London, 1989, p. 131).

In a smaller HRD department, your budget is likely to be smaller. In 1989 I found that budgets of small HRD departments in the financial services industry typically ranged from $10,000 to $500,000. Large companies often spend more than a million dollars annually on HRD programs; you may be lucky to get $100,000. Smaller amounts have a bigger impact in smaller organizations than they do in larger ones. Rick Behring (1987, p. 65) compares Smallco, a hypothetical company with annual sales of $11.85 million and profits of $718,000, to Motorola. Behring suggests that if a training manager at Motorola were to make an error of judgment and lose $200,000 on a training program, this would compare to an error of only $1,950 at Smallco. To state it another way, a training program that saved Smallco $20,000 would have to net $2,050,562 in order to have the same impact at Motorola. On the other hand, a training program that saves $20,000 can make a big difference to a company with only $700,000 in profits.

Whether you are given the budget you request or a predetermined budget, you must learn how to make the best use of the money you have. Let's look briefly at an example in order to understand some of the issues involved in creating an HRD budget.

As HRD manager in the International Consumer Banking Division at Chase, one of my first tasks was to project the annual budget, indicating the amount of money I would need as well as trends in spending. At that time, the closest I had come to managing a budget was asking my previous manager to sign an invoice. I had no idea what a reasonable training budget was, what training activities or facilities cost, or what the consequences of exceeding the budget were. I tried to hide my panic and look at the bright side: this was an important new business, senior management wanted it to succeed and believed that HRD was necessary, and there were no restrictions on the HRD budget. On the down side, I had no idea what to suggest.

Initially, I believed that the most difficult part of budgeting would be finding out what training cost, but in reality the hardest part was creating my plan. I could only project trends in expenses if I first laid out a schedule with all dates and program locations spelled out. On the basis of a preliminary needs analysis, I knew the nature of the training programs that I planned to offer in support of the business plan, but I was not sure of the specific number of people in each country who needed training. I realized that I had to propose a certain number of programs in order to plan my budget. I assumed that I would need to offer all programs twice in the first year. I would make adjustments once I knew the number of potential attendees and the urgency of their need for training.

Another difficulty was deciding where to offer programs given the fact that I was not sure of how many people in each country needed the training. To simplify matters, I proposed offering all the initial sessions in New York. I planned to determine the best locations for future sessions by investigating each country's needs and reactions to the pilot programs. Since travel, lodging, and program costs would have been prohibitively expensive for employees in some of our smaller locations, I recommended that we sponsor these expenses centrally to encourage attendance at programs in the first year. I hoped that once HRD programs proved sufficiently valuable, countries would be willing to pay the cost of sending their employees for further training. Determining who pays for training expenses—your department or the user—is one of the many decisions involved in making an HRD budget.

Other decisions center on whether or not to develop new HRD programs. You can save money by using existing programs or by developing programs yourself. Whenever possible, I planned to use existing Chase programs as part of my curriculum. Several topics, however, were not covered by Chase courses. I believed that I had the expertise to develop some programs internally, but I knew that I needed to hire outside consultants to help me develop or teach others. Attaching a development cost to any particular training program can help senior managers decide what their real priorities are.

Once I'd thought through my objectives and researched the cost of consultants and training facilities, I was ready to develop my plan. Wanting to contribute to the organization's business, I drafted an ambitious training plan that specified program names, dates, and estimated costs for development and implementation. Our senior business managers, not familiar with the costs of training programs, trusted my expertise. In negotiations, we jointly agreed to eliminate some low-priority programs and to combine some others in order to reduce travel expenses. We decided that in the first year my department would sponsor most of the costs of training but that travel expenses would come from the budgets for the different countries. Overall, senior management endorsed my plan and approved a healthy budget — around $450,000 — for general operating expenses and for development and delivery of HRD programs. After the first two years of operation I had developed or purchased most of the programs we needed, and the budget was reduced to $200,000.

Now let's consider what's involved in creating a budget for any small HRD department.

CREATING A BUDGET

An HRD budget is not much different from any other type of budget. A sound budget requires a plan. You need to establish priority objectives to be accomplished in the coming year. For example, are you planning to design or buy a new management training program or are you planning to offer existing programs? In general, it is much cheaper to offer existing programs than to develop new ones. Also, what is your strategy for program development: do you plan to design programs yourself or hire consultants to design them? While it may cost more to hire a consultant to develop a program than to develop one yourself, you may be able to offer more programs and meet a business need more quickly if you make wise use of consultants.

Projecting HRD Costs

Accurately estimating HRD costs involves making decisions about what you plan to do, doing preliminary research, and monitoring and adjusting your spending throughout the year. You need to estimate the categories of expenses you will have, to research how much typical items cost, and to consider different strategies for delivering HRD so that you will know how costs might be cut if senior management wants you to do so.

It is essential that you develop your budget plan in partnership with the organization so that you understand what problems merit investment of HRD dollars. Then, considering both your department's mission and the needs of the organization, you need to translate these problems into an HRD plan. To propose a sound budget you will need to decide the following:

- What programs or services you plan to offer and how frequently you will offer them

- Which programs will provide for the greatest return on investment; which programs are essential versus merely nice to have

- Which programs are readily available, and which ones need to be developed

- Who will instruct programs, and whether you will need to pay for internal trainers or consultants

- What equipment you will need to develop and deliver programs, and whether you have the equipment on hand or will need to buy or rent it

- Where you plan to offer programs and what facilities are available; whether you will need to pay for external or internal training facilities

- Whether people need to travel to the training sites, whether they require housing, and who will pay the participants' travel expenses

Although senior management may be interested only in tracking the "bottom line" of HRD expenses, you will need to divide expenses into meaningful categories so that you will be able to track your performance. Table 5.1 and Worksheet 7 (in Resources) should help you create your budget. Be sure to include the following categories:

- *Salaries and benefits of HRD staff.* Your salary may or may not be included in your budget. It is common for small HRD departments to share their administrative staff with other departments.

- *Data processing equipment.* You may decide to purchase or rent equipment. I strongly recommend purchasing a computer with good word processing,

Table 5.1. Sample Training Budget.

Category	Monthly budget	Annual budget
Salaries and benefits of HRD staff (HRD manager and administrative assistant)	$7,500	$90,000
Data processing equipment (computer, printer, software)	$417	$5,000
Supplies (office supplies; training materials such as binders, tabs, books, videotapes, memento gifts)	$417	$5,000
Shipping, messenger, and telephone	$167	$2,000
Consultants and professional fees (design and instructor expenses)	$2,500	$30,000
Training facilities (conference rooms, meals, equipment rental)	$1,000	$12,000
Travel and entertainment (airfare, ground transportation, lodging for training manager and staff)	$417	$5,000
Training/professional development (attendance expenses of training manager and staff at conferences, workshops; professional society memberships)	$250	$3,000
Overhead (corporate charges for space, furniture, and so on)	$417	$5,000
Total gross expenses	$13,085	$157,020
Service recoveries (charge-backs to participants for programs)	$3,917	$47,000
Net expenses	$9,168	$110,020

spreadsheet, and graphics programs, and a laser printer. You can use your computer to produce professional-quality training materials, such as participant workbooks, visual aids, reports, course catalogues, and program announcements; to project your budget; and to create data bases that help you market programs and track program participation.

■ *Office supplies and training materials.* This includes office supplies and materials that you need to develop, market, or conduct programs, such as overhead projectors, videotaping equipment, flip charts, and markers. Include projected costs of developing a brochure or catalogue of courses, as well as participant and instructor materials. Be sure to include the cost of designing, reproducing, and binding materials. Even if you produce materials on your computer, you will probably want to use a professional graphics designer and printer for covers and tabs or dividers for some of your materials. Finally, be sure to set aside some money to pay for memento gifts to program participants.

- *Shipping, messenger, and telephone.* This includes charges for telephone, fax, and electronic mail, as well as expenses for shipping or sending materials between offices and to and from vendors. If you have many remote or overseas locations, this item may be fairly large. You can usually determine a reasonable amount for these items by checking with other departments.

- *Consultants and professional fees.* Estimate the number of days you will need consultants to help you develop or teach programs. Daily consultant charges range from several hundred dollars up to $2,000 or $3,000 a day for specialized experts. Renowned guest speakers may earn fees of $3,000 or more per lecture. Make sure that you include some money for activities not covered in your current plan. For example, you may have underestimated the amount of money required to develop a program, or you may want to develop a program that explains a new product or service or supports an organizational change.

- *Training facilities.* These include costs for programs conducted off-site. Include lodging, meals, and fees for training rooms and rental of training equipment. Try to negotiate preferred rates for conference centers. Be sure to include room tax and other miscellaneous fees in your projections; taxes and other fees can substantially inflate the cost of off-site training and are frequently not included in the rates quoted by conference center managers.

- *Travel and entertainment.* Estimate the number of people to come from each location and the cost of travel expenses. If there are enough people, consider negotiating a group rate with your company's travel agency. If you have a small budget, however, you will probably want to have participants pay for their own travel expenses. Make sure that you allow for travel and entertainment expenses for your staff's trips to remote sites to conduct needs analyses, to facilitate meetings or teach programs, or to attend HRD programs.

- *Training/professional development* for the HRD staff. Be sure to include funds for your staff's development, including memberships in professional societies, trade publications, and attendance at HRD conventions and training programs for yourself and your assistant. Setting aside money for the professional development of your staff not only ensures that money will be available for such activities but also reminds management of the importance of your staff's professional competence. If any members of your staff are new to HRD, you will need to allocate more money. Chapter Eleven discusses professional development in greater depth.

- *Overhead.* If you work for a large organization, you may be charged for items such as office space, furniture, supporting equipment, and other items. You can usually determine a reasonable amount for these overhead expenses by checking with the company's finance representative for your department. Beware of overhead expenses. Carefully review the items you are expected to carry to see whether they are justified; many companies are somewhat arbitrary in how they allocate overhead charges. You may be able to successfully challenge some of the items for which you are charged (Lloyd, 1989, p. 60).

- *Service recoveries.* Indicate the amount of money you expect to charge back to departments for your programs and services. Determining what to charge back is discussed in more detail later in this chapter.

Clarifying Your Assumptions

In preparing a budget you need to spell out clearly the assumptions you are making. You will not have time to call airlines for the airfare from every location or to collect many proposals from consultants before you submit your budget. You may therefore have to assume, for example, that travel expenses from a certain area will be roughly $2,000, and that it will cost $50,000 to have a consultant develop a workshop. Clarifying your assumptions helps you negotiate your budget with senior management, make adjustments to your plan, track your performance, and provide more accurate forecasts in the future. Knowing the cost of a particular program will help you determine whether or not the program will provide an adequate return on your investment. You can use Worksheet 6 in Resources as a guide to calculating the cost of a training program.

Estimating Expense Trends over the Year

Be sure you understand your company's budget cycle—when the annual forecast is due and how often you will be expected to submit a forecast. Consider the following in forecasting HRD expense trends:

■ *Determine how often forecasts are expected.* Do you need to give monthly, quarterly, semiannual, and annual projections of expenses and variance from plan?

■ *Plan to spend enough money early on so that you do not lose budget money later in the year.* If you do not spend the money you projected you would spend, you may lose that money if cutbacks are called for midway through the year.

■ *Project when spending will occur so that all bills are paid during the quarter or year budgeted for.* Have you allowed for a lag in payment of bills when projecting expenses? Depending on the size of your company bureaucracy, there may be a considerable lag between the time you submit expenses for payment and the time they are actually paid. This can determine in which quarter or year expenses "hit" the budget. Be careful that you don't fall under budget for the current year and then go over budget for the next.

SHOULD THE BUDGET BE CENTRALIZED OR DECENTRALIZED?

The decision of who pays for HRD reflects the organization's values and influences how people view and make use of HRD programs. What is the best budget strategy for a small HRD department? Should you carry HRD expenses in your budget, or should you charge these expenses to the user departments? Each approach has advantages.

Advantages of Centralization

Carrying the entire HRD budget may make it easier for you to keep track of HRD expenses. Centralization may provide you with easier access to a larger sum of money, which can be applied to the development of programs, than you would have if the HRD budget were dispersed among a group of departments or business lines. Centralization of program development costs may send the message that senior management wants to make programs available to everyone. It may also encourage user departments to send employees to programs instead of not sending them in an effort to save money.

Let's look at an example. When I met with senior management to discuss my budget, we talked at length about who should pay for training.

We finally decided that during the first year my department would sponsor most of the cost of human resource development, including the cost of program development, instruction, training facilities, and lodging. This would send a message that senior management felt that HRD was important and would help ensure that all countries participated in appropriate HRD opportunities. We decided that the countries would pay for their participants' travel expenses because trips to training programs in New York could be combined with other business activities.

This budget strategy successfully encouraged a large number of people to register for HRD programs; however, many who registered failed to attend. Potential attendees often canceled at the last minute because their departments were not penalized in any way for cancellations. Once I revised my cancellation policy to include a penalty, people who registered for programs were more likely to attend.

Advantages of Decentralization

Having the user pay for HRD programs can enhance their perceived value. With a decentralized HRD budget, managers in user departments may feel more responsible for the training, education, and development of their employees. Furthermore, when all expenses are covered decentrally, user departments may be less likely to withdraw people from programs because they are paying for them anyway. This can alleviate the nightmare of scheduling and filling programs. Furthermore, when user departments are held accountable for travel and lodging expenses, they are rarely lax in seeking the most economical arrangements.

Continuing with the example introduced above, in the second year of operation my department no longer centralized all program expenses: we began charging countries program fees to cover the cost of instruction, materials, and facilities. This change in strategy encouraged countries to be more selective in sending people to the programs. Furthermore, because their own countries were willing to sponsor them, people chosen to attend the programs perceived human resource development as a reward and an indication that they were valued.

Projecting Service Recoveries

If you decide to charge participants for attending your programs, you will need to project a total for service recoveries or charge-backs in your budget.

The first step involves determining what to charge for each program. Consider the following factors in deciding what you will charge for your programs.

- *Recovery costs.* How much will you need to charge to recover the costs of a program? You may want to include consultant expenses, participant materials, food and lodging, facility expenses, and equipment rental expenses in your program costs.

- *Competitiveness.* Make sure that your prices are competitive with other possible sources of training.

- *Relative value.* Decide what you think a program is worth to any potential participant. You may want to charge back only part of the actual program cost in order to make the program price attractive or even feasible.

- *Overall price structure.* Be sure to price clerical-level programs at lower rates than executive programs. You may be able to cover the costs of your clerical programs by charging more for programs offered to higher-level employees, such as senior managers.

- *Current program price.* If you have inherited an ongoing curriculum, a price may already be set for each of your programs. In some cases you may need to raise the price to cover your expenses, or you may be able to reduce program costs by exploring less expensive consultants and so on. For example, when I assumed my current responsibilities at UNUM Life Insurance Company of America, I found that my department had been offering a consultant-instructed, one-day writing skills program for $475. This was too expensive for most employees. After investigating other consultant options, we were ultimately able to offer a two-day writing skills program for $325.

Once you have priced your programs, you need to decide how many times you will offer each one and estimate how many people you expect to attend each session. For each program, multiply the program cost by the number of sessions by the projected number of participants per session. Then add the numbers for all your programs to get your service recovery total. For example, let's say you plan to charge $300 for a program on managing change, which you will offer two times during the year. If you expect twenty people to attend each session, your total recoveries for that program are $300 times two programs times twenty participants, which equals $12,000 in expected recoveries.

If it is your first year of operation, make fairly conservative attendance estimates to avoid putting yourself under the pressure of trying to fill classes before you have had a chance to build a track record of success. Projecting service recoveries in your second year of operation is much easier, because you will have previous attendance records to use as a baseline. See Table 5.2 for sample service-recovery projections. You can use Worksheet 8 in Resources to project recoveries for your department's budget.

NEGOTIATING THE BUDGET

If you have developed your plan and budget in partnership with the business and your HRD objectives are tied to business objectives, negotiating your budget should not be that difficult. The best way to sell a budget to senior management is to tie HRD results closely to the bottom line. Your budget presentation should include the following:

■ The business rationale for your plan

■ What you plan to accomplish and what it will cost

■ The potential benefits of the plan

■ The risks and costs of not conducting human resource development

■ A backup proposal in case your initial proposal is not approved

Calculating the Return on Investment

The major benefit of human resource development is that it increases the value of an organization's most important asset—its people. Sometimes this increase in value is intangible. Lloyd (1989, p. 58) suggests that gathering "meaningful numbers on return on training, added margins, decreased costs" can be very persuasive. His motto in negotiating HRD budgets is "You can never give them enough numbers." You need to determine which functions will be affected by HRD programs and services and then try to show what comes back for each HRD dollar spent.

Placing a cost on performance problems can be difficult and sensitive, but it can be very helpful in convincing senior management of the impor-

Table 5.2. Estimating Service Recoveries: Sample Projections.

Program	Program fee	Projected number of participants[a]	Number of programs	Total number of participants per program	Total recovery per program
Managing change	$300	20	2	40	$12,000
Communication skills	$350	15	2	30	$10,500
Selling skills	$150	15	4	60	$9,000
Total recoveries			8	130	$31,500

[a] This projection represents a conservative but reasonable number of participants. If you project too large a number of participants per program, you will be constantly below your plan in service recoveries.

tance of spending money on human resource development. Be sure to emphasize both current problems and the possible loss of opportunities due to untrained or underdeveloped employees. Laird (1985, p. 231) recommends the following four steps in calculating the cost of performance problems:

1. *Identify a single unit of defective performance*, such as a customer complaint, a lost customer, a defective manufacturing unit, or a mishandled employee who leaves or sues the company. You can also use positive indicators of performance that HRD would be expected to increase, such as average sale size, number of sales calls, repeat customers, and customer referrals.

2. *Calculate or estimate the cost of one unit.* It is helpful if the data you use are readily available through normal reporting channels and meaningful to management.

3. *Calculate the number of defective units for a year.* You can obtain estimates of this number from managers.

4. *Multiply the unit cost by the number of defective units* to show the annual cost of the performance problem.

To determine the return on investment of any particular program, you need to calculate the cost of the solution. You can use Worksheet 6 in Resources as a guide.

Once you have planned what you would like to do and what you think it would cost, it is helpful to create several different HRD strategies for use in handling different scenarios. Explain to senior management that choices have to be made. My colleague Bob Browning puts it this way: "You can get it good, fast, or cheap—you can have two of these but not all three" (interview with the author, Apr. 15, 1991). You will want to explain the advantages of spending an adequate amount of money—skimping on the budget may incur greater problems and expenses later on. Remember the wise words of Bob Jendusa: "You can't fix a year-old problem with a one-day program. You can't fix a $100,000 problem with a $10 program" (interview with the author, Feb. 14, 1990). On the other hand, you need to do a cost-benefit analysis to determine whether solving a problem is really worth the amount of money required. You don't want to spend $100,000 on a $1,000 problem. For example, the senior management team of one company rejected a proposal to do $200,000 worth of critical renovations on an old training facility because the ultimate resale value of the building would not be worth the $200,000 investment.

Supporting the Business Plan

Human resource development should support the business plan and business priorities. In preparing to negotiate your budget with senior management, you need to be flexible and have ideas for reducing the budget in case the business strategy changes or the money that you want is not available. Changes in the business plan will usually require changes in your HRD budget. For example, let's say that your company had originally planned to pilot test a new service strategy in three test markets. You realize that for the strategy to succeed all customer service representatives would need to be trained in customer relations, new procedures, and cross-selling. You calculate the amount of money you need on the assumption that the business will need X number of service representatives to handle customers in the test markets. If the business were to cut back the number of markets in the pilot test, you might only need to train half as many people.

Cuts in the company budget may lead you to reprioritize training activities. Perhaps the original business plan called for aggressive growth in revenue because of the introduction of a new product. You plan a budget that assumes you will offer product training and selling skills to the sales force. A dramatic downturn in the economy may lead to a more conservative business strategy with an emphasis on containing costs. In light of the changed environment, you may decide to develop programs that teach risk management and expense control rather than selling skills. Make sure you prioritize needs and identify what is essential to do versus nice to do so that your cuts will be based on reason, not on emotions stirred up in the heat of negotiation.

Trimming the Fat and Preparing for Cutbacks

How much money should you ask for? Should you request more money than you need, assuming that management always asks for cutbacks? Or should you request exactly what you need, assuming that management would see an inflated budget as a sign that you are out of touch with organizational reality? The answer depends on how the budgeting process usually works in your organization. To find out, speak to other department managers who have experience in the process.

Before you present your budget, perform your own budget review to determine whether there is any fat in it. There are numerous ways of cutting costs in HRD budgets.

- *Reduce the number or length of the programs offered.* The easiest way to cut expenses is to offer fewer programs. Shortening the length of programs may reduce expenses for program development, instruction, training facilities, and housing for students. Consider cutting down on classroom time by requiring trainees to complete readings or assignments before coming to the program.

- *Increase the number of students per program and discourage cancellations.* Nothing wastes HRD dollars as much as poorly attended programs. One HRD department minimized cancellations to programs this way: students were not charged for attending programs; they were charged only for canceling out of programs without sending a qualified substitute.

- *Combine several subjects into one program or offer programs back-to-back rather than separately.* For geographically dispersed employees who must attend classroom training, meetings, or conferences, you can greatly reduce travel expenses by offering several programs consecutively.

- *Conduct the programs at a less expensive training facility.* Taking the time to research facility costs can save you money. If you plan to use one facility for several training programs, you may be able to negotiate a preferred rate.

■ *Cut travel costs.* Choose a more convenient training site, conduct programs during the off season, try to arrange for volume discounts on travel expenses through a travel agency, or substitute AV-based training that can be sent cheaply to remote locations.

■ *Use outside consultants selectively.* Whenever possible, instruct trainees yourself or have other internal experts do so.

■ *Use less expensive methods of delivery.* For example, use flip charts or overhead projections, instead of slides or videotapes as audiovisual support.

■ *Share the cost of programs.* Whenever possible, find other companies or departments that might share costs with you. You may be able to sponsor programs jointly with other companies or departments. Local companies in noncompeting industries may be willing to share the costs of guest speakers or generic programs.

SUMMARY: STRATEGIES FOR BUILDING AND NEGOTIATING A BUDGET

1. Link your HRD objectives to business objectives. Be sure your plan focuses on business priorities.

2. Research training costs.

3. Make sure you accurately project the budget required to implement your vision, including the costs of

   ■ Training staff salaries and benefits

   ■ Consultant fees for program design and instruction

   ■ Training supplies; production of training and marketing materials

   ■ Travel and entertainment for instructors, developers, and participants (if appropriate)

   ■ Facilities (room, equipment) for training programs and meetings

   ■ Professional development of training staff (professional publications, seminars)

■ Equipment (purchase or rental of audiovisual equipment, computers, and so on)

4. Plan how to sell your budget to senior management. That is, prioritize your projected programs, and focus on the return on investment in HRD, the benefits to be gained, and the costs of doing nothing.

5. Review your plan to ensure that you are using the most cost-effective approach to HRD. Consider a range of budget options, and be prepared to trim the fat from your budget.

6. Determine the impact of centralizing or decentralizing HRD expenses on the way employees participate in HRD activities. (Centralization—not charging for programs—encourages managers to send their employees to programs. Decentralization—charging for programs—encourages managers to be more selective in whom they send to programs.)

7. Carefully project service recoveries on the basis of conservative attendance estimates.

2

Turning Your Vision into Reality

Managing Program Development

*I*mplementing your plan with little or no staff is challenging. Sometimes you can use an off-the-shelf program taught by an outside consultant, but the demands are different when a customized program is required. This chapter examines guidelines for developing programs, building an internal resource network, and effectively managing consultants.

As HRD manager, you are responsible for developing programs. You will probably have to design some of them yourself, but you can also achieve a great deal through the wise use of internal and external resources. As manager of new programs, you are responsible for the following:

- Preparing a project plan and managing the project

- Gathering the information needed to develop useful programs

- Developing design guidelines for the programs

- Managing the design process

- Creating a design team using internal resources

- Finding consultants to design the programs and managing the consultants

- Reviewing and testing program design and materials

Let's look at each of these steps and at your role in the program development process.

PREPARING A PROJECT PLAN AND MANAGING THE PROJECT

Whether you work alone, with a consultant, or with a team of internal resources, you are the project manager for any new program developed. This involves creating a project plan, finding resources, monitoring and adjusting the plan, seeing the project through to completion, and evaluating the effectiveness of the program once it has been delivered. A written project plan, including key tasks, responsibilities, resources, and deadlines, enables you to see the whole picture at once and to make adjustments as changes occur. Such a plan helps keep a project on track, especially when you must juggle several projects at once and manage other people who are unfamiliar with the tasks, resources, and time required in designing a program.

It is important to establish clear accountabilities and deadlines for everyone involved in the project. Your plan should lay out the major phases of program development: conducting the needs assessment, identifying resources, writing the design specifications document, selecting a consultant, designing the program, creating and testing program materials, delivering the program, and evaluating it. For each phase you should list

Major tasks (in order of completion)

Resources required (budget, people)

Who is responsible

Time frames, including starting dates and completion dates

Exhibit 6.1 shows part of a sample project plan to develop a two-day training program with the help of a team of internal subject-matter experts (the design team) and an outside consultant in a period of four months. It is also helpful to lay out tasks in a readable format, such as a Gannt chart, a horizontal bar chart that depicts the tasks in order and shows the time relationship between tasks. Exhibit 6.2 shows a Gannt chart for the same program. There are other types of project-planning formats. You can create your own format or use project-planning software. See Worksheet 11 in Resources for sample steps to include in a project plan; see also Thompson (1990), a helpful resource for the novice project manager.

Exhibit 6.1. Project-Planning Chart for Program Development in Four Months.

Tasks/Activities	Resources	Responsibility	Starting date	Completion date
Needs assessment				
Plan assessment	HRD manager/ HR manager	HRD manager	1/7/93	1/11/93
Conduct assessment	HRD manager/ HR manager		1/14	1/28
Write report	HRD manager/ HR manager		1/28	2/1
Determine design group	HRD manager/ HR manager	HRD manager/ HR manager		
Plan team requirements	Business executives		1/14	1/28
Gain commitment	Business executives		1/14	2/4
Develop design specifications	HRD manager/ design group	HRD manager		
Write specifications			1/30	2/8
Consult with design group			2/11	2/12
Revise on basis of input from design group			2/12	2/15
Hire consultant	Budget: $30,000			
Determine selection criteria	HRD manager/ design group	HRD manager	1/30	2/4
Source candidates	HR division directors		2/4	2/15
Send design specs and requests for proposals	HRD manager		2/15	2/18
Review proposals		HRD manager/ design group	2/26	3/1
Have consultants present proposals	HRD manager/ design group		3/6	3/8
Check references	HRD manager		3/7	3/8
Select consultant	HRD manager/ design group		3/8	3/8
Create and sign contract	HRD manager	HR manager/ business executives	3/11	3/12
Design program				
Design learning objectives	Consultant	HRD manager/ consultant	3/13	3/13
Determine content	Design Group		3/13	3/15
Determine methods			3/13	3/15
Prepare annotated outline			3/18	4/1
Create materials				
Write materials list	Consultant	Consultant	3/27	3/29
Produce materials	Consultant	Administrative assistant	3/27	4/12
Review materials with design group	Design group/ HRD manager	HRD manager/ design group	4/15	4/22
Revise materials	Consultant		4/22	4/26
Test materials	HRD manager		5/1	5/1
Produce final materials	Consultant/ HRD manager		5/2	5/5

Exhibit 6.2. Sample Gantt Chart for Program Development.

Activities	Week 1	Week 2	Week 3	Week 4	Week 5	Week 6	Week 7	Week 8	Week 9	Week 10	Week 11	Week 12	Week 13	Week 14
Conduct needs assessment														
Plan assessment	xxxxxx													
Conduct assessment		xxxxxx	xxxxxx											
Write report				xxxxxx										
Determine design group														
Plan team requirements		xxxxxx	xxxxxx											
Gain commitment			xxxxxx	xxxxxx										
Develop design specifications														
Write specifications				xxx	xxxxxx									
Revise specifications						xxx								
Hire consultant (if appropriate)														
Determine selection criteria				xxx										
Source candidates				xxxx	xxxxx									
Send out design specifications and requests for proposals						xxxx								
Review proposals							xxx	xxx						
Have consultants present proposals									xxx					
Check references									xxx	xxx				
Select consultant									xx	xxx				
Create and sign contract										xx				
Design program														
Define learning objectives											xxxxxx	xxxxxx		
Determine content												xxxxxx	xxxxxx	
Determine methods													xxx	
Prepare annotated outline													xxxx	
Create materials														
Write materials list													xxx	
Produce materials													xxxx	
Revise materials													xxxxxxx	
Test materials													x	xxxxxx
Produce final materials														xxxxxx

When creating plans and managing projects, consider the following five guidelines:

1. *Be as complete as you can.* Identify all the steps and activities needed to complete the project. Err on the side of being too detailed rather than too vague.

2. *Plan early for possible delays.* Check with others to make sure time frames are realistic. Be sure to build in slack time for others' review because you cannot control the time it takes senior managers to review and approve materials.

3. *Keep the plan current and the project team informed.* Schedule a process to update the plan to reflect the current status of the project. It is very common for milestones to change as complications arise, especially when you work with subject-matter experts who do not report to you or even work in the same department or business unit. Keep all members of the project team informed of the latest developments and their impact on the project plan.

4. *Don't get discouraged when inevitable complications arise.* Don't throw out the entire plan when milestones are missed. Look for ways to get the project back on track. Remember, you have some leverage in getting consultants to meet tight deadlines: they want to keep your business.

5. *Learn from your experience.* At the completion of a project, take time to review your plan and learn from what happened. With experience, you'll get better at projecting time frames and identifying critical deadlines.

· ·

GATHERING INFORMATION ON HRD NEEDS

As discussed in Chapter Two, a sound needs assessment underlies any effective HRD program. When you are ready to develop a specific program, you normally need to perform a more detailed assessment of needs. Make sure that you know that a training program is the best solution to a problem and that management supports your development of a training program. Be sure that there are enough trainees to justify developing a formal program for your organization as opposed to coaching people, using an off-the-shelf program, or sending people to a program outside your company.

Your assessment should tell you what the audience needs to learn and any constraints, such as audience and environmental characteristics, deadlines, or budget, that should influence your selection of a training approach. For example, if your audience is widely dispersed and cannot afford to travel to a central location, you may want to buy or develop a video-based program that can be sent to each location. If the information to be taught is likely to change frequently, you'll want to avoid instructional methods, such as video, that are expensive and difficult to alter.

DEVELOPING WRITTEN DESIGN GUIDELINES

Once you know what a program must accomplish and that it is needed and supported by management, your next step is creating a design-specification document outlining your guidelines for the program.

Benefits of Written Design Specifications

Well thought out design specifications increase your chances of success. A design document helps you obtain sponsorship and funding by delineating why the program is necessary and what it will do for the business. Its description of business issues and of how HRD can help achieve business goals also builds your credibility with managers, employees, and consultants.

Moreover, written specifications help you manage the design process. They make it easier for others to help since people tend to offer more suggestions when they are given ideas to which they can react. Documenting what you want makes it easier to hold developers accountable for producing a program that meets your needs and standards.

Written design guidelines also help in soliciting proposals. A clear program description eliminates the need to repeat details to each consultant and helps consultants determine whether they can deliver what you want within the required time and at the specified cost.

Guidelines for Writing Design Specifications

What should you cover in a design document? Your guidelines should describe the following:

- Need for the program: an explanation of the business reasons for developing a formal training program

- Target audience: characteristics that may affect program design—for example, number of participants, level of education, age, attitudes toward training, language capabilities

- Learning objectives: specific skills and knowledge to be acquired as a result of the training

- Requirements or constraints regarding program development and instruction: budget, deadlines, desired program length, methods to be used, and delivery requirements such as training location or the language of the training materials

- Tentative program topics or modules

A flexible design document encourages creativity. Your preliminary specifications will often change on the basis of the subject-matter experts' suggestions. You may decide to change the target audience or to shift your approach. For example, if a business manager asks for training for a very small population, you might decide to expand the target audience, or you might decide to work with a supervisor to develop a coaching plan instead of a formal training program.

Review the final design specifications with your sponsor before proceeding. Requesting help from internal resources or soliciting proposals from consultants without first obtaining management's commitment to developing a program is frustrating, time-consuming, and damaging to your credibility.

Refer to the design specifications document on the ICB Credit Card Training Program in Exhibit 6.3 for a sample document that was used to develop a customized program. The information in this document was prepared by the ICB training manager to use in leading a design meeting with a team of subject-matter experts who were to develop and instruct the program. Since the designers were familiar with the background and rationale for the program, the design specifications did not include a background statement.

Exhibit 6.3. Sample Design Specifications: ICB Credit Card Training Program.

Target Audience. This program is intended for card center managers, area and regional card center managers, managers of key departments within the credit card business, and members of credit card project teams.

Program Purpose. The purpose of this program is to present an overview of the credit card business, its organizational structure, and strategies used to manage the business in the United States. While there are business, regulatory, and cultural differences between the United States and the international marketplace, the program will stress common concerns, risk mitigation, and standard operating procedures.

Managers will have an opportunity to observe advanced processing methods, controls, and risk-mitigating tools used to manage the business. Managers will also discuss strategies for building a quality customer base, including market research, solicitations, credit scoring, and data base management. Emphasis will be given to understanding controls required to identify, correct, and monitor potential problems.

Through close interaction with line managers, program participants will be able to establish a key resource network with U.S. and other international card managers. Time will be set aside for problem-solving sessions where U.S. managers and international participants can address specific problems concerning management of the card business overseas.

Program Objectives. As a result of the Credit Card Training Program, participants will:

1. Understand the dynamics and key strategies of the credit card business
2. Understand the work flows of Chase's cardholder operation
3. Be able to evaluate staffing needs and develop an efficient organizational structure
4. Be able to develop quality assurance techniques and measure key quality indicators and staff performance levels
5. Understand the importance of monitoring and evaluating business performance and addressing problem areas by

   ■ establishing techniques to identify, control, and manage risks

   ■ creating appropriate MIS (management information system) reports to track performance

6. Establish key relationships with domestic and international card managers

Design Constraints and Requirements

1. The program must be designed and ready to implement in one month.
2. There should be substantial program materials that participants can use to help them follow presentations and to serve as a reference on the job. People will need a glossary of terms and samples of key forms and written procedures.
3. Whenever possible, participants should observe actual work flows to gain an understanding of business logistics.
4. Teaching methods will need to be straightforward, for example, lecture, discussion, observation, since the program will be instructed by subject-matter experts, not professional trainers. Each unit will have unit objectives and review questions and answers to ensure that participants learn the required material.
5. The program will be two weeks in length.
6. Time will need to be built in to allow participants to travel to different work sites and to spend more or less time in given departments, depending on their personal learning needs.

· ·
MANAGING THE DESIGN PROCESS

No matter who actually designs the program and creates the materials, you need to manage the process because you are ultimately responsible for the quality of HRD. For the novice designer, Kay Abella's *Building Successful Training Programs* (1986) is an excellent guide to designing and developing training programs.

Let's take a brief look at several crucial steps in the design process.

Defining Learning Objectives

The first step in program design involves defining the learning objectives—what people must become able to do, know, or appreciate as a result of the program. Usually your subject-matter experts will help you refine the learning objectives identified in the design specifications. This process helps people focus on what must be learned and develop a sense of ownership of the program. For more information about learning objectives, see Mager (1962) and Gordon, Zemke, and Jones (1988).

Determining Content

Once you have written the learning objectives, you are ready to determine appropriate topics, learning units, and the best topic flow. Again, your subject-matter experts can be very helpful in refining content.

Determining Learning Methods and Time Frames

Only at this point are you ready to select the best teaching methods given your audience, budget, and time constraints. Beware of the temptation to skip to selecting methods before you think through what it is that must be learned. Should you use lecture and discussion, role plays, case studies, or some other method? With adult learners, it is best to vary learning methods and to include interactive activities that actively involve people in the learning process. Numerous books on training methods are available. See, for example, Abella (1986), Craig (1987), Gordon, Zemke, and Jones (1988), Margolis and Bell (1986), Pfeiffer (1987–1992), Pfeiffer and

Goodstein (1982–1986), Pfeiffer and Jones (1972–1981), Silberman (1990), and Warshauer (1988).

Once you have chosen your teaching methods, you can estimate the time required to accomplish the objectives. Review your methods, considering the time of day, the time required for each activity, and the flow of methods. For example, participants usually have more energy in the morning than they do in the late afternoon, so it may be advisable to schedule lectures early in the day.

Preparing an Annotated Outline

You are ready to write an annotated outline or leader's guide. If you will be doing all the training, you can take shortcuts with your outline. If others will instruct, you need to provide more details. For each unit of the program, the guide should describe the following:

- The purpose and learning objectives of the unit

- Learning activities, including time frames

- Topics and points to be covered

- Materials required to accomplish each activity

When time is short, it may not be possible to develop both participant materials and a leader's guide before launching a program. You may not need a detailed leader's guide if your training population is so small that you will only run a program once or twice. You can run an effective program using line instructors without a leader's guide. Expert resources can usually deliver lectures using the participant guide, especially if you provide visual aids such as flip charts or slides that highlight the main points to be covered. If time is a problem, focus your energy on the materials needed by program participants.

Developing the Materials

Once you have completed an annotated outline, prepare a list of materials needed to carry out the program. Whether you create or buy materials, it is helpful to keep a list of the materials, who is responsible for them, and dates when you will need them. This is invaluable, especially when you are managing a complex program or several programs at once. Include on the list the materials used by the instructor, those given to participants, and any audiovisual aids, such as flip charts, overhead transparencies, videotapes, slides, or games. In selecting materials, consider your budget, deadline, audience, company norms, trainer's skill level, and your own resourcefulness.

■ *Budget.* Determine whether you have the budget to produce slides or overheads. Producing slides is more expensive than creating flip charts. With today's PC software you can develop professional-looking overhead transparencies and handouts at minimal expense. You may also need a participant manual, which costs considerably more than handouts.

■ *Deadline.* Determine how much time you have in which to produce the materials. Outside and inside resources may have different time constraints in their production capabilities. Producing slides takes more time than creating flip charts, and developing participant manuals or producing videotapes requires considerable time and planning.

■ *Audience needs.* Decide which audiovisual aids are needed to reinforce main points and to keep the program on track. Identify materials participants will need in order to learn what is taught in the program. For complex material, you may have to produce a participant manual. With simpler material, you may only need an outline or agenda and a few handouts. If people will be using the materials as a reference source for a job aid, you may need to provide more detail.

■ *Company norms.* What types of training materials do people expect? Is it customary to use professionally developed slides, tapes, or flip charts? Make sure that training materials do not fall below company standards. If the norm is professionally developed slides, then flip charts will probably be inadequate.

■ *Trainers' skill level.* Experienced trainers may be able to teach from a participant manual or an outline, whereas novice or line trainers may require a detailed leader's guide. If you are using nontrainers, try to simplify the materials that they develop. Be sure to provide visual aids that help instructors stay on track when teaching.

■ *Your own resourcefulness.* Many successful HRD department managers are masters at mixing and matching whatever program materials they already have on hand. Your materials may not require much customization to fit the needs of your audience. For example, you may be able to tailor an off-the-shelf customer service or supervisory skills program by creating customized role plays that reflect your company's products or some typical work situations.

Now that we have reviewed the major steps involved in program design, let's look more closely at how you can go about finding and managing internal and external resources.

CREATING A DESIGN TEAM OF INTERNAL RESOURCES

More and more HRD managers are learning the value of using line employees to develop and instruct training programs. Even when consultants are designing your programs, you need internal resources as subject-matter experts. They play an important role in developing the design document, and they also help the writers by describing realistic work situations that can serve as the basis of training activities. But first you need to find these people.

Finding the Right Internal Resources to Help You

Think about the types of people you need on your design team. Be sure to include the sponsor's representative — someone who understands the scope and intent of the project — as well as experts who know the details of what must be learned. It is essential that your internal resources have the business knowledge and company experience to be credible experts.

People are more likely to help when they understand a program's value, and a well-planned design document demonstrates how a training program can benefit the organization.

Having a senior manager who believes in the need for the program makes it much easier to find willing resources. For example, Ann Barkey, who was introduced in Chapter One, was able to meet extremely tight deadlines when she was developing a program at Fred the Furrier's because of the CEO's active sponsorship: he made it clear to everyone that he wanted the program. Some senior sponsors may want you to ghost write a letter, to be sent out under their signature, asking people to assist with program design or instruction.

Frequently, HR managers know of credible experts who have an interest in training, and they can often recommend the best way to request help. Be sure to ask these managers whether an employee is the most appropriate resource. Because employees who are good at training are often asked to help, create a backup list to avoid unreasonable demands on certain individuals' time.

As you conduct your needs assessment, you may meet knowledgeable employees interested in supporting training. Coaching on how to design or instruct training programs can be very motivating to them. Participating in training projects can help managers build skill in developing job aids, teaching employees, and making effective presentations; it may even help them make a transition into the HRD field. For example, I worked with a manager, Janet Sliasky, who was considering a career in training after sixteen years in the credit card business. She helped me develop a training program about credit cards, which further fanned her enthusiasm and led to her taking a permanent training position. You can read more about the credit card training program later in the chapter.

Working with Internal Resources

To work well with employees who do not report to you, you need to recognize their contributions, be sensitive to their needs, make it easy for them to help, and follow up with them to ensure completion of tasks.

Although employees who assist with training may find the experience rewarding in and of itself, it is important to acknowledge their contributions. Write thank-you letters and send copies to their supervisors. Thank-you letters from the program sponsor can be even more effective. Make sure that an employee's having been nominated to help design or teach a program is perceived by the business manager as a mark of recognition. Designers and instructors need to know that they have been chosen because of their expertise and credibility.

Consider giving thank-you gifts. You may wish to invite contributors to receptions hosted by sponsoring senior managers. Holding the program in an attractive location can also be a reward. If you work in an international department, you may be able to offer overseas travel opportunities to those who assist with HRD.

Managing a team of people who do not report to you requires strong interpersonal skills. Flexibility and sensitivity are crucial. Line managers and employees in nontraining jobs have responsibilities more pressing than your project. This is especially true when they work for other lines of business. For example, when I worked with managers in our domestic credit card and mortgage business lines to develop training programs for our managers overseas, I had to adapt to their schedules. While managers were enthusiastic about helping, they had to give priority to their departments' needs over my training needs.

When working with line managers as designers and instructors, you need to adjust your expectations, particularly if you are used to working with professional trainers. Developing training materials may be a completely new skill for line managers. They will benefit from your patience, coaching, and tact. Give them encouragement as well as constructive criticism. Remember, you are counting on their technical expertise, not their HRD experience.

Make it as easy as possible for nontrainers to help by providing them with samples of what you want and by simplifying what they have to do. For example, when Ann Barkey asked two experienced salespeople to help develop and teach a sales module, they were reluctant at first because they did not know how to develop a lecture. When Ann changed the module's format, making it a panel discussion in which predetermined questions were to be asked, the salespeople participated enthusiastically and added much to the module's value by sharing their extensive sales experience with less experienced sellers.

Despite good intentions, your internal resources sometimes lack the time or knowledge necessary to produce the training materials you need on schedule. In some cases, a gentle reminder can put them back on track by showing them that you care about deadlines. In other cases, they need more guidance. When a person continually fails to meet deadlines because of other work priorities or lack of commitment, don't hesitate to change to another resource.

FINDING AND MANAGING CONSULTANTS

When you are pressed for time and lack internal expertise, you may want to hire consultants to design customized programs. They can be extremely helpful provided you have the budget and know consultants who have the credibility and skills to get the job done. Hiring and managing consultants to teach an off-the-shelf program are fairly straightforward; working with them to develop a customized program can be more challenging. Finding the right consultant and ensuring that he or she delivers what your organization needs are skills you will need to develop.

Choosing the Right Consultant

The following steps can help you select the right consultant for your project.

1. *Provide clear program guidelines in advance.* When possible, show your design specifications document to potential consultants. A good design document helps consultants decide whether they can deliver what you want and within your budget constraints. The more guidance you provide, the better you can assess the quality of consultants' proposals.

2. *Determine criteria for selecting the best consultant.* It is helpful to identify the skills, attributes, and characteristics needed in a consultant. Consider the following:

- Background and experience with similar projects
- Relevant technical knowledge
- Ability to produce AV and professional materials
- Credibility within your organization
- Availability of staff to design and teach the program
- Geographic location and ease of contact
- Company stability and financial soundness

Refer to Worksheet 5 in Resources for sample criteria to use in selecting a consultant.

3. *Interview and screen consultants.* Consultants are everywhere. The trick is finding the one that you specifically need. You can call on training associates both within and outside your company or use ASTD's consultant service. You can also refer to the *ASTD Buyer's Guide and Consultant Directory* (American Society for Training and Development, 1992). When

possible, interview consultants before requesting proposals. Try to find out the consultants' fit with your company, their availability, and your level of comfort with them. Screening is crucial, especially if consultants charge a fee for writing a proposal.

4. *Solicit proposals from more than one consultant.* Soliciting proposals from several consultants allows you to choose the best approach. Proposals provide work samples, help clarify what it is you want, and stimulate new ideas. Comparing proposals helps you assess the reasonableness of the proposed budget, which increases your chances of gaining funding. Finally, soliciting several proposals ensures that you will have on call consultants who are familiar with the project in the event that your first choice falls through.

5. *Meet the project team before selecting a consultant.* After screening the written proposals, ask the two leading candidates to present their proposals in person. Be sure to find out if the consultants assigned to your project have the requisite skills and experience. In a large firm, the person who presents the proposal may not lead the project team or even work on the project. You may choose a consulting firm because of its reputation for quick turnaround, only to find out later that your project has been assigned to a new consultant unfamiliar with the company's procedures and hence unable to meet deadlines. Try to meet with or at least speak to the project manager and the consultant who will teach the program. To preview instructors, you may be able to observe a videotape of a training presentation or actually observe a live training session.

6. *Ask questions and check references.* Once you have selected a consultant based on the proposal and final presentation, check references. Some consultants make excellent sales presentations, but fall through when it comes to meeting deadlines or quality standards.

Guidelines for Working with Consultants

There are several keys to working with consultants to produce a useful customized program.

- *Allow time to guide and manage consultants.* It is tempting to think that a consultant will do *all* the work for you. In fact, consultants' contributions will vary tremendously, depending on how you manage, guide, and monitor them. Make sure they understand your business so that the programs they devise will meet your needs. And keep in mind that even though consultants are outside your organization, they need not be out of touch.

■ *Introduce consultants to the organization.* Consultants need to be introduced to your subject-matter experts. Go with them to a few meetings to observe how they interact with company employees. Don't allow new consultants to roam around your organization unsupervised. Consultants with poor interpersonal skills can damage your reputation — they are representing *you.*

■ *Follow up when consultants fail to meet deadlines.* You have a right to insist that consultants deliver what they promise on schedule. If they miss deadlines, move quickly to find out why. Perhaps internal resources have not provided the information the consultants need to produce materials. In such situations, you or someone else who has influence over your resources must intervene. Consultants usually have more difficulty exercising authority over your company's employees than someone within the company would. Sometimes consultants miss deadlines because of conflicting work priorities or production problems. You must convince them of the importance of sticking to the schedule. If a consultant fails to improve, speak to a senior member of his or her firm. If your department represents only part of the business the consultant does with your company, you have additional leverage. As a final resort, switch to the consultant who submitted the next best proposal.

REVIEWING AND TESTING PROGRAM MATERIALS

Monitoring the quality of training materials is as important as managing the completion of the project plan. Nothing undermines your credibility faster than sloppy or inaccurate training materials. Quality checks are especially important if you do not have time for a materials test or a pilot program. Be sure to clarify up front what materials you expect, how detailed you want them to be, and when drafts are due so that you will have time to make changes. When it comes to producing materials, don't assume that a consultant's standards are the same as yours.

Testing Materials

When you are unsure of how well specific training materials or activities will work, perform a materials test in which you try out the program activities or materials on a small group. Materials tests can have many benefits. For example, they may help you avoid the following problems: misleading or unrealistic practice situations, unclear instructions, confusing or incomprehensible materials, and poorly timed activities. Your materials test can also reassure the program sponsors that you are making progress and are on the right track. It often generates enthusiasm and anticipation for the program. (See the UNUM Life Insurance example given later in this chapter for the successful use of a materials test of a communication skills survey.)

Pilot Testing a Program

If you expect to run a program several times, conduct a pilot test to check out the entire program design. It is best to delay production of the final leader's guide for teaching a program until after the pilot test. Allow people to attend a pilot program at no charge in return for their tolerance and help.

Select your pilot audience carefully. Choose people who represent the major business units or departments and who can tolerate imperfections, make constructive suggestions, and serve as advocates or champions for the program. Make sure that pilot program participants understand the expectations and responsibilities of participating in such a program. People who are unaware that they have signed up for a pilot may resent the program's unfinished quality. Some managers enjoy the opportunity of helping shape the direction of future training programs, while others prefer to attend more polished programs. Refer to the success stories about Joanne Rogovin and Ellen Kamp in Chapter Seven for examples of how pilot programs can be used to test concepts and build sponsorship for programs.

SUCCESS STORIES

Let's look at how several small HRD departments have approached finding resources to develop and administer customized training programs in managing a line of business, orienting new employees, building communication skills, and introducing a new computer system.

Building Skill in Managing a Credit Card Business

When I was the HRD manager at the International Consumer Banking Division of Chase, I was faced with the challenge of training our business managers to manage a growing credit card business. Because our international managers were coming to New York within a month, I had to develop a program within that time. There was no time to hire a consultant, and our division lacked the expertise to develop the program. Fortunately, the organization had a successful domestic credit card business line whose executive supported the need for training. I explained the resources I would need: secretarial support and a credit card expert to work with me to identify speakers, to help develop materials, and to coordinate implementation. I was given a secretary and a line manager, Janet Sliasky, an ideal resource who had managed several credit card departments and was interested in training. Janet and I developed tentative program design specifications to help us in leading a design meeting. (See Exhibit 6.3.)

I conducted a design meeting with subject-matter experts, representatives from major credit card departments, who knew the needs of our division. We brainstormed program objectives, topics, time frames, and a topic flow, and we agreed that department managers should teach the program. Janet and I worked closely with these managers to develop the content. We stuck with simple teaching methods: lecture, discussion, and observation of operations.

Despite the tight deadline, we developed a participant manual because we wanted to convey complex information, keep discussions on track, and provide a reference guide for managers. For each segment of the program, we included objectives, an outline, relevant exhibits, a glossary, and review questions. We did not need a separate leader's guide because the managers were to develop their own material and would be using the participant manual as their guide. By developing the material jointly with line managers, we helped structure their presentations and created a sense of ownership and pride in the program.

Thanks to the high level of sponsorship, we received excellent cooperation. People from every level of every department contributed to the program. We sent out more than fifty thank-you letters and memento gifts to those who had helped and held a cocktail party hosted by division executives. The program provided needed technical knowledge, created a network of people to assist in resolving problems, and helped launch our division's credit card business. It also helped Janet make the transition from line manager to trainer.

Developing an Orientation for an Insurance Brokerage

Ellen Kamp, introduced earlier, worked as a one-person HRD department at Corroon and Black, a large insurance brokerage firm, now known as Willis Corroon. The company has a strong entrepreneurial culture and believes in decentralized management: each subsidiary has its own CEO, operating procedures, and culture. Because of rapid growth and decentralization, senior managers wanted to orient employees to the Corroon and Black way and to the scope of its operation.

Ellen was asked to create an orientation program. With a budget of $40,000, she decided that a video and job aids would be the best ways to teach people who were spread out over more than one hundred locations. She hired a consultant to gather information from senior executives and to write a video script. The initial script was cumbersome and disjointed because people focused on their lines of business rather than on the corporation as a whole. Ellen sent the script to the managers to get their comments and to raise awareness of a problem—the lack of a collective vision. The orientation program became a "culture-building" project that inspired senior managers to examine what they needed to do to set out the environment of the company.

Ellen worked closely with the senior managers to create a common vision. What she expected to be a quick project took more than a year to complete, but it was time well spent. Ellen developed close relationships with senior managers and produced a program that was used to orient all Corroon and Black employees until the merger that resulted in a new organization, Willis Corroon.

Developing a Communications Program for a Disability Insurance Company

UNUM Life Insurance Company of America is a leading disability insurer with divisions in the United States, Canada, and the United Kingdom. The company's goal is to be the worldwide leader in disability insurance. Business challenges and company values require strong communication skills and collaborative working relationships; however, a survey conducted by the Communications Department indicated a need to improve face-to-face communication skills throughout the company. As director of corporate training, I was charged with jointly developing a communication skills program with the Communications Department.

I held an initial meeting with the department to determine members' interest in the project and get their ideas on what would be an effective program. Together we decided that the program would be open to all employees and that everyone attending the program would receive anonymous feedback on his or her communication skills before and after training. This necessitated the development of a communication skills survey. We would use the survey to diagnose learning needs and then teach specific skills measured in the survey in the training program.

I assigned the task of managing the program's development to one of my two trainers, who had an interest in communication skills but no experience in creating communication skills surveys. We had the in-house expertise to design a training program but not the communication survey. Consequently, we decided to hire the consultant who had conducted the companywide communication survey the previous year. We worked collaboratively with the consultant to develop a draft of the survey that was reviewed by key people in each major division. We then hired another consulting firm to process the surveys because we did not have the administrative capability to collect all the information and keep a data base.

Since the communication survey was so integral to the success of the program, we conducted a materials test with a dozen people. The test group completed the self-assessment survey and also asked six other people (colleagues, subordinates, superiors) to complete a parallel survey regarding their communication skills. We invited this test group to come in for a two-hour session at which we reviewed the survey data and asked for their comments and suggestions. In this way, we checked the clarity of the survey questions, the usefulness of the feedback report, and the processing capabilities of the consultant before we actually ran the program. The materials test showed that the survey worked well but that the survey feedback report was confusing. We adjusted the survey report and made some refinements in how we worked with the survey processing firm.

The materials test generated tremendous interest and enthusiasm for the full-scale pilot program that we conducted for representatives for each major division at no charge. During the pilot program we received numerous ideas on how to improve the program and then made changes in the next program offering.

To reach many people as quickly as possible, we decided to offer the program both centrally and decentrally. The Corporate Training Department offered a central program for individuals who wanted to attend with people from different divisions. We also ran a train-the-trainer session to train people within the divisions to teach the program. Division trainers learned how to use the leader's guide, how to customize the design to best meet their business needs, and how to improve their training facilitation skills. Within a few months, trainers within the division taught the program to several hundred employees in the customer service unit who were learning to work effectively in self-directed teams.

Developing Business-Focused Systems Training

Mindy Taylor was hired as the human resource director, a generalist position, for an independent insurance brokerage and real estate development company with 150 employees. Her initial challenge was to help improve employee morale and reduce turnover. "The company had a typical sales culture with a 'do-it-now' mentality that focused on immediate results. There were no human resources policies in place, and people were unhappy with minor pay inequities" (interview with the author, July 23, 1992). After revamping the compensation program and developing human resources policies and procedures, Mindy was ready to tackle a training challenge. She describes the situation this way: "The company had committed to installing a computer for policy and information accounting to reduce the cumbersome manual process. Unfortunately, the systems group was isolated from the business and did not figure out a better process; it merely copied the manual one in the computer system. The system was perceived as an accounting system, not a business system. Business people did the technical training in isolation of systems training, and the systems people did not know the business."

As a first training intervention, Mindy helped the systems group work in partnership with the heads of the three main business units. She formed a steering group of business and systems people to create modularized training for customer service representatives to teach people how to use the system more effectively. Mindy's role was that of an internal consultant who had expertise in instructional design. She helped the design group develop learning objectives and an overall design and training philosophy and also helped determine the sequence of the training modules and appropriate prerequisites for each module. The business and systems experts' role was to develop the technical material and to do the actual teaching. Mindy reviewed the material they developed, and helped build their skills in instructional development, job analysis, and instructional techniques.

As a result of the joint project, business and systems people started to communicate more with each other, and systems training was more effective in getting people to actually use the system. This was partly because of the improved instructional design but mostly because of the joint ownership of the training—both groups were committed to making the training succeed rather than blaming each other for its ineffectiveness.

SUMMARY: STRATEGIES FOR MANAGING PROGRAM DEVELOPMENT

1. Maintain control of program development. Play an active role in developing the project plan, creating the design specification document, marshaling resources to design and teach the program, monitoring program design, testing program materials, and evaluating the program's effectiveness.

2. Develop the necessary skills to manage the design process. These include project management skills, knowledge of instructional design, and specific expertise regarding subjects to be taught.

3. Find internal resources to serve on a design team.

   - Demonstrate senior management's sponsorship.

   - Identify the best possible experts who can help you.

   - Obtain the approval of your experts' managers before approaching the experts for help.

   - Be sure that experts are committed to assisting you with your project.

   - Plan to recognize the contributions of internal resources.

4. Ensure that external consultants meet your qualifications and will complete the project as planned.

- Provide consultants with design specifications as part of the request-for-proposal process.

- Request proposals from several consultants.

- Determine that consultants have the credibility to be effective within your company.

- Check consultants' references.

- Ask consultants for written project plans.

- Set aside time to manage the consultants.

- Follow up when deadlines are missed.

5. Review and test program design and materials.

▲ ▲ ▲ ▲ ▲ ▲ ▲ ▲ ▲ ▲ ▲ ▲ ▲ ▲ ▲ ▲ ▲ ▲ ▲ **Chapter** *7*

Attracting
Your Customers

*E*ffectively marketing human resource development is a major challenge. With pressure to produce and deliver programs, HRD managers can easily become isolated from the customers they are trying to serve. The manager of a small HRD department may think: "I have to develop and teach programs; I don't have time to market HRD—that's for those large HRD departments." This attitude can inadvertently undermine the success of a small HRD department.

Why is marketing so important? A good marketing strategy may avoid problems that many small HRD departments face: programs canceled or run with too few participants, the wrong people attending programs, and people arriving at programs late or unprepared for training. What good are excellent HRD programs, if employees don't know what your programs are intended to do, who should participate in them, when they are offered, and what is involved in making them successful? In the words of the renowned marketing expert Don Schrello (1984, p. 7): "The best course or program in the world won't do anything until someone else knows about it. And not just any 'someone, but the *right* someone.'"

The foundation of good marketing begins with a solid understanding of the organization's business and the role that HRD plays in its success. You will have a much easier time attracting customers when your programs and services really do meet vital business needs. To do that, you must perform a sound needs assessment as described in Chapter Two. You must also be clear about the following:

■ *Key customer constituencies that will need to be informed about HRD.* As Schrello (1984) points out, there are four major constituencies that you must deal with in marketing HRD: (1) those who influence HRD decisions, (2) those who make the decisions regarding use of HRD, (3) those who pay for HRD, and (4) those who attend HRD programs. One person often handles more than one of these roles. It is essential for you to be aware of who your constituencies are—especially the people who make decisions about whether or not to support and fund an HRD effort. A senior manager who endorses an HRD program may be reluctant to provide the necessary money if he or she has not been adequately informed or involved in the decision-making process. Finding funding is particularly critical in HRD departments with small budgets because programs are often paid for by other departments.

■ *Information your key customer constituencies want.* Try to find out what type of information people need before they decide to participate in or advocate HRD activities. People usually want to receive information about program goals and learning objectives, the target audience, learning methods, length, cost, location, and dates. Many want to know who is sponsoring the program, who has already attended, and who is planning to attend a specific offering.

■ *The best way to reach your customer constituencies.* Schrello recommends that you make a list of all the people you need to communicate with, including their names, positions, addresses, and phone numbers. This directory is invaluable when you want to promote or advertise any HRD program. Which media should you use to reach them? We'll explore this question in the next section.

WAYS TO PROMOTE YOUR PROGRAMS AND SERVICES

There is a wide range of options you can use to inform your customer groups. You may be able to use a variety of face-to-face approaches, printed materials, or even in-house television to publicize events. Some of your alternatives include individual meetings with managers, advisory groups, business meetings, newsletters, flyers/announcements, electronic mail, bulletin board notices, a catalogue, program previews, and evaluation reports. Let's look more closely at each of these.

Individual Meetings with Managers

The best way to learn about senior and middle managers' values and opinions regarding HRD is to stay in close communication with them. Communicating frequently with managers can help you discover their most pressing business problems, how HRD could help, and how well they understand the requirements for effective HRD. This also allows you to recognize any biases and preferences they have about HRD, and how they would like you to keep them informed. Some managers, for example, prefer brief memos that highlight progress and plans, while others prefer more informal or more detailed information.

One-on-one meetings are an excellent way to learn who your allies are and to build new alliances. Meetings can help you build rapport with key influencers and decision makers because you can tailor your remarks to deal with their concerns and highlight benefits most salient to them.

Advisory Groups (Task Forces)

As discussed earlier, you can use advisory groups to assess needs and develop programs. Such groups can also provide ideas about how to market HRD; and often they will actively promote your programs, especially when members have played a role in developing them. Forming a task force to develop a program or series of programs is an excellent way to encourage joint ownership and to ensure that the programs are tied to business needs. Remember the example of Mindy Taylor's steering committee to develop business-focused systems training in Chapter Six. Be sure to choose advisory committee members who are well respected within the company and active supporters of HRD. We will examine Joanne Rogovin's use of an advisory group at Kidder Peabody later in this chapter.

Business Meetings

You may be able to present your HRD plan, schedule, and upcoming events at business meetings. When appropriate, try to see that HRD is part of the agenda, especially when you are working with managers who are widely dispersed geographically. A well-prepared, professional presentation can help build your credibility with senior managers and encourage them to view you as a business partner rather than an overhead expense. Distributing handouts that summarize key points helps reinforce your message and may enable people who do not attend the meeting to learn about your plans and progress. Make sure that your visual aids and handouts are appropriate for your audience. For example, the manager of a one-person training department discovered that Japanese managers, unlike many Americans, prefer to receive full-scale reports prior to meetings rather than executive summaries and handouts during a meeting.

Even if you cannot formally present your plan at a business meeting, talking with key decision makers at breaks and social activities may help you build relationships. Listening to discussions of business issues during the meeting or during breaks can give you insight into important topics and company politics.

Newsletters

A company newsletter may provide you with free advertising and publicity. You can use newsletters to publicize upcoming HRD events or to describe successes; nothing sells HRD programs better than testimonials from opinion makers in a company. If possible, include a regular column on HRD plans and progress in the newsletter. If your company does not have a newsletter, you may be able to start your own. It is possible to produce attractive and inexpensive newsletters with the computer software available today.

Flyers/Announcements

Flyers and announcements are an excellent, inexpensive way to promote programs. Be sure to use a descriptive title, provide complete information, and highlight benefits in your flyers. You can get ideas on how to write catchy titles and program descriptions from catalogues and flyers produced by outside training vendors. Schrello (1984, p. 29) suggests that your announcement should include the following:

■ The program title and a clear description of the program

■ A complete agenda, including topics with start and end times

■ Benefits of the program

- Your audience (their level, experience, and any prerequisites)

- The cost of the program and how to pay for it

- How to register and get more information

You'll want to vary the amount of detail you present in flyers according to the needs of your audience. Refer to the program announcement for Chase's ICB credit card training program in Exhibit 7.1 for an example. Carolyn Balling (interview with the author, June 20, 1990) believes that simple flyers work best for marketing internal programs. A sample flyer developed by Carolyn is shown in Exhibit 7.2 (on page 139). We'll look at this and at how to use flyers effectively later in this chapter.

Exhibit 7.1. Sample Program Announcement: ICB Credit Card Training Program.

August 6, 1986

To: Distribution
From: Carol P. McCoy, Training Manager
Re: Credit Card Training Program October 6–17, 1986

We are pleased to announce that a second session of the ICB Credit Card Training Program will be held October 6–17, 1986, on-site at Chase locations in New York and Delaware.

The program is intended for card center managers, regional card managers, department managers in the card business, and key members of credit card project teams.

Building on feedback from the June pilot session, the training provides an overview of Chase's credit card business. Managers will also have an opportunity to observe work flows, documents, and phone calls in various areas to help them understand Chase's performance requirements, standards, and risk-mitigating procedures. Time will be set aside to discuss current business problems and application to overseas markets. Refer to the enclosed program description for the objectives and agenda. To ensure that speakers are prepared and discussions are relevant, we are asking participants to complete the enclosed questionnaire.

If you have candidates for this program, kindly have them complete and return the enclosed nomination form by August 29. Please note that we are asking that the candidate's direct manager and the ICB country consumer manager approve the nomination.

All program expenses, except airfare, will be paid for by International Consumer Training. I will be glad to answer any questions you have about the program. I can be reached on Chase net X.

I look forward to hearing from you.

131

Electronic Mail Communications

If available at your company, electronic mail enables you to market programs with virtually no paperwork and with minimal cost. When Banker's Trust cut back their corporate training department, Ron Carter (interview with the author, March 4, 1991) became a one-person HRD department. Ron relied heavily on electronic mail to market his management programs. Building on relationships he had established as a trainer, Ron sent "E mail" notices to human resource managers and alumni of his programs to obtain nominations for upcoming programs. He sent lists of individuals who had already attended and of those who had been prior nominees to "seed" people's nomination lists. To generate interest in HRD in divisions where people had not participated in programs before, Ron sent short, "teaser" E mail messages that sometimes triggered phone calls and meetings where Ron discussed programs in person.

Bulletin Board Notices

Posting announcements or flyers describing upcoming events on a bulletin board in the cafeteria or other prominent locations can publicize your programs. Bulletin boards may be the fastest and simplest way to reach many people. Try to catch people's attention with attractive flyers or with photographs of employees participating in various HRD activities. Do not, however, rely solely on bulletin boards for publicity because many people do not look at them.

Program Catalogue

While program catalogues require money, time, and effort to create, they have several important benefits.

- *Announce a change in direction.* When your HRD department is new or different from a previous department, a catalogue lets people know of your existence and your strategy. Joanne Rogovin used her catalogue to publicize an expansion in the scope of HRD—the beginning of HRD programs above the supervisory level.

- *Provide a framework.* You can provide a clear framework for HRD by the way in which you structure or sequence your courses in a curriculum. Your framework can identify core competencies needed by all employees and show how specific programs teach these needed competencies. This can help people select courses to attend at various points in their careers.

■ *Increase awareness of a range of programs.* If you only publicize programs through flyers, one course at a time, people may not realize the range of available programs. You might even include programs offered outside your company in your catalogue to let employees know which ones you recommend.

■ *Inform people of other HRD services you offer in addition to programs.* A catalogue may describe your mission, philosophy, and range of services. This can help educate people about potential HRD activities other than training programs and provide them with ideas about how to use your department. A catalogue may also include useful planning tools, such as a guide for selecting training, development, and educational activities.

■ *Demonstrate professionalism and commitment.* A well-crafted catalogue sends the message that HRD is a professional function and that the department is there for the long term. Ellen Kamp, who is discussed later in this chapter, published her catalogue because she wanted to let people know that "HRD was here to stay" (interview with the author, March 13, 1991).

Program Previews

Involving managers and key decision makers in a program preview can build support for a program. You may be able to preview films, videos, or computer-based training at little or no cost. Previewing audiovisuals allows you to evaluate their usefulness, to build support, and to begin the process of training. One HRD manager's video demonstration impressed senior managers so much that she obtained funding to purchase several videos.

Previews of classroom training can generate a great deal of excitement. Consultants, who want to sell their programs, may be willing to conduct brief program overviews for free. I used this technique in working with a customer service project team. To build a greater understanding of how customer relations training could help, I invited a consultant who had already taught two successful programs inside our company to give an overview of his program. He explained research supporting the need for customer relations skills and then reviewed the skill model taught in the training program. He demonstrated the difference between excellent and poor customer relations by playing audiotapes of role plays that were created in the training, and then he illustrated the skill improvement that occurred with each role play. One manager, who strongly believed in the program, mentioned that several customers had recently written to the company president to praise service representatives who had just completed the training. The presentation increased the project team's commitment to improving customer relations skills through training.

Summary Evaluations

Distributing summary evaluations of successful programs can be an excellent way to promote your programs. Be sure to include quotations about insights learned as well as any business ideas gained from the programs. Ron Carter, mentioned earlier, found that managers frequently gained ideas for new products or services in a cross-business leadership development program. He publicized them in evaluation summaries that he gave out to managers and program alumni. A sample evaluation report that I used at UNUM Life is included in Chapter Nine, Exhibits 9.1 and 9.2.

MAKING SURE YOU MEET CUSTOMER NEEDS

To be successful in attracting customers, you need more than good marketing techniques: you need sound HRD programs that meet critical business needs and provide appropriate solutions to problems. Make sure that a training program is the best solution to the problem. There are limits to what training can do. Do not suggest a training program if you know that it will be an ineffective or extremely costly solution. Performance problems may be caused by something other than lack of knowledge or skill; for example, they may be caused by a lack of clear standards, unattainable performance goals, insufficient feedback when standards are not met, or insufficient recognition or reward for competent performance. Position yourself as a "performance improvement consultant, not as a peddler of training courses" (Nathan and Stanleigh, 1991, p. 41).

For your marketing strategy to succeed, your programs must be worthwhile, convenient, and cost-effective. This involves planning and ongoing communication with the managers who will decide whether or not to send their people to your programs. As a safeguard, check to see that your programs meet these criteria:

- The program meets a clearly defined business need.

- The dates are convenient for your target audience. Avoid conflicts with important events, such as domestic and international holidays, meetings, other programs, or key events in the strategic planning or budgeting cycle.

- The program location is convenient for your target audience. Choose a location that participants can get to easily and that has affordable lodging nearby.

- The program is of appropriate duration given business constraints. Offer the shortest possible programs that achieve learning objectives. When appropriate, consider breaking programs into modules that can be taught in shorter segments. For example, Joanne Rogovin offered a finance course for three hours once a week over a thirteen-week period. This made it easier for line managers to teach and for employees to attend the program, complete homework assignments, and absorb complex information.

- The program is reasonably priced. Make sure your rates are competitive with the marketplace. Consider offering programs for free until you have established their value.

FOCUSING ON WHAT YOU CAN DO

Successful marketing may actually lead to more work than you can handle. When you are bombarded with too many requests for help, you have two choices: you can try to meet everyone's needs, sacrificing the quality of your work as well as your health, or you can focus your efforts on business priorities, doing fewer things very well. Ron Carter recommends: "Do less, but do it better" (interview with the author, March 1, 1991).

When I began my assignment as a one-person HRD department in Chase's International Consumer Banking Division, I sometimes told managers who wanted my help: "I'm only one person; I can't do everything." While I couldn't do everything, I would have been wiser to say: "Let's look at your situation more closely to see what you really need and how I can help. I'm sure we can find some way to solve your problem." Just because you are a "single contributor," does not mean that you do everything yourself. Draw on the relationships that you build with other resources inside and outside the company, and find ways to share responsibilities for developing materials and teaching programs. Work toward a joint solution where both you and the client take some responsibility for solving the problem.

Be careful not to undermine your own effectiveness by calling attention to the shortcomings of your work because you have been used to having a large staff to help you. Create a positive, realistic mind-set in the eyes of your customers, and then exceed their expectations. There is always room for improvement: ask the users of your services for their suggestions, and incorporate their ideas wherever possible. Don't fall into the trap of apologizing for what you cannot do; focus on what you *can* do.

SUCCESS STORIES

To get a better feel for how attracting customers really works in a small department, let's take a look at several different approaches taken by successful HRD managers.

Attracting Customers Through Direct Marketing

Carolyn Balling, former director of HRD for AMEX Life, learned the hard way how to market her programs to the company's six hundred employees. Carolyn sent a program catalogue to all employees, yet most people did not read it or use it to register for courses. She also tried sending flyers to managers to announce upcoming programs. The managers often neglected to share the information with employees who were the target audience for the training programs. Flyers also proved inefficient because they referred people to the catalogue for more information and for registration forms. And Carolyn ended up creating more work for herself by having to continuously send out copies of the catalogue.

Carolyn decided to take advantage of her company's expertise in direct marketing—selling products directly to people through the mail. She invited a marketing manager to critique her catalogue and flyers. Her revised flyers became so successful in attracting the right people to programs that Carolyn no longer needed to produce a catalogue. She learned so much that she now frequently speaks about internal marketing at national conventions. Here are Carolyn's recommendations (interview with the author, June 20, 1990).

■ *Maintain a good data base.* As HRD manager, you have an enormous advantage over outside marketers—access to an excellent and manageable data base for mailings at minimal cost. Carolyn attributes her success to her mailing list: "We had a great list of people, including what they did, and where they sat. We kept the data base really 'clean' and up-to-date."

■ *Mail directly to potential program users.* Go right to the target audience and send flyers directly to people who might use the program. Let managers know that you are going to send their employees an invitation, but do not go through the managers because they often forget to give program flyers to their employees.

■ *Personalize your mailing list as much as possible.* People are much more likely to respond to a program directed specifically at their needs. As Carolyn puts it: "You can slice up your data base in as many ways as make sense to you—by level, by function, by years of experience. Then you can tailor your sales pitch to fit the needs of that particular group." You might, for example, modify the name or content of the program so that it reflects the specific audience.

■ *Make your flyers attractive and highlight benefits.* Make the content and look of your flyers appealing. According to Carolyn, "We needed a recognizable look, one that was more pleasing to the eye and easier to read. We found access to a Macintosh computer and a better printer in another department. We featured benefits by describing 'what's in it for you' and the results that training would bring. And we highlighted advantages, such as the fact that programs were free. We charged for programs only if people canceled within less than forty-eight hours before the start of a program."

■ *Make it easy for people to respond and register.* Simplify the registration form and process. Carolyn states, "Asking for too much information from people may become a barrier. Do not ask for information already in your data base; only ask for changes since your last mailing. Make it easy to return your registration form." For example, Carolyn used peel-off mailing labels that employees could use on the registration form. She included the return address on the back of the registration form so that employees could

137

easily mail it back. And to maintain good customer relations, she allowed people to sign up for later sessions of programs if they could not make the upcoming session, and they could check off a box if they did not want to receive mailings on particular topics.

■ *Use bulletin boards to post flyers.* Carolyn used a bulletin board in the main floor of the company headquarters to post announcements of internal and external programs. She discovered that photographs of people participating in HRD activities helped to grab people's attention.

See Exhibits 7.2 and 7.3 for the sample flyer and registration form that Carolyn used for interviewing and selection training at Collagen, where Carolyn now works as HRD manager.

Using Task Forces, Meetings, and Newsletters at Kidder Peabody

Joanne Rogovin, formerly of Kidder Peabody, took a different approach from Carolyn Balling's. Joanne made extensive use of task forces to develop and market programs. Because she worked closely with line managers in developing and implementing her training programs, marketing was done primarily through progress reports presented in newsletters and at meetings. She publicized her programs through a catalogue, a department newsletter, and bulletins that described what was happening with programs in progress. Here are Joanne's recommendations for marketing HRD (interview with the author, Feb. 7, 1990).

■ *Develop business relationships.* "Keep the network going within the company. Build key contacts so that you can stay current in the business and provide business-relevant solutions to problems." Once you have established relationships through meetings and HRD events, you can communicate more effectively through more impersonal methods, such as newsletters and memos.

■ *Use a catalogue to publicize offerings.* A year after Joanne joined Kidder, she produced a catalogue because this was the first time that HRD was being offered for managers and executives. Joanne sent the catalogue, which included course descriptions and a six-month schedule, to line managers and human resources managers across the firm. Four to six weeks before the programs, Joanne sent reminders or called people to let

Exhibit 7.2. Sample Flyer: Program Announcement.

If you have a staff vacancy . . .

. . . chances are that you want to fill it fast and fill it well. You want to interview people who have what you want and need, and select the best candidate. Chances are, too, that you will want to attend:

INTERVIEWING and SELECTION
a one and a half day workshop for hiring managers:*

APRIL 14–15, in manufacturing facility

APRIL 21–22, in corporate offices

Each session is limited to 12 participants

INTERVIEWING and SELECTION will:

- help you **determine who**, exactly, you need for the job, so you will both succeed;

- give you an **approach** for interviewing and decision-making that increases your odds of making the right choice;

- enhance your **questioning skills**; and

- let you **practice** new interviewing techniques in a low-risk setting before putting you and your department on the "hiring line."

Others who have attended **INTERVIEWING and SELECTION** have said:

"It's a darn fine course. I think anyone can benefit."
"Having these skills will save me valuable time."
"My confidence and the questions I ask have improved—no more 'give-aways!'"

To enroll: Complete the attached form and return to Training and Development by **April 3**. Your enrollment will be confirmed. *Space is limited to 12 participants in each group.*

INTERVIEWING and SELECTION is free! Your investment of 10½ hours now can save you time later, and potentially save your department and the company several thousand dollars!

* If you involve your direct reports in your hiring process by having them interview key candidates, you'll want them to attend a new, one day course, **DEVELOPING INTERVIEWING SKILLS**, to be offered in mid-May. The course is intended for those who interview who are not hiring managers.

Source: Reproduced with permission of C. Balling. All rights reserved.

Exhibit 7.3. Sample Program Registration Form.

INTERVIEWING and SELECTION
Enrollment

Name _____ Extension _____

Dept _____ Division _____

Position _____ Length of time in position _____

Immediate Supervisor _____ Initials (to approve enrollment) _____

Directions: *Complete all information and return to Training and Development* **by APRIL 3.** *Space is limited.*

1. **Check one:**

   ☐ Sign me up for the workshop on **April 14–15 in manufacturing.**

   ☐ Sign me up for the workshop on **April 21–22 at corporate offices.**

   ☐ I am **unable to attend** either workshop. Please keep me informed of future course offerings.

   ☐ I completed a similar course in (year)_____, sponsored by _____.
   You do not need to let me know about future offerings for this course.

2. **Current** (or anticipated) **openings** in my area:

   title   *exempt or non-exempt*   *anticipated hire date*

3. In the past 12 months **I have filled the following openings:**

   title   *exempt or non-exempt*   *start date*

4. By attending this workshop I am hoping to **find out more about, or improve my skills** in these areas:

5. Send these people from my staff the **enrollment information** on DEVELOPING INTERVIEWING SKILLS:

fold and staple—no envelope needed!

Source: Reproduced with permission of C. Balling. All rights reserved.

them know of upcoming events. Joanne believes in the value of a catalogue: "A catalogue is a tangible product. I sent it out after a year because up to that time we had mostly worked on two major projects and had not concentrated on other courses. After sending out my catalogue, I got calls from managers telling me that they were not aware that we offered courses in writing skills or presentation skills. Some people did not even know that the HRD department existed."

■ *Use a task force to develop and market programs.* To understand how to use a task force to develop and market programs, let's look at The Best of the Best, a twelve-module self-study program for sales assistants. When a branch productivity study indicated that the highest-performing branches had the most knowledgeable sales assistants, Joanne met with the national sales managing director to discuss how to improve the skills of sales assistants. In her words, "We decided the way to have a successful program was to create a broad-based task force of sales, administration, operations, and systems people to work with an outside firm. We did this out of respect for the program user. If we were going to take people off their jobs, we needed to have practical, relevant, useful information. We needed input from users and from people who received their services." The managing director nominated the branch manager to work on the task force. An operations manager, who was part of the original study, joined the task force and nominated others to participate.

■ *Recognize accomplishments and make people feel important.* "We made task force members feel very important so that they would work hard on the project, go back to their regions, and talk up the program. We flew them into heaquarters, wined and dined them, and worked them very hard." They identified content and wrote volumes of technical material that the consultant put into an instructional design format. The group members reviewed all material and discussed their reactions with Joanne in conference calls. Joanne also recognized the accomplishments of people who successfully completed the program by giving out attractive certificates bearing The Best of the Best logo to program graduates. The program had an impact on the business—it reduced errors made by sales assistants as well as the time needed for them to become proficient in their jobs. According to Joanne, "We wrote up the program in the company newsletter, and even included a photo of one of the train-the-trainer sessions. We personally recognized everyone involved in the effort."

■ *Demonstrate sponsorship.* Sponsorship is key to attracting customers, especially when you use self-study programs that require monitoring by line managers in remote locations. According to Joanne, as sponsor of The Best of the Best program, the managing director sent a letter stating his excitement about the project to the entire division. He explained that a consultant had found areas where the company could improve, that they were going to design a training program to accomplish this, and that they would keep everyone informed of progress. He also made an introductory video that was used at the program launch and whenever anyone began the program.

■ *Communicate progress and build anticipation.* Joanne wanted to build a sense of anticipation about the program; she communicated regularly to everyone about progress in the project, beginning with the sponsor's letter to the division and following up with newsletters from HRD. Joanne gave regular updates, including outlines of chapters, an overview of the design meeting with the consultant, and samples from the audiotapes and videotapes.

■ *Pilot test material.* Part of meeting customers' needs is making sure that your materials work. Joanne ran a pilot test with thirty-seven sales assistants in five branches to make sure that the content and process worked before rolling out the program to everyone. The program was tested with inexperienced sales assistants (the target population) and with experienced assistants who could verify the program's accuracy. The task force had been so meticulous that Joanne needed to change only a few words of more than six hundred pages of materials. Pilot participants were impressed with the program. Joanne encouraged them to tell others of the program's value because employees are usually more influenced by their peers than they are by announcements from the HRD department.

■ *Build ownership.* One way to ensure widespread program participation is to include many people in the development and implementation of a program. Even though The Best of the Best program primarily involves self-study, managers play a strong administrative, motivational, and coaching role in supporting it; Joanne trained more than eighty facilitators to implement it. She conducted facilitator training with the consultant on a regional basis. Explains Joanne, "We made a big deal of being a facilitator. We did the training at nice hotels and took the facilitators out to dinner. They felt valued. We did the training a month and a half prior to launching the program so that they would go back to their offices and 'talk it up' and prepare the brokers to support the program. We wanted the brokers to be part of the process. We used communal events to build interest, deal with their questions and concerns, and make everyone feel included. We kicked off the program with a lunch with the brokers and the sales assistants. All but a few of our twelve hundred brokers eagerly supported the program and allowed time for their assistants to complete the program. The reluctant brokers were quickly turned around."

Marketing Through a Catalogue and Ongoing Communication at Corroon and Black

Ellen Kamp built Corroon and Black's HRD department from scratch. Since HRD at Corroon had had several false starts, Ellen wanted to send a message that HRD was there for the long term. Shortly after joining the company, Ellen published a schedule and list of courses in a slick booklet that, in her words, "looked more like an annual report than a catalogue." She included programs that she would offer as well as self-study programs whereby employees could obtain advanced degrees in insurance. She sent all senior officers in each division her catalogue along with a cover memo from the CEO announcing the importance of professional development to the success of the company. Ellen suggests taking a business-focused approach to marketing to ensure that you have management's support (interview with the author, March 13, 1991).

■ *Position HRD as an integral part of the business, not just an ancillary service.* According to Ellen, "Talk about the business in business terms, not training terms. The key is knowing everything that you can about your business and organization. Everything we do is tied to the business objectives. As training professionals we need to make it a major part of our job to understand the business needs and issues, how training ties into the business plan, and why training is a valid investment."

■ *Find opportunities to learn about the organization's business and to communicate your mission.* During the six months before launching her programs, Ellen worked on several projects that allowed her to talk with key managers and regional executives. She got invited to as many meetings as she could in order to talk about her vision of HRD and the role of management in professional development. At these meetings, Ellen also had the opportunity to listen to business issues and learn about Corroon's strategy of differentiation through quality service rather than through low pricing. Ellen discovered that as competitive pressure increased, some sales representatives were compromising this strategy, rushing in to make bids to clients but failing to close on sales. She recognized the need for a strategic selling program to increase sales and retain existing accounts.

■ *Conduct pilot programs to build involvement and sponsorship.* Ellen rolled out the strategic selling program in a two-phase process. In the first phase, she held several pilot programs to obtain local "buy-in." She asked the CEOs of Corroon's subsidiaries to send well-respected sales leaders to pilot programs to evaluate the programs' effectiveness. While the pilot audiences were very enthusiastic about the training, they realized that a workshop alone would not change the operating culture. They needed the involvement of the CEOs and sales managers in each subsidiary to do this. In phase two, Ellen explained to the CEOs that establishing a strategic selling process in their subsidiaries required their commitment. They needed to commit to sending themselves, their sales managers, and producers to the workshop and to conducting follow-up meetings with Ellen to prepare an action plan of how to make the selling process work in their office. Ellen worked with a dozen subsidiaries to make the process happen. Managers know that the workshop is a management tool to help them meet their revenue goals.

■ *Publicize successes.* Once Ellen's programs were launched, she compiled evaluations that summarized participants' comments about the programs and sent them to senior managers so that people would be aware of the level of HRD activity and how people valued the programs. As a result of the quality of Ellen's programs and of her marketing efforts, her department has grown to meet the needs of the company.

· ·

SUMMARY: STRATEGIES FOR ATTRACTING YOUR CUSTOMERS

1. Create a marketing plan for attracting your customers. Through a needs analysis, determine your target audience and the products that best meet their needs. Make sure programs meet a real business need. Using a task force or advisory group can ensure relevance to the organization's business.

2. Demonstrate senior management's commitment to human resource development. Make sure you have management's commitment before developing programs. Publicize your sponsor's support through memos and newsletters,

and invite your sponsor to host events that launch new programs. If you are using self-study methods, consider having the sponsor create a video announcing each program's importance.

3. Make sure that the right people know about your programs and schedules, who should attend, and what they will get out of the programs.

4. Use a variety of methods to promote your programs. Consider informal meetings and talks with key managers, advisory groups, business meetings, newsletters, flyers, electronic mail communications, bulletin board notices, a catalogue, program previews, and evaluation reports.

5. Try to ensure that program dates do not conflict with other important events and that program logistics (timing, duration, and location) are the most convenient for your target audience.

6. Focus on what you can do rather than try to do everything. Focus on the benefits of what you have to offer, avoid being defensive about how little you can do, and don't be overly critical of yourself because you think that your programs are not perfect.

Mastering the Art of Program Logistics

A s HRD manager you are responsible for program delivery and administration, quality control, and implementation of your plan. With all the pressure, it is easy to become bogged down in administrative details and lose focus on your customers. You may even start to feel: "If only I didn't have to deal with all these customers, I could get my job done." How well you handle program logistics contributes greatly to an HRD program's success and can make or break your credibility. As Scandinavian Airlines president Jan Carlzon puts it, every customer contact is a "moment of truth" when customers form an opinion of your organization (Albrecht and Zemke, 1985). Chapter Eight will help you stay focused on your customers and build processes to ensure that you have effective program delivery and administration, registration, and tracking procedures for your department.

MANAGING LOGISTICAL TASKS

Some of the best HRD programs fail because of inattention to logistical details that can have great impact on your customers' experience of HRD. Here is a small sampling of potential problems caused by administrative oversights:

- *Scheduling problems.* People initially scheduled to attend your programs fail to attend when important meetings or events are changed after you publish your schedule.

- *Instructor problems.* Instructor credibility is undermined because scheduled presenters send unprepared, last-minute substitutes.

- *Training facility and equipment problems.* Training sessions run over time because rooms and equipment were not set up properly or checked before hand.

- *Difficulties in travel arrangements.* Programs are disrupted when participants come late or leave early as a result of poorly planned travel arrangements.

- *Material production difficulties.* Program participants fail to listen to a lecture because they are distracted by errors in the participant materials.

You can avoid these problems if you pay attention to logistical details such as program scheduling, management of training facilities, program setup, participant registration, travel arrangements, production and distribution of training materials, and record keeping. Perhaps key to all of these is streamlining and automating the process while keeping the customers' needs in mind. Let's look at each of the foregoing logistical tasks and how you might handle them in a small HRD department.

Scheduling Programs

Construct your schedule with the needs of your customers and instructors in mind. As a small department, you need to schedule programs so that you have enough time to develop program materials, arrange for instructors, and manage program logistics. In the early stages you may need to allow more time between programs. Once you have been operating for awhile, you may be able to offer several programs at once provided you use outside instructors for some of them. Consider the following factors as you plan your schedule:

- The company's strategic planning or business planning cycle
- Quarter-end business activities

147

- Holidays, including local, national, and religious holidays

- Peak volume or production periods such as the beginning or end of the week or month

- Availability of nearby training facilities

- Tie-ins with other significant company events that require prospective trainees to be in one location

- Travel time for most people to the location (considering the impact of late arrival times or jet lag on participants or instructors)

Managing Training Facilities and Program Setup

Training facilities have a great impact on program effectiveness and ease of program administration. If you are lucky, you may work for a company that has on-site training facilities or be able to use a high-quality conference facility. As the HRD manager, you need to decide where to conduct your programs. The lower your budget, the more likely it is that you will have to offer programs at company facilities not designed for training and have to take care of many details handled by experienced staff members at training conference centers—for example, providing meals and snacks; setting up the training rooms; stocking supplies such as flip-chart pads, markers, and masking tape; supplying equipment; repairing or replacing defective equipment; and serving as a message control center.

Consider the following factors when choosing a training facility:

- *Cost.* If there is a fee for using the facility, can you afford it?

- *Location.* How convenient is the facility to program participants and speakers?

- *Services provided.* Can you arrange for meals and breaks? Are there people who can help you set up the training room?

- *Training equipment provided.* Will there be appropriate equipment and space to show movies, videotapes, or slides? To videotape training activities, or to use computers? Are easel stands and flip-chart pads available, and is there adequate space to tape flip charts to walls?

■ *Room environment.* How well ventilated and lighted is the training room? Can you adjust the temperature? People do not learn well when they are falling asleep because of a poorly ventilated, overheated, or dimly lighted room. Will you be able to control the lighting so that it will be dark enough for showing slides, videos, and overhead transparencies and yet light enough for taking notes? Can the room accommodate all your participants comfortably? Are "break-out" rooms available for small group activities? See Laird (1985) for a discussion of training room requirements.

■ *Distractions.* How distracted will participants be by the demands of their office? Can distractions of phones, faxes, and electronic mail be minimized or eliminated?

■ *Cancellation penalties.* When using training facilities that you don't own, you may be charged for rooms and services you don't use if you cancel a program or change your reservations after a stipulated deadline. Be sure to find out how late in the process you can inform the facility of the number of program participants. Dates range from a few days to several months in advance of the program.

Managing Program Registration

Program registration is a customer-intensive process with many "moments of truth." If you have been used to the luxury of having someone else handle registration while you concentrate on designing and instructing programs, managing the details of program registration may be tedious, burdensome, or even overwhelming. Careful planning can simplify the registration process and also ensure that you focus on the needs of your customers. What are the critical steps you want to manage regarding registration?

■ *Provide timely program announcements.* The registration process begins when customers start to consider the possibility of attending one of your programs. Even if you have sent out a program catalogue and schedule, you may want to remind people of upcoming programs by sending announcements. Be sure your announcements include enough information so that potential participants and their supervisors can decide whether courses are appropriate. At a minimum, provide information on the program's purpose and objectives, audience eligibility, cost, date, and length. Remember to mention registration procedures and deadlines as well as where to send forms and whom to call for more information. Refer to Chapter Seven for a discussion of how to use HRD announcements.

■ *Establish and publicize the registration process.* Having a clear-cut procedure that is well understood by all your customers greatly simplifies program registration and reduces misunderstandings and phone calls. You will need to establish eligibility requirements, an approval process, deadlines, forms to complete, and cancellation procedures.

■ *Create a simple registration form.* As the manager of a small HRD department, you may be tempted to avoid registration forms. However, registration forms collect vital information that may be difficult and time-consuming to obtain in other ways. Registration forms can help you determine eligibility to attend programs, send mailings to the correct addresses, make confirmation calls, develop a participant list with pertinent information, charge back costs of programs, and build your own data base to market future programs.

Consider carefully the information that you request on registration forms; lengthy, detailed forms may discourage people from attending your programs. (See Exhibit 7.3 for a sample registration form.) Design or borrow a form that is easy for participants to complete and that provides all the information you need to register and track participants. Be sure the form asks for the following vital information:

■ Participant's name, work location, mailing address, and phone number

■ Program name and date

■ Participants' social security number or an expense code that allows you to charge back program expenses

■ Employee's department, title and/or level (helpful in determining eligibility and in tracking attendance by business unit or level)

■ Supervisor's signature indicating approval (especially important if the department is charged for the program)

■ Other information such as participant's date of hire, reason for attending

■ *Inform people promptly of the status of their registration.* People want to know whether they are registered, on a waiting list, or not permitted to attend a particular program. See Exhibit 8.1 for a sample confirmation

Exhibit 8.1. Sample Confirmation Form.

Date: April 9

To: INTERVIEWING AND SELECTION Enrollees
cc: Immediate supervisors of enrollees

From: Carolyn Balling, Training & Development

Subject: **YOUR UPCOMING WORKSHOP**

I look forward to seeing you at the INTERVIEWING AND SELECTION workshop:

> Tuesday, April 21, 8:30 a.m.–4:30 p.m.
> AND
> Wednesday, April 22, 8:30 a.m.–noon
>
> Training Room
>
> *If you find your schedule has changed and you are unable to attend,*
> *please contact me immediately at x4658.*

Please plan to arrive a few minutes early to get a cup of coffee and to get settled, so that we may begin promptly at 8:30 a.m. We'll take an hour break for lunch.

The INTERVIEWING AND SELECTION workshop will enable you to effectively interview job candidates and make appropriate hiring decisions. During the 1½ day program, you'll have an opportunity to practice a variety of interviewing skills and to conduct a short interview on videotape.

PREPARATION
Please bring with you to the workshop:

____ Job description and requisition form for a current open position in your area (or a job description of an anticipated or likely open position in your area)

____ Pen or pencil—a binder or workshop materials will be provided.

MESSAGES
During the workshop, others will be unable to contact you except for true emergencies. Please let your staff and others know you'll be unavailable during workshop hours. Messages can be left in Training (ext. 4870), to be delivered to the Training Room during breaks.

QUESTIONS?
If you have questions about the workshop, please contact me (x4658).

I'll see you at the workshop! Please come ready to participate and learn!

Source: Reproduced with permission of C. Balling.

form. Carolyn Balling uses this form to confirm people's attendance at a workshop on interviewing and selection. In designing your registration form, you may want to include a section where you indicate the action taken on each person's application. If your program is full, let people know of alternative programs they may attend. If you think that a person has registered for an inappropriate program, contact the person or his or her manager by phone to explain why the program is inappropriate and suggest alternatives. You can make exceptions to policies if there are good reasons why people want to attend a program. For example, individual contributors may want to attend a management skills program because they frequently manage project teams or because they expect a promotion soon. An advantage of managing a small HRD department is your ability to make exceptions to rules. You can win friends and build your credibility by creating flexible policies and taking the time to follow up on unusual requests to attend your programs.

■ *Allow people to register by phone or electronic mail.* Make it easy for people to sign up for popular programs by phone or electronic mail. Be sure to obtain their mailing address and phone number so that you can send them registration forms later.

■ *Create a file or folder for each program.* Having all the registration forms and other correspondence for a program in one place is especially helpful if you are offering several programs around the same time. Being organized makes it easier for you to manage your assistant or any temporary helpers when it comes time to create lists, mail program materials, or charge back for programs.

■ *Confirm attendance shortly before programs are offered.* Be sure to ask people whether they plan to attend a program before you send them any preparation work. Confirming attendance saves you from spending time and money on useless mailings and also allows you to resolve some problems over the phone. For example, you may be able to convince a reluctant participant to attend by explaining how the program personally benefits him or her. If a participant is thinking of canceling because of a last-minute meeting, you may be able to make special arrangements so that he or she can miss part of the program. In cases where participants cannot personally attend the program, you may be able to convince them to send a qualified substitute, thus avoiding cancellation fees or canceling the program because of too few participants. Finally, people who have been contacted by phone are more likely to attend programs than those who have been contacted by mail alone.

■ *Create a tentative participant list and monitor registration.* A tentative participant list serves several purposes. Some people who choose to attend a program on the basis of who else is attending want to see a participant list. Also, your tentative list may signal problems with registration. For example, suppose a department that you expected to participate has not sent registration forms or called with nominations. A few phone calls may encourage registration or clarify why the department cannot send people to your program at this time. On the other hand, you may notice that a department is planning to send both employees and their bosses to the same program. In this case, you'll want to contact the managers to discuss the implications of doing this and to present other options for them to consider.

■ *Prepare a final participant list.* Creating your final list as close to the program as possible helps ensure its accuracy. Inaccurate lists cause confusion and may give participants the impression that people backed out at the last minute. You can use the final participant list for many purposes: to make reservations at a hotel or training facility, to create participant name tags or plates, to distribute to participants as a networking tool, to track attendees and no-shows, to create work teams in the program, to keep a record of attendance, to charge participants for programs, and to update program sponsors on who has attended.

■ *Keep track of cancellations.* Keep a record of people who cancel at the last minute or who repeatedly ask you to change their registration. You may want to contact such people to find out whether they are seriously interested in attending a program or simply going through the motions of registration.

Managing Travel Arrangements

When your trainees or speakers are spread out geographically, you will need to consider travel arrangements in your program logistics. If the program is being offered near you, you may underestimate the impact of travel on training effectiveness. If people are uncertain or worried about travel arrangements, they may arrive at a program late or exhausted, or they may leave early and disrupt their own or others' learning. Imagine how difficult the training logistics might be for someone commuting to the program.

Consider the needs of people coming from another state or country who are unfamiliar with the area and with your normal training setup.

People coming from far away want to know what arrangements you've made for lodging and meals. If you have enough people traveling to a program, you may be able to obtain group rates. If you have not made special arrangements, recommend where they might stay. People need to know costs of hotels and taxis, how to get to the training facility, and what time they need to leave a program in order to make their travel connections. Letting people know the best route, approximate travel time, and the cost of taxis from the airport or train station to the hotel can prevent taxi drivers from taking advantage of out-of-towners.

A customer-oriented administrative assistant can be invaluable in alleviating participants' travel concerns. Even if you do not have an assistant, you can minimize travel distractions and endless phone calls by including relevant information in confirmation packages that you send to participants. A well thought out program logistics package gives participants all the information they need to plan their schedules and avoid confusion in travel arrangements. You may be able to get a travel agency or hotel to put together a packet of information for participants. Consider including the following information in the packet:

- Program starting and closing times

- Recommended hotels, their addresses, prices, and phone numbers

- Maps and directions to the training facilities, airports, train stations

- Travel time to the nearest airports and train stations.

- Any meal arrangements connected with the program (such as breakfast, lunch, and planned group dinners)

- Restaurants and other local attractions that may be of interest

Managing Production and Distribution of Materials

Material production involves designing and producing materials for your HRD programs, for marketing HRD programs, and for preparing HRD reports. If you have never been in charge of developing program materials, you may be surprised at the number of decisions that you have to make.

Planning can simplify procedures and save you money and time. One basic decision is whether you want a standard look to all your materials. If so, you may want to design a department logo and select department colors for your materials. Using a logo on all your correspondence and training materials helps establish your identity and gives a professional appearance to your documents. You may be able to hire a graphics firm, or you may save money by using an in-house graphics department or local art student to design your logo.

You will also need to choose what you will use to hold participant materials for each program. If you will use only a few handouts, you may only require a dual-pocket folder. You can order plain folders and use a stick-on logo to provide a more professional look. When you have many pages of participant materials, you will want to use a binder to hold them. You can obtain a better rate if you order binders in bulk for all your programs. Binders with slip-in pockets on the front and spine can be used for more than one program by inserting covers and spines with the appropriate program name into the pockets. Budget permitting, you may want binders with program names silk-screened on them. Silk-screening creates a sleeker look and eliminates the need for inserting covers and spines, but it is considerably more expensive and sometimes wastes materials.

When using binders, you will generally need dividers to separate sections of the program materials. Many different types of dividers are available. The cheapest, most flexible option is numbered tabs. You can insert a table of contents explaining the material to be found in each section. Numbered tabs are inexpensive and flexible but make looking up information cumbersome. Another inexpensive and flexible option is blank tabs with space to insert topic names. These tabs, however, look somewhat unprofessional and require someone to type or print the labels and insert them.

Customized tabs, once produced, are easy to use and more professional looking. They are an excellent option if you expect to offer a program several times, have the budget, and want a more polished look. With customized tabs, you will need to plan enough time for design, production of a rough draft, proof reading and correction of the draft, production of final copy, and transportation. Customized tabs look professional and make it easy for participants to refer to material, but they are expensive and can become outdated if you redesign a program and change topics. You can circumvent this problem by using fairly generic headings on your tabs.

Another part of material production involves the creation of the materials themselves. Finding imaginative ways to speed up the production and distribution of training materials can relieve you of a time-consuming administrative burden. Here are some possible ways to simplify material production.

■ *Use a computer to produce your materials and automate various processes.* While it may be hard to imagine, some departments have such small budgets that they don't own a computer. Can your department purchase its own computer and printer, or can you use computers in other departments to produce materials? Nothing is more wasteful than typing and retyping materials. With a computer it is easy to create and edit training documents, reports, and mailing lists and labels for use in a variety of programs. Computers are also useful in projecting budgets and in tracking program attendance.

■ *Arrange for another area of your organization to handle word processing, reproduction, and collation of training materials as well as to "stuff" binders for you.* Can you borrow resources from other departments, or can you barter for help? Susan Warshauer (1988) suggests you may be able to trade free attendance at your training programs for administrative help.

■ *Use an outside agency or temporary help to produce materials.* If you have the budget, can you hire outside help to produce training materials? Outside agencies may be able to complete the production of materials much faster than you or another department could. Whenever possible, have instructors be responsible for producing enough training materials for each program. If you use outside resources, be sure that you or your assistant reviews materials before final production to ensure their accuracy. It is costly, time-consuming, and frustrating to redo incorrect materials.

■ *Ask presenters to bring materials with them.* For programs where you use outside speakers, can you have speakers bring materials with them to the program? This approach saves you time and money in preparing materials. When given more accountability, presenters may be more careful in preparing and reviewing materials. Instructors can revise materials easily and stay alert to any last-minute changes in them. This is especially important if presenters sometimes send last-minute substitutions. Finally, when there are several presenters, students are not distracted by material from upcoming presentations. On the other hand, speakers may forget to bring enough materials for everyone, materials may vary in format and quality from speaker to speaker, and participants may form the impression that materials were thrown together at the last minute. You can avoid these problems by providing speakers with guidelines on format, calling speakers to remind them of the correct number of sets of material to bring with them, and reviewing the materials before they are reproduced.

Creating a Checklist and Tracking Logistical Tasks

Because of the wide range of logistical tasks you may have to handle personally, it is helpful to create a checklist of actions and deadlines for each program you offer. A sample of action steps follows and a sample tracking sheet—Worksheet 12—is provided in Resources.

1. *Schedule program.* Choose program dates and tentatively book a training facility. Check feasibility of program date with program sponsors to determine whether timing is best for your customers.

2. *Announce program.* At least two months before the program, send an announcement that includes registration information.

3. *Secure booking of training facility.* Determine the tentative number of rooms/reservations needed for participants, instructors, administrative staff, and guests. Sign and return the facility contract. If required, arrange to send partial payment of the fee in advance to hold your reservation. Make sure that you check to see how much time you have to change the reservations without penalty so that you can confirm the actual rooms required before the deadline.

4. *Arrange for equipment.* Reserve equipment or specify the equipment required with the training facility coordinator.

5. *Plan for meals.* Determine which meals you want to include in the package. Arrange for meals with the training facility manager, the local cafeteria, or a local food delivery service. Adjust the number of food orders when you have a more accurate count of participants.

6. *Collect registration forms.* Review applications and inquiries for eligibility and appropriateness.

7. *Notify potential registrants of status of their applications.* Let people know within a reasonable time that you have received their application and whether

or not it has been accepted. If you are not sure whether there will be enough participants to offer a program, let people know when you will decide.

8. *Create a tentative participant list.* Call to confirm attendance.

9. *Create a program materials list.* Be sure to include materials to be ordered or developed. Indicate materials needed before and during the program.

10. *Design and order binders and tabs.* Identify binder and tab requirements. Call vendors or ask the in-house graphics department to select a vendor. Review options for binders, select best option, and order enough copies. Design cover and tabs, and order enough copies for several programs. If this is your first program, design a logo as well as artwork for the specific program. Review and edit artwork mechanicals. Check binder for quality before payment. If you use binders with slip-in covers and spines, leave enough time to design and produce the covers and spines and insert them into binders.

11. *Create an information package for participants.* Order brochures about the hotel or training facility. Determine participants' transportation options, or arrange for their transportation. Order or create maps. Put together a package that explains program logistics and includes required preparation work, a program description and agenda, and a participant list.

12. *Send confirmation material to participants.* Identify participants; verify intent to participate and mailing address; gather materials to send by mail, messenger, or courier. Be sure to confirm receipt of participants' preparation work, especially if it is sent from overseas.

13. *Reproduce training materials.* Review materials list. Produce photocopies of materials and handouts; reproduce enough copies for participants, instructors, sponsors, and your department files. Be sure to reproduce materials to be inserted in binders on three-hole-punched paper. Collate materials and insert into binders.

14. *Arrange for transport of materials to the training center.* Review materials checklist. Check binders for completion and accuracy. Package materials. Arrange for delivery. If you are sending materials to international locations, be sure to inquire about customs procedures and leave enough time for materials to clear customs. Verify delivery of materials.

15. *Create a final participant list.* Send the list to the training facility or hotel to confirm reservations.

16. *Prepare site for training.* Meet with your facility liaison to review current status. Set up or check setup of the training room. Make sure that the room is set up properly and that all equipment and supplies are there and working. Place name cards at appropriate seats. Place binders on tables. Clean room of excess debris before the program begins. If possible, do all these things the day or night before the program.

17. *Conduct the program.* Even when using consultants to teach a program, you will want someone representing your department to make sure that the program runs smoothly. At a minimum, make arrangements for you or your representative to be there at critical points, such as program kickoff, significant guest speakers' presentations, meal breaks, and program wrapup and evaluation.

18. *Clean the training room and return unused materials.* If you are using your own facility, you are responsible for the condition of the room. Even when you are renting facilities, cleaning up makes for good business relations and allows you to save unused materials and supplies. Be sure to pack supplies and arrange for their return. Participants may also wish for training materials to be mailed to them, especially if materials are heavy and people are coming from long distances. It is helpful to talk with someone from the training facility before the program about arrangements for sending materials to participants.

19. *Conduct program evaluation.* Evaluating the effectiveness of each program helps ensure that you are meeting customer needs and lets people know you are interested in their needs. Write a summary evaluation report.

20. *Take care of finances.* Pay bills relating to the program, including facilities and consultant charges. Arrange to charge participants for the program.

21. *Write and send thank-you letters to guest speakers and sponsors.* Be sure to thank people who helped make the program possible. It is also a good practice to send copies of thank-you letters to people's managers when appropriate. You may want to include a summary of the program evaluation with the thank-you letter.

22. *Maintain program records.* Keep a folder with a record of each program, including the attendance list, registration forms, the agenda, instructors and guest speakers, correspondence relating to the program, preparation work, and the summary evaluation report.

23. *Revise your logistics checklist.* Review what happened during the program administration process. Make any necessary adjustments to your logistical project plan to make sure that the time frames are accurate and to help prevent any future slipups. Plan to replace vendors, training facilities, food services, or messenger services that gave you inferior service.

ROLE OF YOUR ADMINISTRATIVE ASSISTANT

How well you take advantage of your administrative assistant's skills can greatly ease the burden of handling program logistics. It is best if you have a permanent assistant who can develop relationships with your clients and learn the routine of planning for and delivering HRD programs. Use your assistant to manage a variety of behind-the-scene tasks such as booking a facility and making meal arrangements, collecting registration forms, preparing participant lists, producing and mailing correspondence and preparation work, collating materials, collecting and tabulating any preparatory information, transporting materials, setting up the training room, tabulating participants' evaluation forms, paying bills, and charging participants for the program. If you are a one-person department, try to hire someone part-time or borrow someone from another department to help with program logistics. Delegating administrative tasks enables you to concentrate on designing, marketing, and teaching programs.

Your assistant fills an important customer service role by answering questions about program logistics and helping participants with travel arrangements. Be sure that he or she also understands who a program is for and what it is intended to accomplish. A program description, including the program goals and agenda, can help this person respond to some basic questions. In general, your assistant should handle questions about program start and stop times, meal arrangements, and dress code, while you handle questions about program content. Questions about program content can involve helping clients decide whether a program is best for them and whether they should participate in other types of HRD activities. You are best equipped to handle such questions.

If you have hired an assistant primarily for his or her organizational skill in handling back-office procedures, you may need to coach this person to become customer-focused. With all the pressure, some administrative assistants become so involved in administrative details that they view customer calls as an interruption to their real work. Providing your assistant with an opportunity to meet some of the customers he or she serves puts faces to names for the customer and your assistant and helps build good customer relations. Being directly involved with customers also helps to provide your assistant with an appreciation of the complexity of running a program and with a sense of pride in the program and his or her role in its success. It also allows customers to recognize and thank your assistant for his or her help. Consider using your assistant to cohost meals or to serve as the on-site coordinator.

. . . .

SUMMARY: STRATEGIES FOR MASTERING THE ART OF PROGRAM LOGISTICS

1. Take a customer-oriented approach to program administration. Keep in mind that every customer contact is a "moment of truth."

2. Keep logistical procedures as simple as possible. Learn from each program or service you offer how to improve program logistics to provide better customer service.

3. Make the best use of available technology in administering your programs. If you do not already have a computer, make a strong case for getting one.

4. Create a checklist of essential logistical tasks relating to each program.

5. Use a program tracking sheet that includes key logistical tasks, responsibilities, beginning and end dates, and a space to check off tasks when they are completed.

6. Delegate as many administrative tasks as you can to your administrative assistant or to other administrative personnel. Make sure that your administrative assistant understands the full picture of what your department is trying to accomplish.

▲ ▲ ▲ ▲ ▲ ▲ ▲ ▲ ▲ ▲ ▲ ▲ ▲ ▲ ▲ ▲ ▲ **Chapter 9**

Ensuring and Evaluating Program Effectiveness

A common pitfall in HRD departments is neglecting evaluation and other activities that ensure the effectiveness of HRD programs. Senior management needs to know that HRD is making a major contribution to the organization. Evaluating your performance helps you improve your effectiveness, market HRD programs, and build management commitment. This chapter discusses benefits of evaluation, how to evaluate programs, and how to present your evaluation findings to make people aware of the importance of human resource development to an organization's success. It also examines ways to reinforce the effects of training programs to increase the chances that employees actually apply to their work situations the new behaviors they have learned.

BENEFITS OF PROGRAM EVALUATION

When you are busy planning, marketing, designing, teaching, and managing, why take the time to evaluate how you are doing? Thoughtful evaluation provides many benefits. Evaluation helps you to do the following:

■ *Focus on priorities.* Evaluation helps you focus your efforts on meeting priority needs (doing the right things) and providing long-term solutions, not just short-term fixes, to problems.

■ *Manage resources wisely.* Evaluation enables you to determine whether you are spending your time and budget so that you get the best return for your investment.

■ *Provide customer service.* Evaluation helps you provide quality service from your customers' perspectives—a key to credibility. Just because a program runs smoothly does not mean that you have met your customers' needs for service. Evaluation enables you to correct mistakes and shows customers that you care and listen to them.

■ *Strive for continuous improvement.* Evaluation is essential for continuous improvement of your programs and services. It helps you coach others who work with you by identifying what works well and what needs to improve in terms of program design, instruction, and administration.

■ *Energize for change.* Evaluation can provide the impetus and energy needed to change what you are doing. According to Fritz (1989), creative energy comes from awareness of the gap between your goals (where you want to be) and current reality (where you are now).

■ *Market HRD programs and build sponsorship.* Evaluation provides data that help you market programs to potential participants and sponsors. People are more willing to commit time and money to programs that have proven useful to others.

In a nutshell, careful evaluation sends a message to your clients that you want to help the organization and that you are making a contribution and are committed to continuous improvement. How can you approach program evaluation in a small HRD department?

Because your major challenge is providing HRD training that supports the organization's business strategy, you need to ask whether your programs help prepare employees to meet business challenges. Avoid the trap of responding to all requests for training without evaluating how they fit the overall business strategy. As discussed in Chapters Two and Three, conducting a needs assessment and creating a mission help you focus on critical business needs. Evaluation is particularly effective when you consider it before implementing any programs as part of your needs assessment. Once you have determined that your department is doing what it should be doing, then you evaluate the effectiveness of your specific programs. What exactly do you want to measure, and how should you go about measuring it? The next two sections describe and discuss levels of evaluation and how to use them.

· ·

LEVELS OF PROGRAM EVALUATION

Dana Gaines Robinson and James C. Robinson (1989) take a hard-line approach to evaluating training in *Training for Impact: How to Link Training to Business Needs and Measure Results*. Their main point is the need to refocus evaluation from counting training activity to determining training's impact on the organization's business needs. Much of the Robinsons' work derives from Don Kirkpatrick (1987), who introduced the concept of evaluation levels to describe effectiveness of training. Each increase in level measures training effectiveness at a deeper level of change. Let's look at what each level measures.

Level-one (reactions) evaluation deals with initial customer satisfaction—how well participants liked the program. In the words of one HRD manager: "I need feedback and I need to know how satisfied my clientele is at the close of the training experience. If they aren't satisfied, the chance of their using the skills that they were taught is nil." Level-one change is the easiest to measure and therefore the method most frequently used.

Generally, people will not change their behavior as a result of training that they did not like. Liking a program, however, does not mean that behavior change will occur. People may believe that they have gained new knowledge or skills, but they may not really understand the new concepts or be capable of using the new skills. You obtain a more accurate assessment of change in a trainee's skill or knowledge level by directly measuring learning.

Level-two (learning) evaluation deals with change in skill or knowledge level as a result of training. Level-two change indicates that trainees have actually improved their ability to perform certain tasks. It can be measured by various types of paper-and-pencil tests or skill demonstrations.

Managers differ in the value they place on testing to measure change in critical behaviors or competencies. One senior manager told me: "We should test everyone on core competencies taught in every training program that we offer." Another said: "You cannot measure really important change. Change is subtle and takes place over time like the erosion of the seashore by the ocean. You know it happens, but you cannot measure it meaningfully in a single instance." While level-two evaluation indicates a change in skill or knowledge level, it does not indicate whether or not the change will be implemented effectively on the job.

Level-three (behavior-performance) evaluation deals with measuring behavior on the job. At this level, evaluation assesses whether there was an increase in skill or knowledge as the result of training and also whether there was any transfer of learning to the job. Quality of training is only one factor that influences on-the-job application of skills learned in training programs. For level-three change to occur, the people and processes in the work environment must reinforce the newly learned behaviors. To support level-three change, the HRD manager must work closely with business managers to determine whether the new behaviors are really desirable. We will consider ways to reinforce the effects of human resource development in more detail later in this chapter. For now, let's look at an example that illustrates the importance of the work environment.

Consider a training program that teaches bank tellers to cross-sell products to customers in order to increase products sold and ultimately profitability. For tellers to cross-sell products, they need selling skills, knowledge of available and appropriate products, and a supportive environment. Since cross-selling takes more time than simply completing transactions requested by customers, managers of busy branches may discourage tellers from doing anything that increases the time that customers must stand in waiting lines. In some branches, tellers may have actually learned cross-selling techniques and product features but not tried to cross-sell products to customers because the branch manager does not want them to. While on-the-job behavior change is the goal of training, level-three evaluation still does not tell whether the organization has received an adequate return on your training investment.

Level-four (results) evaluation, the hardest and most critical, deals with return on investment—the impact of training on business results. While you cannot prove that training is the major factor in influencing business results, you can show that people who have been trained in critical skills are more successful than those who have not been trained in accomplishing bottom-line results.

There are cases where trainees do apply newly learned skills on the job, but the impact on business results does not justify the cost of the training. Where budget dollars are becoming increasingly scarce, you need to know the potential economic impact of your programs. In some cases the behaviors taught in programs may actually work against business performance. For example, referring to the previous cross-selling example, let's say that the branch manager supports tellers in their cross-selling attempts. If tellers take time to apply new cross-selling skills, waiting lines may become so long that customers take their money to banks with faster-moving lines. To avoid teaching unproductive behaviors, be sure to explore with your sponsors all the possible outcomes that might result from training.

Now that we've discussed levels of evaluation, let's look more closely at how you can measure HRD's effectiveness.

. . . .

METHODS OF EVALUATING TRAINING

Level-One Evaluation Methods: Program Evaluation Forms

At a minimum, evaluate all your programs at level one. Level-one evaluation indicates that you care enough about customer satisfaction to ask people what they thought about your programs. You can measure this by having program participants complete evaluation forms at the end of training. The sample program evaluation form in Resources, Worksheet 13, illustrates questions typically asked in a level-one evaluation. Forms such as this provide useful data in an easy-to-tabulate format, and they can elicit invaluable ideas for improving the effectiveness of your programs. Explain that you will use the information to improve future programs and modify programs in light of suggestions when appropriate.

While level-one evaluation forms do not accurately measure behavior change, they do indicate customer satisfaction and can indicate perceived learning as well as intent to use new skills on the job. Here are some tips on using level-one evaluation forms.

■ *Have participants complete evaluation forms before they leave a program.* You are most likely to have evaluation forms returned if you ask participants to complete them before they leave the training room. People frequently forget to return forms, lose them, or complete them so long after the program that they cannot accurately report their opinion at the time of training.

■ *Keep evaluation forms for all your programs as similar as possible.* Doing this saves time in creating new forms and enables you to compare programs to find out what works best. Comparability helps if you want to determine the impact of changing training activities or instructors on a program's effectiveness or to rank order your programs in terms of customer satisfaction.

■ *Use a variety of questions on your evaluation forms.* A combination of closed- and open-ended questions works well. Likert-type scales, asking people to rate effectiveness on a 5-point scale ranging from 5 (excellent) to 1 (poor), enable you to tabulate averages and compare different programs. Open-ended questions, on the other hand, allow people to express themselves more freely and completely. Qualitative comments often provide more useful ideas on how to make programs more effective. Moreover, you can use quotations as testimonials to help in marketing programs.

■ *Focus questions to obtain specific information.* While you will want to ask some questions about the overall value of a program, you should also ask questions that focus on specific aspects of the training. In pilot programs especially, be sure to ask questions about specific topics or units. Try to get people to be specific in their responses so that you will know what action you need to take. For example, it is better to ask people to rate pacing as too fast, too slow, or just right than as excellent, very good, or needs improvement.

■ *Request some participant background information on your form.* Background information helps you understand people's perspectives and decide how to change your programs. Factors that may have an impact on how trainees perceive programs include management level, years of experience on the job, business unit, and reason for attending ("desire for personal growth" versus "my manager told me to attend"). Program evaluations grouped by management level or length of experience may reveal that different audiences have distinctive reactions to your programs. This may, in turn, lead you to offer separate, customized programs.

Level-Two Evaluation Methods: Tests and Simulations

Level-two change reflects a difference in level of skill or knowledge. You can measure level-two change through formal written or oral tests and behavioral simulations such as role plays. For example, trainees who are to undertake a self-study program on principles of consumer lending could complete a pretest before training and a different but comparable posttest after the training.

Formal written tests can be useful in measuring increase in knowledge. For jobs where skills are essential to successful job performance, consider assessing level of knowledge before allowing trainees to "graduate" from training. Passing a test may be a requirement of training. Key to effective level-two assessment is the validity of any tests you use to measure change. Does your method really measure what you want it to? For example, can you determine competence in analyzing loans through multiple choice tests? Is recognizing the correctness of an item on a list comparable to knowing what to do on the job? If not, create a test that more accurately assesses ability to analyze loans. See Rosenberg and Smitley (1990) for ideas on test construction.

In some training programs it may be possible to test trainees' learning by having them demonstrate a skill during a simulated job situation. For example, in a telephone skills program for customer service representatives, participants can be tape-recorded during role plays at the beginning and at the end of training. You can rate a trainee's greeting to customers, handling of customer questions, telephone etiquette, proper use of transfer procedures, and so on. A rating form measuring presence of key behaviors can help you determine the amount and type of follow-up coaching that each participant needs. In another example, in a presentation skills training program, you can videotape trainees giving initial and final presentations and compare changes in behavior such as eye contact, gestures, vocal projection, use of visual aids, and so forth.

Level-Three Evaluation Methods: Observation and Questionnaires

You can measure level-three change by observation and the use of questionnaires and interviews. Level-three evaluation requires a time lapse between the end of the training program and the time you gather data. You may choose to observe performance on the job yourself, if you have time. On the other hand, you can observe on-the-job performance through the supervisor or a more neutral party, such as a hired consultant or a "mystery shopper." Some consultants who teach skills such as customer service include follow-up evaluation and on-the-job coaching as part of their services. In some cases departments may use a mystery shopper, an outside person pretending to be a customer, to evaluate on-the-job performance. Using a hired observer can be an extremely effective approach.

Let's look at an example of how level-two and level-three evaluation was used in teller training. As training coordinator in a regional bank, Mary (whom we met in Chapter Three) was asked to spearhead a major effort to retrain all five hundred tellers within six months. Prior to retraining, tellers did not understand their job responsibilities and policies and consequently failed to implement procedures or balance books consistently. Mary led a small project team who designed and implemented a revised teller training program for all tellers and measured the results of the retraining process.

Prior to the retraining effort, tellers were not rigorously tested since they were given open-book exams. Furthermore, tellers were not rigorously evaluated on the job either since there were no clear performance standards. Mary instituted serious level-two testing during training so that tellers could not look up answers during tests. She also set the stage for level-three evaluation by redesigning performance evaluations on the job and measuring teller performance against the standards. The evaluation process involved testing during and after training, including review of performance evaluations and feedback from supervisors. Mary's evaluation indicated that tellers implemented human resource practices more consistently, balanced their books more quickly, and committed fewer fraudulent actions. Mary's ability to demonstrate the results of retraining helped her win a promotion.

Let's look at another example of level-three evaluation. A small specialty insurance company wanted to improve the way in which employees communicated with each other in order to encourage cross-level and cross-business collaboration. To measure communication skills, the HRD manager worked with an outside consulting firm to design a communication skills questionnaire that was sent as a preparatory assignment to all participants in a communication skills training program. Participants evaluated themselves and received feedback from six other people. The outside consulting firm tabulated the results, which were then presented anonymously to participants. The feedback report helped participants determine communication strengths and areas to focus on during the training. The report is now also being used to measure the overall effectiveness of the program in changing on-the-job behavior. Three months after the program ends, all attendees complete the feedback process again to see whether there has been a change. Frequently, simply telling people that you will be measuring their behavior leads to an improved performance. By using this method the company can track whether or not the program is helping improve overall employee communication.

Level-Four Evaluation Methods: Business Success Indicators

It is important to determine critical indicators of success, such as increased sales or productivity, reduced errors or customer complaints, before conducting a program. You should identify critical success indicators during your needs assessment, not during postprogram evaluation.

How can you measure the bottom-line impact of training? To measure the impact of a selling program, you could document an increase in the number of sales and multiply that number by the dollar amount of an average sale. It is best if you can compare trained and untrained groups who have comparable territories and products. You can examine the difference in selling skills on revenues generated to determine whether the benefit of the sales training justifies its cost. You may not need to perform the financial analysis yourself since business managers may have sales data for their salespeople.

Let's look at an example of level-four evaluation in a brokerage firm. Amy Lampert worked with an assistant as a training and recruiting manager for a regional sales division of a major brokerage firm. Her goal was to improve the performance of new brokers, who as a group were not productive in generating revenue. Amy's target was 110 brokers with less than three year's experience. She conducted performance management programs for managers and sales training for brokers. By implementing a performance management system and skills training, Amy tried to influence business results.

Amy's programs were successful. In her words: "We made a significant impact. There was a 30 percent increase in revenue per broker, and our division went from last to first within six months, largely through the efforts of our performance management system. Managers monitored performance daily, gave immediate feedback, and set performance goals. As a consequence, brokers either improved their performance or, in rare cases, resigned voluntarily when they recognized that the company was serious about performance" (interview with the author, June 22, 1990).

HRD works best when you can influence the entire human resource process—from selection to training to performance management.

· ·

USING EVALUATION TO BUILD YOUR CREDIBILITY

Katie O'Neill (inteviewed by the author on Feb. 20, 1990) has been a training manager in small HRD departments in both the newspaper and banking industries. Katie understands the importance of results-focused training in building credibility. She points out the need to understand what results the client, or sponsor, wants: "It's a mistake to design only for the consumer instead of the client. You need to get the results the vice president wants. There's a danger of going overboard with an elaborate design that may not be necessary." Evaluating your effectiveness is critical. Katie comments: "You have to do a good job of evaluation. Evaluation gives you leverage when requesting money for the budget. People did not require very sophisticated data at the newspaper—they were satisfied with self-reported data and 'smile sheet' results. I had expected pragmatic results from an interviewing program since there was discrimination in interviews. Unfortunately we did not do a study to illustrate its impact. This was a missed opportunity."

Katie learned from this experience in her next assignment at a small savings bank. She advocates translating training's impact into real business results. "For example, we did a workshop on telemarketing at the bank to support a direct mail project. In the workshop we taught branch managers how to develop guideline scripts for different points in the project. Since we expected a 3 to 5 percent response from mailings, a response rate of more than 5 percent was seen as a success. We measured success by actual business results, not by the number of scripts managers produced."

Know Your Audience

Many HRD managers perform evaluations but fail to present results that impress senior management. You need to learn how your sponsors will determine the effectiveness of human resource development. Some HRD sponsors are only interested in "activities" and "numbers" of participants.

These managers may measure success by looking at whether you conducted X number of programs for X number of people, met quarterly deadlines, and kept expenses under budget. Other, more sophisticated sponsors may be interested in results-based evaluations at levels two, three, or four. Senior managers may have never seen an impressive training evaluation report that focuses on the impact of HRD on the organization's business. Tying program results to business strategy helps build your credibility as someone with business savvy; it also helps educate others in evaluating HRD's success in a constructive way.

Besides understanding how your performance will be evaluated, you need to know how much and what types of information senior management wants regarding evaluation. Since it is difficult to gather meaningful numbers at the last minute, set up tracking methods early to help you collect the data you need for evaluations.

Present Information on New Initiatives

You can use evaluation summaries of new initiatives to maintain the involvement of your program sponsors. It is helpful to provide summaries of the pilot program and first offering to show that your program is meeting customer needs. Even if your pilot program does not receive the ratings that you would like, you can turn poor ratings into success by demonstrating improvement from the pilot to the next offering. Important information to include in the summary report on a pilot program is the target audience for the program, the level of participation, program quality and how it has improved from the pilot to later sessions, the initial impact of the program, and next steps for program implementation. See the sample evaluation report, with summary, in Exhibits 9.1 and 9.2 for ideas on how to present such information to your sponsors. You can use Worksheets 14 and 15 in Resources to help you prepare a report.

Learn from Experience

The most constructive use of evaluation is to learn from it. Try to determine which criticisms of your programs are valid and make adjustments to later programs on the basis of participants' suggestions. If you learn from experience in pilot programs, your future programs should be more successful. Whenever you make improvements based on a pilot group's sug-

Exhibit 9.1. Sample Evaluation Report on Pilot Program.

To: Human Resources Management
Re: Understanding the Impact of Change Pilot

I am pleased to report the results of the initial rollout of *Understanding the Impact of Change*. This program is a prerequisite for *Leading in a Changing Environment*, to be offered first quarter next year. See the attached evaluation summary for details of program content and participant evaluations.

Target Audience. The audience for the pilot was Customer Service, which is undergoing major changes. This unit decided to send pairs of managers and employees to the program so that they could learn about coping with change and take the concepts back to their work teams.

Participation. In October, seventy managers and employees attended the program. A member of HR Training and someone from Customer Service conducted the first two programs. Two members from Customer Service conducted the third program and plan to conduct two more sessions for underwriting and systems managers.

Program Quality Improvement. We received excellent suggestions during the pilot and were able to make changes to the program within a week. As a result, program quality improved from 3.2 to 4.2, "personal value to me" improved from 3.4 to 4.3, and appropriateness of topics improved from 3.4 to 4.3. We added a number of guidelines on coping with change and sent these guidelines to pilot participants.

Initial Impact. As a result of the program, Customer Service has become more aware of how different people respond to change. They have also learned to help people separate from the past so that they may focus on the future. In a recent Customer Service meeting, the unit conducted a tribute to the past that helped people celebrate the past so that they could move on.

Next Steps. Next year we will offer this program as well as train-the-trainer for line managers. We are currently refining final materials for broader delivery. The follow-up program, *Leading in a Changing Environment*, is being designed with input from line managers to ensure that content is relevant to the business. I'll keep you posted on progress.

cc: Customer Service Management

gestions, consider sending revised materials to the pilot participants. Showing people that you have taken their ideas seriously builds their involvement and increases the chance that they will continue to give you honest, thoughtful suggestions.

For example, in a pilot program on understanding the impact of change offered at UNUM, participants said that they wanted more infor-

Exhibit 9.2. Sample Program Evaluation Summary.

Program: ___Understanding the Impact of Change___ Date: ___10/28/92___

1. How has the program been helpful to participants?

   "It has given me a method for working wtih my employees during change."

   "It helped me to understand what my role is in helping my people through change."

   "Gave me knowledge that I need to be able to help my peers feel more confident with change."

   "Helped me develop personal understanding of how change affects people. Also will help me relate to fellow employees who feel differently than I do concerning change."

   "Provided tools to help identify behavior in others and will allow me to be an effective leader for my team."

   "Gave me information on where my people are in the change process, and ideas on how to help them cope."

2. What was of most value to participants?

   "Knowing that what I'm feeling is normal."

   "Learning how to deal with other people going through change."

3. What suggestions did participants have for improvement?

   "Provide more guidelines on how to manage change."

   "Spend less time on the participant introductions."

Category	Excel-lent 5	Very good 4	Good 3	Needs improve-ment 2	Poor 1	Pilot average 10/15	First session average 10/28
Program quality	7	12	2	0	0	3.2	*4.2*
Relevance to participants' job	7	10	4	0	0	3.5	*4.1*
Personal value to participants	8	12	1	0	0	3.4	*4.3*
Program objectives met	6	11	3	1	0	3.5	*4.0*
Speaker knowledge	11	7	3	0	0	4.0	*4.4*
Training activities	5	11	4	1	0	3.3	*4.0*
Written materials	7	11	3	0	0	3.2	*4.2*
Appropriate topics	9	9	3	0	0	3.4	*4.3*
Topic flow	7	11	3	0	0	3.4	*4.2*
Preprogram information	3	6	11	1	0	3.1	*3.5*
Length of program	Just right	*19*	Too long	*1*	Too short	*0*	
Recommend to others?	Yes	*21*	Maybe	*0*	No	*0*	

mation on how to deal with change. We wrote guidelines for dealing with people in various stages of change for use in later programs and sent the guidelines to pilot participants via electronic mail. This gave people the guidelines they wanted, allowed them to make suggestions on the guidelines, and showed them that their ideas would improve future programs.

REINFORCING PROGRAM EFFECTIVENESS

Evaluation of program quality is one way to ensure that your programs are effective in teaching new behaviors. As we saw earlier, program quality is only one factor that influences application of learning to the job. What happens before and after people attend training can have just as much impact on the application of new skills as what happens in a training program. Following are some guidelines to ensure that training has a positive impact on the business.

Build Relationships

Part of successful HRD delivery involves making sure that you are plugged into the organization. Being connected to influential people helps you learn the requirements for HRD to succeed and makes it easier for you to educate others about activities that must occur for training to have an impact. Being in touch with key people in the organization allows you to identify potential program sponsors. People take training more seriously when it is endorsed by important managers in an organization. On the other hand, some people may try to undermine a program's effectiveness if they believe that it is not endorsed by the people who count.

Having good relationships with people who conduct the organization's business can help you identify and avoid potential obstacles that can impede training's effectiveness, such as scheduling conflicts or ineffective instructors. For example, knowing key business managers may help you schedule programs at the right time when people perceive a need to learn new skills and have time to apply what they learn to their jobs. Moreover, your relationships with important decision makers may help you select credible instructors that are respected for their knowledge. Working closely with managers can also help you determine whether the right behaviors are being

175

taught in your training programs. As we saw earlier in the cross-selling example, some behaviors taught in training programs may actually run counter to what managers want to happen. Make sure that you do not teach counterproductive behaviors and that you gain managers' support for what is taught in your programs.

Take the time to determine the key players with whom you must build relationships to maximize the effectiveness of training. Be sure to stay in touch with sponsors of programs, potential program participants, managers and supervisors of participants, and other human resource professionals. Being a player on the human resource team can help you influence other necessary processes for HRD effectiveness.

Encourage Processes That Support Training's Effectiveness

As Robinson and Robinson (1989) point out, quality of training is only half of the equation for training effectiveness. The other half is the work environment. No matter how good your programs are, behavior will not change unless the organization supports behaviors taught in training. Think of the other efforts that have to take place to ensure that training is effective.

Let's consider, for example, what else besides sales training is needed to increase sales. The company's products must be competitive. Sales support, such as advertising programs, needs to increase the public's awareness of products and encourage their desire to purchase. The organization's norms should encourage spending time selling products versus completing paperwork. Supervisors must have a way to track individual sales performance. Sales managers must monitor sales and provide the sales force with feedback on how members are doing. Compensation or incentive programs need to reward sales. As we saw in Amy Lampert's case earlier in this chapter, you can help ensure that these other processes are in place.

Allow Time for People to Practice and Improve New Skills

To learn new skills, people must be allowed time to practice. Make sure that your training design builds in adequate practice time so participants can "try on" new skills and receive feedback about how they are doing. Encourage supervisors and managers to allow time for employees to apply new skills on the job as well. Most people cannot learn many new skills at once. Some organizational change efforts fail because people who are expected to learn new behaviors attend so much training in such a short period of time that they are not able to absorb what was learned or practice new behaviors in a safe environment. Encourage managers to allow for a "learning curve" of new behaviors.

Involve Participants' Supervisors

You can involve supervisors before, during, and after a training program. Involving supervisors in the needs assessment process begins to build their commitment early on. It is also wise to involve supervisors in the process of selecting trainees to attend particular programs. You can do this easily either by asking supervisors to nominate potential program participants or by having them approve of participants' attendance by signing a registration form.

There are several ways you can involve supervisors during a program. Try to include supervisors of potential trainees in pilot programs. This helps raise supervisor awareness of program concepts and build supervisor commitment to a program's success. You may want to have supervisors attend a condensed version of a program to familiarize them with content, or you may have them attend parts of training programs with their employees or invite them to a graduation luncheon at the end of a program. An important way to involve supervisors before and after training is to encourage them to become involved in coaching their employees.

Train and Encourage Managers and Supervisors to Coach Their Employees

Employees benefit greatly from coaching and constructive feedback when they are trying out new skills on the job. When you help managers to become better coaches in skills taught in training programs, you can create a sense of ownership and accountability for the success of a training program. Encourage managers to have developmental planning sessions with trainees before and after training. Supervisors can help employees understand why they are attending the training and set learning goals for programs they attend. After training is complete, supervisors can encourage transfer of training by talking with employees to find out what they learned and how they plan to use new skills and by providing recognition for the use of new skills and guidance on how to improve.

Encourage Managers to Reward Successful Newly Acquired Skills

Using new skills can be awkward. According to Michalak and Yager (1979, p. 125), the single most important factor in encouraging the use of newly learned behavior on the job is positive reinforcement by the immediate supervisor. People tend to apply new skills in their jobs when the current job environment, their manager, and the reward structure all support the new behaviors. If the trainee's manager does not encourage new behaviors, the trainee will behave in ways that are rewarded by the manager.

Create Job Aids to Increase Retention of Learning

Even if management supports new behaviors, trainees may not adequately remember all the skills or knowledge taught in your programs. Job aids can be an inexpensive, effective way to help trainees remember what they learned and reinforce skills taught in training. See Chapter Four and Harless (1985) for more information on job aids.

Plan Follow-Up Activities After Training

You can build in planning for follow-up activities as part of your training design. Warshauer (1988) discusses several ways to do this. One technique is to allow time at the conclusion of a training program for participants to write memos to themselves that capture key skills and techniques they plan to apply. You can mail these memos to participants thirty days or so after training to remind them of what they wanted to do. You can also have participants select a training partner who plans to meet with them after training to discuss how they are doing at trying out new skills. Both these methods encourage use of skills without requiring you to have direct contact with participants. You can also follow up informally with trainees to see how they are doing.

On the other hand, you might consider planning a follow-up session in which participants discuss ways in which they are applying new skills and any problems they are having in doing so. This method can present scheduling difficulties, but it allows you and participants to encourage the use of skills on the job. Another follow-up technique involves sending reminders, such as relevant readings, additional guidelines, or summary lists of ideas generated by participants during training, to trainees some time after training. Sending change guidelines to people who participated in UNUM's pilot program on understanding change is a good example of a follow-up strategy that reinforces learning. Typing up lists of participants' ideas preserves useful, relevant ideas for participants and also builds a repertoire of realistic examples for your use in future sessions.

SUMMARY: STRATEGIES FOR ENSURING AND EVALUATING PROGRAM EFFECTIVENESS

1. Evaluation has enormous benefits—giving you information needed to ensure and increase effectiveness and to demonstrate the value of HRD programs to sponsors and clients.

2. Evaluation works best when you consider key success indicators as part of your needs assessment.

3. Make sure you evaluate the curriculum against business needs, periodically testing current offerings in light of those needs. Consider the overall value added by each program or service, not just the quality of any particular program.

4. At a minimum, evaluate all your programs at level one, using well-planned, easy-to-tabulate evaluation forms that give you customer service data. Use this information to improve future programs.

5. When possible, also evaluate your programs at levels two (learning), three (behavior-performance), and four (results).

6. Present your evaluation findings to senior managers in a way that influences them to perceive the value of human resource development.

7. Reinforce the effectiveness of HRD on the job by doing the following:

    ■ Involving managers and supervisors in HRD programs

    ■ Encouraging other processes that reinforce new behaviors

- Training supervisors to coach and reward new behaviors

- Allowing time for practice both during and after programs

- Providing job aids

- Planning for follow-up activities

PART

3

Keeping
the
Department
on
Track

Managing Your Budget

N ew HRD managers frequently lack experience and training in managing budgets and may be unenthusiastic or anxious about the prospect of dealing with them. As a new HRD manager I was so relieved to have successfully negotiated the funding I wanted that I thought I could ignore my budget for a while. My philosophy was to keep expenses to a minimum so that I would never go over my budget. Every month the finance area would send me unintelligible summary budget reports to review. I would immediately file them in my desk drawer and forget about them. One day I was asked to explain deviations from my plan and to reproject my numbers. Panic set in. I had been so busy designing, teaching, and administering programs that I had neglected to track expenses systematically. What had I actually spent? What did the numbers and variances on the report actually mean? Soon I discovered what my department had spent and how my expenses actually appeared on the report. I finally began to ask all the budget questions I had previously been too embarrassed to ask and to track expenses so that I stayed on top of the situation.

The moral of my story is "You had better understand senior management's budget requirements and actively track your budget throughout the year, not just at annual budget planning time." This chapter will help you manage your budget so that you meet your HRD and finance goals and help ensure that your department continues to be funded adequately in the future.

· ·

UNDERSTANDING YOUR COMPANY'S BUDGET PROCESS

Key to successful budget management is understanding the budget process and tracking your budget so that you can provide the information that senior management needs. Knowing what you have projected for the month and how you are doing in terms of your plan can build your credibility and help prevent HRD budget cutbacks when the company's expense belt tightens during hard times.

Understanding budget reports and reporting requirements is crucial to your success. You need to organize a system that allows you to monitor your budget in categories that are useful to you and to senior management. This may not be a simple task because most companies' budget reports are created to monitor profit centers, not staff units such as HRD departments. You must be able to translate your budget categories into those used on the organization's reports. You will want to build a good working relationship with your organization's finance staff so that you can find out the following information:

1. *What you need to track for the company's budget.* What does senior management expect from you regarding the HRD budget? Even if you do not currently control the budget, you will be in a better position to win control of it if you understand budgeting requirements.

2. *When you need to provide information regarding your budget for the current year, the upcoming year, and the more distant future.* Do you need to give monthly, quarterly, semiannual, and annual projections of expenses and variance from plan?

3. *The amount of detail you need to provide in explaining variance from your plan.* Do you need to explain variance from the overall plan (the bottom line) or from specific budget categories, such as the following?

    ■ Salaries and related expenses

    ■ Computer and data processing expenses

    ■ Consulting and professional fees

    ■ Travel and entertainment expenses

    ■ Service recoveries (charge-backs) for training?

Whether or not senior management requires a detailed explanation on a monthly basis, you will want to know how you are doing in each of these and other categories.

4. *The degree of latitude in adhering to your original budget.* Don't assume that simply staying under budget is the best strategy. Being continuously under your budget can give senior management the impression that you lack business savvy. Senior managers may conclude that you don't know what you really need, that you are purposely asking for more than you need, or that you are not accomplishing what you promised since you are not spending what you requested.

5. *The time of year when management pays serious attention to your forecasts.* Usually senior management tolerates some variance from plan in the beginning of the year as long as you have a reasonable explanation for the variance, such as a delay in payment of bills. Later in the year, management will expect you to get your budget in line or to reproject your budget so that it more accurately reflects expense trends. Senior management cares about the company's overall economic performance and needs to be able to predict profitability and expenses on a periodic basis. When you are under your budget plan, senior management wants to know whether this reflects "real savings" or inaccurate prediction of expense timing. When you are over your budget plan, senior management wants to know if you can get back on track by saving on other expenses.

CREATING A BUDGET TRACKING SYSTEM

Tracking Budget Variance

Armed with the answers to the foregoing questions, you can create a budget tracking system that works for you and for senior management. I recommend setting up a budget notebook with tabs for each month. Use the notebook to store your monthly budget reports as well as your forecasts and explanations of your expenses. It is helpful to use a spreadsheet program, such as Lotus-1-2-3 or Excel, to track expenses. Tracking and forecasting expenses manually is time-consuming and more prone to error than tracking on a computer. It is fairly easy to create a spreadsheet to track variance from your plan. Once you have entered the amounts budgeted as well as what you have actually spent for specific categories, a simple program can automatically calculate variance from plan and total sub-categories on a monthly, quarterly, and year-to-date basis. Each month you simply need to update your actual expenses, and your variance is calculated in a few minutes. Table 10.1 shows a sample tracking report for HRD department expenses. Refer to Worksheet 9 in Resources for a blank copy that you can modify for your own use.

Tracking Program Expenses

It is also helpful to keep a record of expenses for each program that you offer. You may want to record specific expenses for consultants, materials, training facilities and equipment, food, and travel, as well as charge-backs

Table 10.1. Sample Budget Tracking Report.

Budget category	Month March			Quarter 1st			Year to date Thru March			Year 1993		
	Plan	Act.	Var.	Plan	Act.	Var.	Plan	Act.	Var.	Plan	Fore.	Var.
Salaries and benefits	7.5[a]	7.5	0	22.5	22.5	0	22.5	22.5	0	90	90	0
Consultants	2.5	2.0	(.5)	7.5	6.5	1.0	7.5	6.5	1.0	30	30	0
Training facilities	1.0	0.8	(.2)	3.0	2.4	0.6	3.0	2.4	0.6	12	12	0
Travel and entertainment	0.4	0.5	.1	1.2	1.0	0.2	1.2	1.0	0.2	5	5	0
Training	1.0	0.7	(.3)	3.0	2.5	0.5	3.0	2.5	0.5	12	11	(1)
Computer	0.4	0.5	.1	1.2	1.5	0.3	1.2	1.5	0.3	5	6	1
Materials and supplies	0.4	1.0	.6	1.2	3.0	2.8	1.2	3.0	2.8	5	6	1
Other operating expenses	0.4	0.4	0	1.2	1.2	0	1.2	1.2	0	5	5	0
Total expenses	13.6	13.4	(.2)	40.8	40.6	(0.2)	40.8	40.6	(0.2)	164	165	1
(Recoveries)	3.9	3.0	(.9)	11.7	9.0	(2.7)	11.7	9.0	(2.7)	47	50	3
Net expenses	9.7	10.4	0.7	29.1	31.6	2.5	29.1	31.6	2.5	117	115	(2)

Note: If a monthly forecast is required, you can substitute forecast (Fore.) for actual (Act.) when you submit your forecast. At the end of the month, you may want to look at variance (Var.) from your budget plan, from your monthly forecast, or from both.

[a] Numbers are in thousands.

to program participants. Tracking expenses on a per program basis enables you to test the expense assumptions that you used in projecting your budget and to make more accurate forecasts in the future. It can also help you determine where to cut back on program expenses. Don't assume that your company's budget reports provide enough data to track program expenses. Frequently, organizational expenses are classified in different categories from yours, and expenses from different programs are lumped together. You can overcome this problem by tracking expenses and purchase orders for programs as they occur. Tracking program expenses on an ongoing basis may seem obvious, but it may be difficult to do as pressures to design and teach programs mount. I learned the hard way how much longer it takes to unravel program expenses after the fact than to plan to track them beforehand.

Managing the Spending Cycle

As HRD manager, you are responsible for managing the spending cycle: the more accurately you can predict when you will spend money, the better you can indicate specific monthly budget money needed. If you budget for the same amount of money on consultants every month even though you know that you won't spend that money until the last six months of the year, you may lead the company budget managers to a wrong conclusion. Be careful that you spend enough money early on so that you do not lose budget money later in the year. In some companies, when you have not spent the money you projected you would spend, you may lose that money if cutbacks are called for midway through the year. In my first year in the International Consumer Banking Division of Chase Manhattan, I was so afraid of exceeding my budget that I failed to spend what I had planned on consultants and worked overtime myself during the first half of the year. Senior management then concluded that I did not need the money and substantially reduced my budget. This restricted my training options for the remainder of the year.

You also need to monitor spending actively to avoid mistakes or quickly resolve any problems in processing expenses. Many mistakes can occur if you are not careful. For example, consultants may submit more than one invoice for the same work; the expense processing department may delay bill payments or charge or credit a wrong department for an HRD expense. You will need to be sure that bills are paid on time and that you are not paying inaccurate bills or duplicate invoices or paying for something that should be charged to other departments. It can be an eye-opening experience to discover how often consultants' bills are inaccurate and how often expenses are charged to wrong departments. Getting to know the manager of the expense processing department and learning about documentation requirements can make processing expenses and charge-backs for programs proceed more smoothly.

You will want to watch out for delays in bill payment because this may cause expenses to be paid in a quarter or year later than you predicted. Quarterly delays are a nuisance, but payment in the wrong year can be disastrous. For example, when I conducted a training program in mid December, the hotel and consultant bills were not paid until the following month. When expenses hit the following year, I lost $50,000 from that year's budget. If I had notified the finance area in advance, I could have requested special processing or accrued the expenses so that they would have been included in the year I projected. Another solution would have been to plan that December expenses would be part of the next year's budget. In either case, you will want to be aware of expenses coming at the end of the year and their consequences for your budget.

Involving Your Assistant in the Budget Process

If you have an assistant, be sure to involve him or her in the budget process as soon as possible so that he or she understands the information you need and when you need it. As your assistant processes HRD expenses, you can instruct him or her as to what to track for each budget category to simplify monthly calculations that you have to make. You can also sensitize your assistant to the budget implications of conducting programs with too few participants or of canceling programs.

Managing Charge-Backs of HRD Expenses

In Chapter Five you learned the advantages and disadvantages of charging participants for the costs of HRD. If your company charges back for HRD, you will need to forecast and track service recoveries. Table 10.2 shows a sample service-recovery tracking report. See Worksheet 10 in Resources for a blank form that you can use to track recoveries. Setting up a spreadsheet to monitor recoveries saves time and tells you the number of participants

Table 10.2. Sample Service-Recovery Tracking Report.

Program	Cost per participant	Planned number of participants	Actual number of participants	Planned recoveries	Actual recoveries	Variance
Management skills	$500	15	16	$7,500	$8,000	$500
Communication skills	$300	15	13	$4,500	$3,900	($600)
Orientation	$100	20	18	$2,000	$1,800	($200)
Sales skills	$450	15	16	$6,750	$7,200	$450
Total		65	62	$20,750	$20,900	$150

you need to break even on each program. Tracking projected and actual attendance and service recoveries by program can help you manage your service-recovery budget. You can create a formula that indicates the charge for each program multiplied by the minimum number of people to reach your service-recovery target for each program. If you don't have enough participants to meet your target, you can sometimes make up for the deficit by increasing the number of participants in your other programs.

One way to get back on track is to involve your administrative assistant in aggressively marketing your programs to ensure that you have the maximum number of participants. As my assistant became aware of the impact of canceled or undersubscribed programs on our service recoveries, she worked harder at trying to fill programs with participants. Make sure you put your energy into marketing your $1,000 programs, not your $100 programs. Don't assume that people who register early will actually attend. Depending on your company's attitude toward your programs and your cancellation procedures, you may need to register thirty people to ensure that twenty people attend a program. When people cancel early enough to avoid a cancellation penalty, you or your assistant may be able to convince participants to find substitutes who can benefit from the training and save you lost service recoveries.

Be especially careful to avoid canceling programs. Canceled programs can damage relationships with the people who want to attend and can wreak havoc with your service-recovery projections. Canceled programs may save some consultant or facilities expenses, but they usually lead to lost service recoveries that are difficult to make up. Even worse, low service recoveries may suggest to senior management that HRD programs are not valued enough for people to participate in them.

Making Choices When Your Budget Is Cut

In tough economic times you can probably count on being asked to cut back on your expenses. Requests for cutbacks may occur at the beginning of the budget cycle or midway through the year if your company discovers that it is below its profitability targets. The best way to prepare to deal with such requests is to know your priorities—what HRD activities are essential versus merely nice to offer—and to have ideas on how you can save money on lower-priority efforts. To ensure that you do not cut the wrong programs, consider asking an advisory group to help you to prioritize your activities.

In some cases you can save money by taking a different approach. For example, you might use a task force of internal resources rather than external consultants to help you design or teach HRD programs. You might scale back your use of audiovisual support, such as videotapes or slides, or participant materials. You may also be able to cut expenses by sharing the cost of program development or delivery with other areas in the company that have not been as hard hit by budget cutbacks. For example, I was able to share the cost of developing a communication skills survey to be used in a communication skills training program with our Communications Department.

One target for cutbacks could be expensive, optional programs taught by external consultants on your company premises. If enough people do not attend these programs to cover the cost of consultants, you continuously lose money. Perhaps you could publicize public seminars or workshops rather than arrange to sponsor them in-house.

MEASURING YOUR BUDGET PERFORMANCE

One of your objectives as an HRD manager is to manage your budget effectively. Following are some criteria you can use to evaluate your effectiveness at budget management.

■ *Accomplishment of objectives.* Did you accomplish your HRD objectives to senior management's satisfaction, or did you spend money without accomplishing your objectives? Even in an expense-controlled environment you are expected to produce results. Be careful that you do not cut back on expenses so much that you jeopardize the value of your department.

■ *Accuracy and timeliness of forecasts.* Provide senior management with timely budget information in an acceptable format. Be careful to ask for the money you need rather than for substantially more or less than you really require. Be organized and up-to-date in tracking and projecting HRD expenses. Make sure that your monthly and quarterly forecasts are accurate and that you accurately trend expenses within an acceptable limit. Did you expect to see the numbers on the tracking reports or were you often surprised by them?

■ *Expense management.* Spend money on the right things, and manage expenses wisely. Negotiate the best possible prices from consultants and vendors. Try to ensure that your budget comes in on or under your plan. If senior management asks you to cut back, make sure you limit spending wisely. If you exceed your budget, make sure you have good business reasons for spending more money, and make senior management aware in advance that you expect to be over your budget.

■ *Problem resolution.* Establish good working relationships with the finance staff and with the expense processing departments to prevent problems. Follow up quickly to resolve any problems that do occur.

SUMMARY: STRATEGIES FOR MANAGING YOUR BUDGET

1. Set up a tracking system so that you can monitor budget performance in categories that are useful to you and to senior management.

2. Learn how to read your organization's budget reports and how to translate your budget categories into those used on the organization budget reports.

3. Find out what you need to track as it relates to the overall organization's budget in terms of monthly, quarterly, semiannual, and annual projections of expenses and variance from plan.

4. Determine the critical dates and reporting requirements of your organization's budget cycle regarding the current year, the coming year, and the more distant future.

5. Find out the types of forecasts you must make and the amount of detail required in expense tracking in your organization. Determine whether you need to explain variance from the overall plan or from specific budget categories such as salaries and related expenses, consulting and professional fees, and service recoveries (charge-backs for training).

6. Be accountable for the accuracy of your forecasts. Learn how to stick with your original budget. Discover at what point in the year senior management starts to take forecasts more seriously.

7. Even if you are not accountable for your budget, track costs anyway to help win control over the budget in the future.

8. Set up a computer tracking system to monitor service recoveries so that you know where you stand when programs are canceled or undersubscribed.

9. Track and monitor payment of bills to ensure that they are paid on time. Avoid paying inaccurate bills, such as duplicate invoices or expenses belonging to other departments. Follow up to ensure that expenses are charged to appropriate departments when errors occur.

10. Allow for time lag in bill payment when projecting expenses so that all bills are paid in the projected year.

11. Plan to spend enough money early on so that you do not lose budget money later in the year.

12. Involve your administrative assistant in helping you project the budget and track expenses so that he or she understands the importance of keeping accurate and timely records of the information you need.

13. Test the accuracy of assumptions that you have made about HRD expenses so that you can make more accurate forecasts in the future.

14. Investigate the exact cost of projects. Be able to stress benefits and results on a specific line-by-line or item-by-item basis.

15. Present quantitative information based on research conducted with other HRD departments in comparable companies to back up your arguments.

16. Be prepared to reprioritize HRD activities to stay focused on business priorities in the event that your budget is cut. Ask for input from management or an advisory council to approve of what you continue to do and stop doing.

Making Time for
Your Own Learning

According to Peter Senge (1990), the key to any successful organization is continuous improvement through learning. The pressures of work can lead you to isolate yourself and to avoid learning activities essential to your personal growth and to the well-being of your department. As Jon Barb of Olin Corporation warns: "Be careful that you don't neglect your own development. For the first three years I did not develop my professional training skills. You can lose touch with the marketplace. You need to network with other trainers and find out what they're using" (interview with the author, February 6, 1990). Managing a small HRD department requires special competencies. This chapter identifies experiences that can help you prepare for such an assignment and ensure that you continue to grow on the job. The chapter also looks at selecting the right assistant and helping him or her develop necessary skills.

HRD MANAGER COMPETENCIES

To plan your own development, consider the qualities and competencies you need to manage a small department and implement your vision of human resource development, as well as your own strengths and weaknesses. To be a successful HRD manager of a small department you need business skills, managerial skills, HRD skills, and certain personal qualities. Let's look at each of these in turn.

Business Skills

Business skills include knowing your organization's business as well as making the most of business tools, such as a personal computer. A business focus is essential to your credibility. To manage your department so that it supports the overall goals of the organization, you need to understand its goods and services, marketing strategy, financial performance, competitive standing, regulatory pressures, and other industry-related issues. To have a business focus you need to know how to develop a mission and strategy for your department, determine and find resources needed to carry out your mission, manage your budget and resources wisely, and evaluate and explain HRD's impact on the organization's business.

Computer skills can greatly enhance your productivity, especially if you are a one-person department and must provide your own administrative and secretarial support. Knowing a word processing program and being able to create documents directly on a computer can save you time, money, and resources. Spreadsheet programs, such as Lotus 1-2-3 or Excel, allow you to project and track program attendance, expenses, variance from plan, service recoveries, and resource requirements. Chart and graphics programs, such as Harvard Graphics, enable you to produce inexpensive, professional-looking overhead transparencies and handouts for use in senior management presentations and training programs.

Proficiency with any electronic mail and office management systems available in your organization can improve your business performance. Some electronic systems allow you to schedule meetings with several people at once directly on the computer. You may be able to handle a great many logistical tasks, including program registration, using a computer and your organization's electronic mail system. By creating distribution lists, you can send promotional announcements to specific audiences who may be interested in or scheduled to attend your programs.

Managerial Skills

Whether managing an administrative assistant or resources outside your department, you need to have solid managerial skills. You must be able to clarify your expectations, monitor what others are doing, and provide feedback and guidance when their performance is not meeting your expectations. The ability to influence people is an especially critical managerial skill because many of the resources you will want to help you will not report directly to you. You have to convince them of the importance and value of helping you sponsor, design, or teach various HRD programs. You also need to coach and teach others to perform tasks that they may never have done before. Other important skills are necessary for managing your budget, projects and time.

HRD Skills

HRD managers who have had experience as HRD program designers and instructors have a head start compared with line managers who have had no HRD experience. Managing a small HRD department requires competence in a wide range of HRD areas, including the following:

- *Assessing HRD needs:* identifying the gap between desired and actual performance, determining the causes of this gap, and proposing appropriate solutions

- *Creating a business-focused HRD plan:* formulating a department mission and developing long-range plans and strategies for accomplishing your mission in your organization

- *Attracting your customers:* promoting your HRD programs and services and explaining what they can and cannot do for the organization

- *Designing and developing HRD programs:* designing programs and managing consultants and other people in the design process

- *Teaching and facilitating HRD programs:* teaching programs yourself and coaching others who teach them

- *Evaluating program effectiveness:* identifying the impact of HRD programs and services on the business, writing evaluation reports, and explaining the value of human resource development

- *Managing logistical tasks:* ensuring that participants are present and that facilities, equipment, materials, and programs run smoothly

Personal Attributes

The most important personal attitudes you will need to manage a small HRD department successfully are energy, confidence, resourcefulness, flexibility, and a learning orientation. Energy is required to juggle many tasks, work long hours under pressure, and persevere when faced with others' resistance.

You need self-confidence to promote your department's value when you feel strapped for resources. When I began my assignment at Chase, I did not want to raise false expectations so I constantly focused on what I could *not* do rather than what I *could* do to help my customers. Projecting a can-do attitude increases your customers' confidence in you as well as your energy and enthusiasm.

Resourcefulness is paramount in managing a small HRD department. You will need to think of alternate ways of solving problems. Consider who else in the organization besides your staff might be able to help you and actually benefit from doing so. Try to simplify procedures and still maintain your effectiveness by eliminating unnecessary steps or doing things differently.

Flexibility is a great asset in helping to gain the support of others who do not have a strong vested interest in helping you. Flexibility is critical when working with line managers to deliver your programs. Finding ways of accommodating others' needs and being flexible about what must be done make it easier for people to help you.

A learning orientation is key to continuous improvement. It allows you to learn from your mistakes and from the suggestions of others. Every day is an opportunity to learn how to do things better. It is easy to become defensive when you are given suggestions about what you could do to be more helpful. Instead of explaining what you cannot do, listen to your clients and incorporate their suggestions whenever possible.

DEVELOPING YOUR BUSINESS AND MANAGERIAL SKILLS

Now that you understand what skills you need, let's look at how you can develop these skills. We begin with business and managerial skills.

Developing Business Skills

Business experience, especially managing a small business, provides a helpful perspective. As one person explained it: "I ran my own business and learned to do everything on a small budget." Experience in your industry or organization gives you a head start on developing business expertise because you are more aware of critical organizational issues and are more likely to focus human resource development on your company's business priorities. One HRD manager believes that her experience as a product manager gave her instant credibility. Business experience helps you visualize training as an integral part of the organization, not an isolated activity but one that responds to business needs.

If you are new to business, consider subscribing to business publications such as the *Wall Street Journal*, *Business Week*, or *Fortune* magazine. You can learn a great deal about your company's business by reviewing its annual report, strategic documents, and company and industry newsletters. Staying in touch with senior management also helps keep you focused on organizational priorities. Interviewing key managers to find out what they do helps hone your business focus. Working lunches to discuss key business issues with managers and employees help you stay abreast of what's happening in your organization. Consider the possibility of "job shadowing" or observing people who work in crucial positions in different departments to get a closer look at the business.

If you work for an organization with field locations, make sure that you take the time to get to know what life is like in the field. Ann Daniells, who worked as recruiting and training manager in the circulation department of a large regional newspaper, faced the challenge of coordinating training for field managers while dealing with the problem of constant management turnover. She stresses the importance of business knowledge: "You have to understand the business to have credibility. Spending time in the field gave me both business knowledge and visibility. Unfortunately, I spent too much of my time in the office because I was working so hard. I didn't go to the field as much as I should have because I feared that people felt I had done it enough and would see it as 'playing.' I denied myself the benefit of exposure and learning" (interview with the author, Jan. 30, 1990).

If your experience has been as a designer or instructor, you may need to develop your business skills by attending a business-planning, strategic-planning, budgeting, or marketing program provided by a local organization or educational institution. See also Chapters Five and Ten of this book for insights into how to gain control of your budget and manage your expenses wisely, Chapter Two to learn more about understanding your organization's business, and Chapter Seven to learn how to attract customers to your programs.

It is also important that you acquire the skills to use various business tools available to you. For example, there are many ways to learn to develop your computer skills. You may want to buy a computer for use at home. This will allow you to improve your skills in a safe, low-pressure environment. The best way to improve your computer skills is to find simple ways to practice using software programs. Learn to develop simple tracking sheets for your own use before you work on budget presentations for senior management.

Most software programs have tutorials that give you a head start on learning to use the programs. You can also subscribe to various technology magazines that provide helpful tips on how to get the most from your software. Your company's data processing department may have advice about technology training available in the company or the local community. Be sure to build relationships with other employees who know how to use the software you want to learn to use. Perhaps you can offer them free training in your programs in exchange for coaching on how to use a computer.

Developing Managerial Skills

Having some prior management experience helps in running a small HRD department. Here is what some managers have said about the value of management experience:

- "Being a supervisor/manager for ten years helped me become very comfortable with interpersonal relationships."

- "Managerial experience helped me learn to consolidate training efforts to respond to business priorities."

- "Managing a customer service department taught me management skills, product knowledge and systems knowledge, and gave me line experience, which built my credibility with the business."

Many small HRD departments are the result of start-up situations. Having experience creating a department from scratch can be a big help.

You learn how to work with few resources and little structure, how to create a budget, how to develop policies and procedures, and how to get things running.

Any management experience in working with minimal support will be helpful to you in managing a small HRD department. As one person put it: "I was previously a corporate trainer for Filenes and was responsible for four stores. I had to work with minimum supervision and minimum resources. This made it easier to manage a small training department." On the other hand, if you have only worked with a large staff, you have a more difficult transition: "One gets used to extra 'pairs of hands.' It is harder to anticipate the lack of resources previously available for support and functions." As another manager put it: "I have always been a firm believer in delegating. I now have no one but myself to delegate to."

You can learn to compensate for your lack of staff by drawing on the help of others who do not report to you. This type of "delegation" requires negotiation and influence skills. Direct experience is not the only way to develop these skills. A course on positive politics or on positive power and influence can help you learn to influence others in a collaborative way. Chapter Six of this book discusses techniques for building a resource network that can help you accomplish your HRD goals while building broad-based support for your efforts.

If you are new to management, attend a management skills workshop. Consider attending a project management workshop that hones your organizational and managerial skills in dealing with people who do not report directly to you. Skills learned there can save you considerable time and errors in managing complex projects such as designing new HRD programs. Participating in a workshop inside your company allows you to build an internal support network of managers who know how to get things done inside your company. On the other hand, attending an external program allows you to speak more freely about people and to gain the perspective of managers in other companies and industries.

Time management is especially important when you must handle many tasks yourself and deal with constant scheduling pressures. There are many workshops and self-study programs that can help you improve your time management skills. Key to all time management programs is learning to create meaningful goals, write a daily to-do list, set priorities, and work on high-priority tasks before tackling less important ones. Make sure you use some sort of calendar and daily appointment book to prioritize monthly goals, daily goals, and essential tasks to help you keep track of what you are supposed to be doing. Franklin Management Institute's time management program offers an excellent planning and tracking system that includes self-study materials and workshops that can help you use their time management tools effectively.

··

DEVELOPING YOUR HRD SKILLS

Having some experience in needs assessment, design, and instruction of training is a big advantage in helping you identify needs and resources and begin to meet needs quickly. In the words of one manager: "Wide exposure to all facets of training and development is essential. One has to have a wider range of knowledge in a small department. You are more like a family practitioner than a specialist."

On the basis of your own background, plan to participate in specific training or activities that can help you learn needed skills. If you have had little HRD experience, concentrate on programs provided by HRD professional societies such as the American Society for Training and Development, the OD (Organizational Development) Network, Training Directors Forum, University Associates, or the Society for Performance and Instruction.

Reading

One of the least expensive and fastest ways of developing HRD skills and knowledge is through reading. *The Trainer's Professional Development Handbook* (Bard, Bell, Stephens, and Webster, 1987) suggests a thoughtful approach to planning an HRD professional's skill development and includes a wealth of developmental activities for HRD managers and trainers. Part One focuses on planning an effective learning strategy for the novice or the experienced HRD professional. Part Two provides a useful catalogue of learning resources and materials. Part Three, which gives an overview of key HRD concepts, theories, and contributors, is a helpful reference for the HRD novice.

Training and Development and *Training* magazine are especially valuable resources. Once you subscribe to them, you'll find yourself on a mailing list that offers you almost infinite reading possibilities. Be sure to keep up with relevant industry publications. I have found the following books and publications to be particularly helpful in my own department:

- Kay Abella's (1986) *Building Successful Training Programs* teaches a step-by-step approach to program design.

- Peter Block's (1981) *Flawless Consulting* can help you learn to say no and set realistic expectations when working with clients.

- *ASTD Trainer's Toolkit: Needs Assessment Instruments* (Allen, 1990) provides relevant articles and samples of needs assessment instruments.

- *ASTD Infoline* series is a monthly publication of hot HRD topics in an easy-to-read format.

- Susan Warshauer's (1988) *Inside Training and Development* is an excellent, no-nonsense guide to developing business-focused training programs and marketing them effectively in today's organizations.

- Robinson and Robinson's (1989) *Training for Impact* presents a framework for evaluating HRD's impact on the business.

- *Training Directors' Forum Newsletter*, produced monthly by Lakewood Publications, contains helpful tips on managing HRD departments of any size.

- Robert Craig's (1987) *Training and Development Handbook*, third edition, is a comprehensive reference book that contains essays on virtually all aspects of training and development.

- J. W. Pfeiffer's *The Human Resource Development Annual Set*, a series published since 1972, includes a wealth of tools, techniques, and design ideas for the HRD professional.

Networking

Networking with other people is a powerful way to develop your HRD skills and learn new ideas. Contact with people outside your company keeps you in touch with the marketplace and provides you with ideas, moral support, and inspiration to meet the challenges you face. As Joanne Rogovin advises: "You need to develop allies with whom you can talk things out and brainstorm. You can tap into your colleagues for referrals and ideas about programs" (interview with author, Feb. 7, 1990). According to Bob Jendusa: "Networking can help you build mentor relationships with others in your industry. Mentors were instrumental in providing support and in helping me gain acceptance of the value of training in the publishing industry. I had real safety valves — close friends who provided a sounding board and support" (interview with author, Feb. 14, 1990).

One of the biggest pitfalls of managing a small HRD department is becoming isolated from people who can help you. Ann Barkey explains the danger this way: "People get wrapped up in the demands of the job and don't keep up with learning and professional development. Be careful you don't create your own vacuum — it's easy to get sucked in. We perpetuate our own vacuum when we fail to network and make excuses why we cannot go to meetings. Because we are a one-person department, we think we have to be the only one doing training. We think we have to reinvent the wheel, when six people have already thought of it" (interview with the author, Jan. 30, 1990).

Abundant sources of networking are open to HRD managers. The American Society for Training and Development, which produces *Training and Development* and newsletters, sponsors national and local conferences. Some conferences focus on HRD in general, while others focus on technical training. The ASTD also has local chapters, special-interest groups, and industry groups. Lakewood Publications, which publishes *Training* magazine and the *Training Director's Forum Newsletter*, sponsors the Best of America conference for HRD professionals. The OD Network also sponsors local networks.

Crystine Mancini, a training manager in a small local bank, describes her experience with networking this way: "I read an advertisement in the paper for a local ASTD chapter meeting. I attended this meeting and felt 100 percent reassured that help was very close at hand. I then joined national ASTD and became very active in my local chapter. ASTD membership has brought hundreds of networking opportunities, and I feel that my employer and myself have benefited greatly" (letter to the author, July 7, 1989).

You can create your own support network by calling HRD managers in companies in similar industries or in nearby locations. I was able to find continuing inspiration for writing this book and to discover new ways to improve my department by asking other HRD managers of small departments to share their success stories with me. My network grew as I asked each person I called for the names of other managers of small HRD departments whom they knew and admired. People generally return your calls when you tell them that a colleague has referred them as an excellent source of ideas. Without exception, HRD managers of small departments were willing to share their ideas and were appreciative of being asked for their opinions. For more ideas on networking, see Bard and Loftin (1987).

DEVELOPING YOUR PERSONAL ATTRIBUTES

A person who is creative, energetic, flexible, and open to learning has a good chance of being a successful manager of a small HRD department. Let's look at how you can develop these attributes.

Increasing Your Creativity

Anyone who manages a small HRD department can benefit from workshops that foster creativity and encourage participants to create their own vision of human resource development. I strongly recommend workshops by Robert Fritz, president of DMA and developer of the Technologies for Creating curriculum. You can learn about Fritz's philosophy in his excellent book, *The Path of Least Resistance* (1989), which explains how to create the results you want in your life. Fritz emphasizes the importance of creative tension in helping you achieve your goals. This tension comes from clearly visualizing what you want while taking a realistic look at where you are in relation to your goals. The gap between your vision and your current state creates a natural tension to close the gap by achieving your vision. Having a clear vision of what you want can help you through discouraging periods.

Increasing Your Energy and Dealing with Stress

Because managing a small department is very demanding, be sure that you take steps to reduce your stress. Robinson's (1987) "Tapping Your Inner Resources and Learning from Yourself" is a helpful source of ideas for dealing with stress in a healthy way. Many people who must deal with the pressures of a small HRD department can draw on personal strengths and habits that they developed in other stressful working environments. For example, one training manager who had been a surgical nurse felt that she had benefited from having had to handle the details, setbacks, long hours, and "doctor-like" executives that she had encountered in the operating room. She found that HRD was truly a "breath of fresh air" compared to surgical nursing.

Take a course on stress management. Be sure to get enough exercise and sleep and eat properly. Consider using relaxation tapes or meditating to increase your energy. Be particularly careful not to overindulge in coffee, alcohol, or sugar, especially when on business trips where you have to fly. Drinking coffee and alcohol may make you feel better temporarily, but they can greatly increase the effects of jet lag.

Find ways to rejuvenate yourself and to reduce stress and pressure. Jon Barb recommends that you "set up enjoyable experiences for yourself and take care of yourself in the organization" (interview with the author, Feb. 6, 1990). Jon suggests finding ways to travel to interesting locations in your company to accomplish important projects. He recommends getting out into the field organization as quickly as you can, making sure that you have a business reason for the trip and leave something of value with people, such as your recommendation for training or a development planning tool. Getting away from the office not only enables you to build relationships with distant customers, but it often restores your energy and enthusiasm for your job.

Increasing Your Flexibility

Learn to be flexible in how you respond to requests for help. As the manager of a small department, you may need to choose a "quick and dirty" solution over an elegant one. One manager felt she had been handicapped by her previous career as a surgical nurse: "I had a need for perfectionism and had trouble with the 'quick and dirty' approach. I was used to having closure on things." Chapter Six offers ideas on how to be flexible when working with resources who do not report directly to you.

Adopting a Learning Orientation

You can find out more about developing a learning orientation by reading books and attending workshops by Peter Senge, author of *The Fifth Discipline* (1990). Senge discusses the importance of learning from your mistakes in order to make changes in the system so that the same mistakes don't happen again. The best way to continue learning is to stay open to feedback. Do not become defensive about what went wrong but focus on what would be more helpful in the future. Whenever possible, conduct pilot programs and listen carefully to participant feedback about what would work best for your customers. Making improvements based on people's suggestions goes a long way in establishing your reputation as a responsive and open-minded person.

EXPANDING YOUR STAFF

If you are a one-person department, hiring administrative help can be a struggle. Let's look at how you can convince senior management that you need another person to accomplish your HRD goals.

Convincing Management of Your Need for an Assistant

Organizations are reluctant to add additional staff unless there are strong business reasons to do so. Adding staff members is extremely expensive. In fact, the major expense in most organizations is salary and benefits of full-time employees, who may receive as much as 30 to 50 percent of their salary in benefits.

Ellen Kamp (whom we met earlier), formerly of Corroon and Black, strongly recommends that you not ask for additional staff until you demonstrate the value of your department and show what you could do with additional resources. You need to provide management with the following information:

- How many more programs you could offer and their impact on business results

- How many more customers you could reach

- How program or service quality would be improved

- What additional services you would be able to provide and their impact on business priorities

Let's say you convince senior management that you require additional staff. Carefully consider the skills and talent you need in an assistant. Having a clear idea of what you need and creating a developmental plan for your assistant are important first steps.

Creating an Additional Position in Your Department

Your first priority is usually hiring an administrative assistant to help you with the many logistical and administrative details involved in running a small HRD department. Depending on your budget and the availability of training resources, it may be easier and more productive for you to use temporary professional training help than to use temporary administrative help. For example, you may be able to hire consultants or use subject-matter experts within your organization to teach or design programs. If you hire a professional trainer and expect the person to handle administration as well as program design and instruction, he or she is likely to become frustrated. While you can use temporary administrative help during heavy work periods, it is difficult for a temporary assistant to understand the goals of your department, your clients' needs, and how to respond effectively to clients' requests for information and help. You will continuously need to orient and train temporary assistants in how your department operates, and you will not have adequate time to do this well.

Selecting Your Assistant

A skilled, permanent administrative assistant provides critical support in a small HRD department. First and foremost, find someone with skills that balance your own. For example, one highly creative HRD manager made sure that she hired an assistant who was more organized and attentive to detail than herself. Also, look for someone who is compatible with your management style. The last thing you want is conflicts with your staff. If you know that you need to be in control, make sure that you find someone who can tolerate this behavior or tell you when your style is interfering with his or her effectiveness.

Aside from compatibility with your style and strengths, look for the following in an administrative assistant:

- *Organizational skills* required to handle registration, materials production, scheduling facilities, budget assistance, tracking, and other administrative tasks.

- *Communication skills* so that he or she can represent your department professionally on the phone and in person. This person needs to be able to provide answers to questions about your department's programs and services, procedures, and program logistics to a variety of audiences.

- *Customer focus* so that he or she can maintain positive relations with customers while working hard to meet deadlines and juggle tasks. Your assistant must care about serving customers and be sensitive to what customers want. Customers see your assistant's treatment of them as a reflection of your customer service orientation.

- *Independence*, which allows him or her to function effectively even while you are away from the office. Your assistant needs to be able to handle ambiguous situations and work with minimal supervision.

- *Ability to handle pressure*, which enables him or her to work on several projects at once and still meet tight deadlines. You cannot afford to hire someone who can only focus on one thing at a time or who crumbles under pressure.

Hiring an Additional Trainer

If you decide to hire an additional trainer, you'll want a trainer to have many of the same competencies you have. Look for the following in a professional trainer:

- *Program design expertise*, or the ability to design and develop HRD programs

- *Instructional skills*, or the ability to instruct and facilitate HRD programs and team-building sessions

- *Consulting skills*, or the ability to work with business units to determine HRD needs and develop appropriate interventions

- *Organizational skills*, or the ability to manage complex projects with minimal guidance

- *Personal confidence, energy, flexibility, resourcefulness, and a learning orientation*, or the same qualities you need for the same reasons mentioned earlier

■ *Program administration skills*, or a willingness and ability to help you with program administrative tasks described in Chapter Eight

●●●

DEVELOPING YOUR STAFF

Beware of the pitfall of overworking staff members. Don't rely so much on your administrative assistant and trainer that you ignore their personal and professional development. This can lead to early burnout. Overloading them with a never-ending stream of administrative tasks or teaching responsibilities allows no opportunity for them to think about how to do things better or to improve their skills. Build in opportunities to learn new skills. Provide time away from the job without the pressure of deadlines and constant customer demands to allow for and encourage their professional development.

Training

Sending your staff to training programs not only teaches them skills but allows them to step back from their work to think of better ways that things can be done. It also provides a much needed, re-energizing break that can keep them from reaching burnout, a constant danger in a small department. Providing training also sends the message that taking time to develop skills is worth a temporary disruption of work flow in a department.

Creating a Team Approach

Make everyone on your staff a significant player on your team. One way to achieve this is by providing a meaningful context for what staff members do—making sure they understand the importance of tasks that they are performing and how they serve the overall mission of your department. You can do this partly by sharing various strategic documents or reports with them. A more effective approach is to take time to explain what your department is trying to do, what is important to senior management and to your other constituencies, and how they contribute to the effectiveness of HRD.

Coaching and Special Projects

You can develop your staff's skills through coaching and through special assignments. For example, you can broaden your assistant by giving him or her expanded responsibilities in helping you to track or project the budget. I worked with one assistant to help me determine the actual costs of a program so that we could calculate the number of participants required to break even on program costs. Prior to that assignment, the assistant had overseen payment of invoices, but she had little awareness of the real cost of programs and of the importance of ensuring full attendance at programs. Following that assignment, she took a more active effort in helping to market programs to improve attendance and avoid needless program cancellations.

Exposure to Clients

You can also develop your staff's skills by giving them exposure to clients rather than only behind-the-scene tasks such as materials production and registration. You might, for example, have them be present during an orientation program to present the program overview and to introduce and coordinate guest speakers. Introducing speakers helps develop your staff's presentation skills. It also helps give them a better understanding of the program's purpose, of what both participants and speakers need for a program to succeed, and of the impact of training logistics on program effectiveness. Most important, it provides them with an increased sense of ownership in your department's programs.

· ·

SUCCESS STORIES

Successful managers of small HRD departments find ways to learn from a wide range of experiences. Let's look at the development of two successful HRD managers.

Learning from Past Experiences

We met Carol Ryan Ertz in Chapter Three. When Carol became training coordinator for a Catholic hospital, it was her first formal training position.

How did she learn the skills that enabled her to succeed as a one-person HRD department? Carol's early work experience involved eight years in public school education, where she designed curricula for students at both ends of the intellectual spectrum—the extremely gifted and the learning disabled. This design experience helped her learn to create a curriculum and to be flexible in how she approached learning methods.

Carol also obtained a master's degree in human resources education. While studying, she worked part-time as a training administrator for a college, where she honed her administrative skills and learned about several vendor programs. In both her public school and college jobs, Carol became adept at coordination with both internal and external customers. She learned to juggle many tasks and to develop key relationships with people whose support or participation she needed in various programs.

One of her most valuable experiences was a three-month internship with a technology company. Here she observed many training programs taught by master trainers. This helped her learn about a wide range of training styles that apply to adult learning and learn the content of a number of programs, such as management skills and communication skills. As part of her assignment, Carol learned to give constructive feedback to instructors on how they were effective and how they could improve their teaching styles. Skill in giving diplomatic feedback is a cornerstone of a successful trainer and a useful skill when you need to explain to people what you can and cannot do for them.

Teaching Yourself New Skills

Debra Shine, whom we met at the beginning of Chapter One, joined a bank right out of high school. Largely self-taught, Debra worked her way through a variety of positions at the bank and up through the bank's holding company. Her first official training assignment, director of product and sales training, reporting to the head of marketing, recognized an organizational need to create a sales culture. Debra replaced someone who had been in the position for only six months. Her mission was to see that every employee had product knowledge and used sales skills. She worked on her own, sharing a secretary with four other people. She saw her challenge as bringing focus to sales and product training, standardizing the process while leaving implementation to local offices.

Debra is a good example of someone with a strong business focus and an understanding of how business operates. She learned all facets of banking through many types of business experiences. When she formally joined the training function, she had twelve years of experience throughout the company as a teller, customer service representative, operations manager, and merger coordinator. As operations manager of several hundred people, Debra learned the fundamentals of business and people management, and she also did some training and course design. To learn more about the fundamentals of adult learning, she became actively involved in the ASTD.

Debra symbolizes the essence of the learning organization. In her words: "I learned that you can teach yourself to do anything." Debra comments on the difficulties she faced when she began her formal training assignment. "I had an open playing field. I was an 'operations person'—I did not know marketing, and it was my first official training assignment and my first assignment with an aggressive corporate headquarters. I did not have a degree and I had to work with people who did. I had to educate myself regarding everything, including computers, producing videos, teaching, designing, writing, dealing with consultants. I never learned more from any other assignment" (interview with the author, June 20, 1990).

Debra also met the challenge of learning from experience. After three years as director of product and sales training, she was named vice president and director of training and development at one of the bank's affiliates. Recently, she spent two years developing her skills as an external consultant and guest speaker, focusing on quality, executive team building and management development. She is currently directing training and development as well as mergers for another aggressive financial institution.

SUMMARY: STRATEGIES FOR DEVELOPING YOUR AND YOUR STAFF'S SKILLS

1. Ensure that you have adequate skills and knowledge to run the HRD function effectively. Determine your strengths and weaknesses, assess how well they match the needs of the business, and decide what skills or attributes you need to implement your vision of human resource development.

2. Plan developmental experiences to ensure that you, as the HRD manager, have adequate business knowledge, HRD skills, managerial skills, and confidence, energy, resilience, and flexibility.

3. Plan to stay in touch with the external HRD community through ASTD meetings, Best of America conventions, the Training Director's Forum, and the OD Network. Call up local HRD managers, and read HRD managers' newsletters.

4. Stay in touch with your internal customers in the organization through phone calls, meetings, lunches, and other gatherings.

5. Use the following information to convince senior management when you need an assistant if you do not already have one:

    ■ Quantity of programs required to meet business needs

    ■ Quality of customer service

    ■ Quality of programs

    ■ Needs that would not be met without an assistant

    ■ Impact on the organization

6. Identify the skills needed by your assistant. Consider compatibility with your style and skills, administrative and organizational skills, communication skills, independence and autonomy, and other skills needed by your department.

7. Ensure that your staff develops professionally through attendance at training programs, special projects, meaningful work assignments that stretch skills, coaching, job shadowing, and customer contact.

▲ ▲ ▲ ▲ ▲ ▲ ▲ ▲ ▲ ▲ ▲ ▲ ▲ ▲ ▲ ▲ ▲ *Chapter* **12**

Preparing to Address Future Challenges

Despite the uncertain economy, the future of small HRD departments looks bright. One of the key challenges of the nineties is to increase productivity without increasing staff. Companies can save money by cutting back on full-time employees, thereby reducing expenses associated with benefits and other office space requirements. As companies "rightsize" staff and flatten organizational structures, small HRD departments are likely to increase in number. Because many companies are trying to do more with fewer resources, small HRD departments now have the opportunity to make an even greater impact on their organizations. In this chapter we will briefly review some organizational trends that may be helpful to you and then summarize what makes managers of small HRD departments effective. Finally, we will consider how to put the information presented in earlier chapters into an action plan to increase your future effectiveness.

. . . .

ORGANIZATIONAL TRENDS AND THEIR IMPACT ON SMALL HRD DEPARTMENTS

Several organizational trends may present opportunities for managers of small HRD departments. For example, many organizations are becoming aware of the need to set priorities in order to meet financial goals and provide quality goods and services to customers. As a consequence, it may be easier for you to focus your efforts on priorities and say no to requests for nonessential services. Other trends that may help make your job easier include the movement toward the involvement of nontrainers in training, a growing recognition of the importance of collaboration between departments and organizations to maximize resources, the rise of technology in human resource development, and the movement to decentralize staff to be close to the organization's business. Naturally, these trends may be more or less prevalent in different organizations. Usually smaller companies and not-for-profit organizations lag somewhat behind larger companies and for-profit organizations in adapting to trends. Even if your organization is not yet engaged in some of these movements, you may be able to increase management's awareness and be a helpful agent for constructive change. Let's look briefly at these trends.

Involvement of Nontrainers in Training

As companies aspire to become "learning organizations," many leading-edge companies are beginning to recognize that teaching and learning are part of everyone's job, not just the HRD department's. The role of manager is becoming more of a coach and teacher who is responsible for encouraging the staff's learning and development. As a result, more nontrainers are getting involved in the design and delivery of training. The job of managing a small HRD department becomes easier when others assume increased responsibility for sharing learning.

Consider, for example, UNUM Life Insurance Company of America, which was first introduced in Chapter Four. Its customer service department was moving from a traditional organization toward self-directed teams. These teams needed to understand how constant change would be affecting them, and they needed to spread this knowledge quickly to the five hundred customer service employees. As a strategy to meet this need, the corporate HRD department developed a one-day training program, Understanding the Impact of Change, and trained two line human resource managers to teach the program. To further speed the dissemination of information, each customer service team sent the team leader and one team member to the training program to learn concepts about change and to take these concepts back to the workplace. By means of this approach, many more people were trained than would have been if the HRD department had provided training directly to the entire department of five hundred people.

In another example, Pacific Gas and Electric made a commitment to increase diversity awareness of twenty-seven thousand employees throughout the organization. Ronita Johnson, diversity planning coordinator for Pacific Gas and Electric, benefited greatly from senior management's commitment to diversity as well as from the willingness of managers to take on more responsibility for training. With the help of an outside consultant, Julie O'Mara, Ronita has trained over one hundred line managers in a rigorous train-the-trainer process to prepare them to deliver diversity training. Furthermore, these diversity awareness trainers have responsibilities beyond training: "they're expected to champion diversity in their day-to-day interactions with others. They're expected to walk the talk and thereby reinforce the messages they teach" (Johnson and O'Mara, 1992, p. 50).

Collaboration with Other Departments and Organizations

In an effort to save money and time, organizations are beginning to collaborate with each other to meet their HRD needs. The previous examples describe the way in which small HRD departments can collaborate with other departments to provide relevant and timely training. Furthermore, companies are collaborating with sources outside the organization, such as local educational institutions or other companies, for free or low-cost training. For example, a local charitable organization that is dealing with an impending reorganization, asked me to present a shortened version of the Understanding the Impact of Change workshop offered by UNUM. The workshop is a way to help a not-for-profit organization provide tools to assist all its employees, from the bus drivers to directors, in coping with wide-scale change. Many companies are willing to provide free training to customers and suppliers as well as to charitable and educational institutions.

London (1989) describes an example of two companies sharing resources to develop a leadership program that neither company could afford on its own. In other instances noncompeting companies may share the expense of bringing in famous speakers to address current topics in human resource development. As manager of a small HRD department, be sure to take advantage of any opportunities for collaboration with external sources in your area. See McDermott (1990) and London (1989) for further details on this trend of collaboration between organizations.

Advances in Technology

Technology can benefit a small HRD department in many ways. With advances in computer software and hardware, you can produce professional, cost-effective, and customized training materials quickly and easily. Marketing, administration, budgeting, and tracking of HRD programs are much easier with computers. As mentioned in Chapters Seven and Eight, you may also be able to use electronic mail to market and administer HRD. According to Bell's prediction of trends for the nineties: "Electronic mail will be as common as the telephone is today" (1987, pp. 14–15).

In an effort to save money and reach geographically dispersed people, organizations are relying less on classroom training and more on technology, such as audiotaped training, video-based training, and computer-based training (Cohen, 1991; London, 1989; Sheridan, 1992). According to a *Training* magazine survey (Lee, 1991, p. 50), 90 percent of companies surveyed used video for some training. Video teleconferencing is becoming a more affordable, realistic option for delivering training to distant locations, especially when local departments help pay the cost of teleconferencing (Sheridan, 1992). Wise use of technology can enable managers of small HRD departments to assume a more strategic role and to train many more people in a cost-effective way than using classroom training as the sole approach to human resource development.

For example, the quality department at UNUM collaborated with the training and executive education departments to hire a renowned speaker on service excellence. The speaker's initial talks reached an audience of several hundred managers who were able to attend one of two sessions. However, because the sessions were also videotaped, more than five thousand employees throughout the United States, Canada, and the United Kingdom will be able to understand the critical dimensions of service excellence by viewing the videotape in their local offices.

Increase in Small, Decentralized HRD Departments

In an effort to improve competitiveness and customer focus, many companies are decentralizing lines of business along with staff (Cohen, 1991). In their early stages, companies are likely to have a small, centralized HRD unit that is responsible for addressing generic HRD needs and teaching corporate values that cut across business units. As different business units form, a centralized HRD department cannot address the specialized needs of all its populations. One solution is to decentralize human resource development. Decentralization can provide business units with clear accountability, build greater expertise, concentrate resources where they are needed, improve decision making, and encourage innovation (Piturro, 1988). A small, decentralized HRD department has several advantages compared with a large, centralized one:

- *Focus on priorities.* Despite fewer resources, you can focus on priorities of the business unit in a timely way. Decision making occurs more quickly and is more responsive to business needs. While the corporate HRD department may address problems eventually, one business unit's priorities may not be the whole organization's priorities.

- *Closeness to the business unit.* As an insider, you have a closer view of the business unit and what employees need to do for it to succeed. You are more in touch with the local culture and how to implement HRD successfully.

- *Ownership.* You have a vested interest in the success of the business unit and the development of *your* people. Business units' specialized developmental needs are likely to be ignored by corporate HRD departments. The decentralized HRD manager is only as successful as the unit itself. This increased accountability often leads to improved performance.

- *Commitment to meeting needs.* In a decentralized department, you usually have stronger management commitment to develop programs for smaller— but critical—populations that the corporate HRD department frequently ignores. You may be able to offer one-shot programs for small populations, whereas most corporate HRD departments must concentrate on broad-based programs.

- *Experimentation.* As a small unit, it is easier to be innovative because there is less risk involved in experimenting on a small scale. If your HRD experiment succeeds, other business units may try it as well.

On the other hand, there are also disadvantages to decentralization. However, many of these may be overcome by careful management of the HRD function.

- *Lack of resources.* Decentralized HRD departments often do not have as many concentrated resources as centralized HRD departments. Consequently, centralized HRD departments can usually offer more "professional" programs more frequently than smaller, decentralized departments. With wise use of resources, you can create good programs that meet clients' needs even with a "shoestring" budget. Flexibility, focus, and getting beyond perfectionism are crucial in a small, decentralized HRD department.

- *Loss of the big picture.* In a decentralized HRD department be careful to stay in touch with important HRD issues facing the whole organization. In some cases, you may need to make an extra effort for employees in your business unit to attend HRD programs with employees from other business units. Also, career planning that involves moving people across business units may be difficult. Staying connected to key people in other departments within the organization can help overcome these difficulties.

- *Need to influence resources not under your control.* As with any small HRD department, your skill in finding and managing indirect resources is particularly important. Decentralization works well only if the HRD manager can focus on business priorities and maximize resources not directly under his or her control.

STRATEGIES FOR SUCCESS: SOME COMMON THEMES

Throughout, this book has discussed strategies for success. While there are as many successful approaches to managing small HRD departments as there are people managing them, some common themes emerge. What are the most important lessons that we can learn from other managers of successful, small HRD departments?

- *Think of yourself as a business: focus on priorities.* Create a clear mission. Let your clients know how you can add value, and continuously evaluate the worth of what you are doing to ensure that human resource development supports the business strategy. Create annual goals and daily to-do lists that relate to those goals. Every day make sure that you work toward accomplishing your goals. Ask yourself: "If I could do only one thing, what would it be?" Learn to say no to unreasonable requests and at the same time help your clients solve their own problems.

■ *Conduct a thorough needs assessment.* Find ways to understand the organization's needs and what is required for success. Don't assume that you know what your clients want. What worked in one organization may not work in another. Taking the time to understand needs can save time spent redoing work or making up for mistakes.

■ *Market, market, market.* Contribute to the organization's business, and make your contributions visible to the people who matter. Make sure that your customers know how they can benefit from your expertise, programs, and services. Provide timely information about human resource development in ways that work for your customers. Keep people informed of your progress rather than wait until you have a finished product. Beware of the trap of "psychic marketing" — don't expect clients to know what you are doing without your telling them.

■ *Build line-manager support.* Involve your clients in a partnership with you. Collaboration creates a sense of ownership so that you are not expected to do everything yourself. Involving others in the development and delivery of HRD programs allows you to offer more programs that meet the needs of the organization. Program attendance is not a problem when people throughout the organization champion the value of human resource development.

■ *Develop your own support network.* Connect with other people with whom you can share ideas, celebrate successes, and learn from mistakes. Build relationships with line managers and employees who will participate in your HRD programs; and create a network within the human resource community inside and outside your company. Include consultants in your network, and try to contract as much work as you can to trusted consultants, within the limits of your budget.

■ *Maintain perspective and a sense of humor.* Keep yourself energized, encouraged, and confident of your value. It is easy to lose heart when you compare your staff or budget to that of a large corporation. At times you may feel like "a tiny speck of dust in the universe" (to quote Lou Grant on the "Mary Tyler Moore Show"). You can have a tremendous impact by focusing on what is really important to the business.

■ *Be open to learning from experience.* Be a learning organization. Step back from fire fighting and crisis management and look at the big picture so you can learn how to prevent future problems. Every day your customers will give you ideas on how you can meet their needs. Welcome their ideas on how to improve your effectiveness. Remember, resolving problems quickly and sensitively helps develop loyal customer relationships.

Managing a small HRD department in a small company or in a decentralized business unit within a larger organization can be a tremendously challenging, exciting, and rewarding experience. You may never learn more from any other assignment, and you may never have more impact on an organization. As we have seen from the success stories throughout this book, you don't need a large department to make a difference. If you have a clear and business-focused mission and build allies throughout your organization, you can be a constructive force for positive change.

Keep in mind the wide variety of approaches that other successful small HRD departments have used. When you feel stymied and discouraged, think of alternative approaches to the situation or reach out to others who may be able to help you. Stay in contact with key people in your organization and with the rest of the professional community, and take the time to network with others who can provide you with encouragement and moral support. Since you may never work harder in any other job, make sure that you reward yourself for all your hard work.

ACTION PLAN FOR FUTURE SUCCESS

All the worksheets in the section Resources, which follows this chapter, are intended to give you ideas and tools to ensure your future success. Perhaps the most important is Worksheet 1, an HRD department planning tool. This tool summarizes the criteria for effectiveness discussed throughout the entire book. It identifies key areas for you to examine in evaluating your own performance and provides space for you to write down action steps, resources, and due dates. You can use this as a planning tool to help you schedule actions needed to accomplish your HRD plan or as a developmental plan to help you improve your skills in each area of effectiveness. Go through the entire list and check off actions that you want to make sure you take. Once you have completed the list, prioritize high-payoff actions. Don't try to do everything at once.

Focus and time management are critical in all aspects of running a small HRD department, including improving how you run it. Remember Pareto's 80–20 rule: 20 percent of your actions produce 80 percent of your results. As stated by Alan Lakein in *How to Get Control of Your Time and Your Life*: "If all items are arranged in order of value, 80 percent of the value would come from only 20 percent of the items, while the remaining 20 percent of the value would come from 80 percent of the items (1973, p. 71). Determine what are high-value activities in your organization, and make changes selectively. Don't get bogged down in low-value activities. Ask yourself if changing a particular behavior or procedure will make a difference to your customers and sponsors. Changing only a few behaviors can increase your effectiveness dramatically.

Remember, the key to success is believing in yourself, staying optimistic, and keeping focused on the organization's business needs. Good luck and enjoy the challenge!

▲ ▲

Resources:
Fifteen Worksheets for
Planning and Evaluation

This section includes worksheets that can help you in managing an effective HRD department. Worksheet 1 can also help you accomplish your HRD plan or plan your own development. Feel free to make as many copies of the worksheets as you need.

1. HRD Department Planning Tool
2. Preparing a Needs Assessment Report
3. Creating a Mission Statement
4. Selecting a First Program
5. Selecting a Consultant
6. Computing Training Program Costs
7. Projecting a Training Budget
8. Estimating Service Recoveries
9. Budget Tracking Report
10. Service-Recovery Tracking Report
11. Project Planning for Program Development
12. Program Logistics Tracking Sheet
13. Program Evaluation Form
14. Evaluation Report on Pilot Program
15. Program Evaluation Summary

Worksheet 1. HRD Department Planning Tool.

Criteria for effectiveness	Action steps	Resources	Dates

Assessing business priorities and HRD needs

Review the business plan for key trends.

Use several data collection approaches in your needs assessment.

Include methods that build the involvement of others.

Include the right people in your needs assessment.

Find out what types of HRD programs and services are most essential to your target audience.

Consider key success indicators when assessing needs.

Ensure that your data reflect real training needs.

Identify gaps and recommend actions in your summary.

Worksheet 1. HRD Department Planning Tool, Cont'd.

Criteria for effectiveness	*Action steps*	*Resources*	*Dates*

Creating a business-focused HRD plan

Create a mission statement.

Clearly define the clients you serve.

Make sure senior management understands and supports what you are trying
to accomplish.

Create a realistic plan with attainable
deadlines.

Address priority business needs and key
populations.

Build flexibility into your plan so you can
make changes.

Ensure that your programs meet real
needs, not just perceived needs.

Consider alternatives to classroom
training.

Source: Managing a Small HRD Department, by Carol P. McCoy. San Francisco: Jossey-Bass. Copyright © 1993. Permission to reproduce and distribute
(with copyright notice visible) is hereby granted. If material is to be used in a
compilation to be sold for profit, please contact publisher for permission.

Criteria for effectiveness	*Action steps*	*Resources*	*Dates*

Creating a business-focused HRD plan, cont'd.

Ensure that training is the most appropriate solution.

Plan early "wins" to build your credibility.

Focus initial programs on an audience with whom success is likely.

Plan to play a visible role in the delivery of successful programs.

Finding resources

Find out what resources you need to accomplish your plan.

Discover how to get needed resources.

Collaborate with other resources to design programs.

Buy programs from consultants when appropriate.

Worksheet 1. HRD Department Planning Tool, Cont'd.

Criteria for effectiveness	*Action steps*	*Resources*	*Dates*

Finding resources, cont'd.

Make use of appropriate programs
offered outside your organization.

Teach some programs so that you stay in
touch with clients and are visible as a
resource.

Use other internal resources (such as line
managers) to teach some programs.

Budgeting

Be responsible for the HRD budget.

Create a budget sufficient to cover your
goals.

Know the costs of your programs and
services.

Estimate spending trends throughout the
year.

Create a charge-back policy with the
impact you want, that is, to encourage
increased attendance or selective
attendance.

Criteria for effectiveness	Action steps	Resources	Dates

Budgeting, cont'd.

Consider how to measure the impact of your programs to see that you have an adequate return on investment.

Trim the fat from your budget.

Plan what you will eliminate in case of budget cutbacks.

Consider cost in planning the length and timing of all programs and meetings.

Examine ways to increase program attendance.

Conduct programs at the most cost-effective facilities.

Examine ways to save costs involved in travel and lodging for participants/ instructors.

Managing program development

Create a project plan for all major projects to monitor progress.

Criteria for effectiveness	Action steps	Resources	Dates

Managing program development, cont'd.

Have written design guidelines for programs that you develop.

Ensure that your programs are an appropriate length to meet needs.

Actively manage the design of customized programs.

Use other internal resources to help design programs.

Recognize contributions of those who help you.

Make it easy for others to help you.

Create a process for choosing the best consultants.

Allow time to guide and manage consultants.

Worksheet 1. HRD Department Planning Tool, Cont'd.

Criteria for effectiveness	Action steps	Resources	Dates

Managing program development, cont'd.

Introduce consultants to the
organization.

Follow up when consultants or other
resources miss deadlines.

Test program materials before offering
them to large audiences.

Attracting customers

Create a marketing plan.

Keep customers informed about HRD
programs and services in ways that work
for your customers.

Demonstrate management's commitment
to HRD projects.

Provide a catalogue describing programs
and giving schedules.

Ensure that programs are conveniently
located for your target audience.

Worksheet 1. HRD Department Planning Tool, Cont'd.

Criteria for effectiveness	*Action steps*	*Resources*	*Dates*
Attracting customers, cont'd.			
Offer programs of appropriate length given business constraints.			
Price programs reasonably.			
Make it easy to register for programs.			
Use meetings to promote HRD programs and services.			
Promote your programs through advisory groups.			
Use newsletters, flyers, announcements to promote your programs.			
Use electronic mail to promote programs and register people.			
Use summary evaluations of programs to promote them.			

Worksheet 1. HRD Department Planning Tool, Cont'd.

Criteria for effectiveness	Action steps	Resources	Dates
Mastering program logistics			
Consider customers' needs in your program schedule.			
Conduct programs at appropriate, cost-effective facilities.			
Create cancellation penalties that discourage costly cancellations.			
Make program registration simple, well-organized, and easy for customers.			
Notify participants promptly of their registration status.			
Keep a file for each program, including information on speakers, participants, and costs.			
Provide participants with adequate logistical information.			
Organize material production procedures.			

233

Worksheet 1. HRD Department Planning Tool, Cont'd.

Criteria for effectiveness	*Action steps*	*Resources*	*Dates*

Mastering program logistics, cont'd.

Use all available help in producing
materials.

Delegate administrative tasks to your
assistant.

Use a program logistics checklist to
coordinate logistics and avoid problems.

Keep useful records to help measure
effectiveness and plan for future
programs.

Ensuring and evaluating effectiveness

Measure your performance in light of
your mission.

Offer essential services, not merely nice-
to-do ones.

Ensure that the "right" people (your
target audience) attend your programs.

Ensure that an appropriate number of
people attend each of your programs, not
just one or two people.

Source: Managing a Small HRD Department, by Carol P. McCoy. San Francisco: Jossey-Bass. Copyright © 1993. Permission to reproduce and distribute (with copyright notice visible) is hereby granted. If material is to be used in a compilation to be sold for profit, please contact publisher for permission.

Worksheet 1. HRD Department Planning Tool, Cont'd.

Criteria for effectiveness	*Action steps*	*Resources*	*Dates*

Ensuring and evaluating effectiveness, cont'd.

Measure customer satisfaction to ensure that your customers perceive you to be responsive to their needs.

Measure learning through second-level evaluation.

Measure application of learning on the job.

Measure HRD's impact on business results.

Present your evaluation findings in ways that impress senior management.

Present evaluation information on new initiatives to show they are worth investing in.

Consider ways to reinforce the effects of training.

Managing your budget

Create an organized tracking system to monitor your budget.

Worksheet 1. HRD Department Planning Tool, Cont'd.

Criteria for effectiveness	Action steps	Resources	Dates

Managing your budget, cont'd.

Read your organization's budget reports.

Be prepared to give budget projections whenever they are needed.

Explain any variance from your budget.

Be accountable for the accuracy of your forecasts.

Monitor service recoveries (charge-backs) so you know where you stand.

Accurately predict spending trends throughout the year.

Involve your assistant in tracking your budget.

Investigate the costs of projects in order to sell them to senior management.

Worksheet 1. HRD Department Planning Tool, Cont'd.

Criteria for effectiveness	Action steps	Resources	Dates

Managing your budget, cont'd.

Be prepared to reprioritize HRD activities to focus on business priorities in case of budget cutbacks.

Seek advice from an advisory group regarding what to continue to do and stop doing in case of cutbacks.

Pursuing professional development

Understand your organization's products, marketing strategy, financial performance, and other business issues.

Develop computer skills that take advantage of available technology.

Seek feedback from others to improve your effectiveness.

Obtain a broad range of HRD skills and knowledge.

Look for ways to recharge your energy and confidence.

Project a can-do attitude.

Worksheet 1. HRD Department Planning Tool, Cont'd.

Criteria for effectiveness	Action steps	Resources	Dates

Pursuing professional development, cont'd.

Be flexible in working with others.

Subscribe to and read HRD publications.

Network with other people in the HRD profession.

Attend at least one external conference or workshop a year.

Explore ways to increase your creativity.

Justify a need for more staff in terms of expanded service.

Develop your staff through training, teamwork, coaching, and projects.

Preparing to address future challenges

Involve managers and supervisors in designing and teaching training programs.

Worksheet 1. HRD Department Planning Tool, Cont'd.

Criteria for effectiveness	Action steps	Resources	Dates

Preparing to address future challenges, cont'd.

Provide train-the-trainer sessions to prepare nontrainers to teach training programs.

Collaborate with other departments inside your company and with noncompeting companies to offer HRD programs.

Take advantage of technological advances in providing HRD.

Experiment and learn from your experience.

Stay in touch with important issues facing the entire organization.

Use the HRD planning tool to identify areas needing improvement.

Focus on a few areas for improvement at a time; prioritize and concentrate on high-payoff actions.

Source: Managing a Small HRD Department, by Carol P. McCoy. San Francisco: Jossey-Bass. Copyright © 1993. Permission to reproduce and distribute (with copyright notice visible) is hereby granted. If material is to be used in a compilation to be sold for profit, please contact publisher for permission.

Worksheet 2. Preparing a Needs Assessment Report.

Business background and business need

Describe the business situation (problem or opportunity) that led you to investigate HRD needs.

Needs assessment approach

- Describe the methods used and rationale for using them.

- Identify who participated in data gathering.

- Identify sources of data and information.

Source: Managing a Small HRD Department, by Carol P. McCoy. San Francisco: Jossey-Bass. Copyright © 1993. Permission to reproduce and distribute (with copyright notice visible) is hereby granted. If material is to be used in a compilation to be sold for profit, please contact publisher for permission.

Worksheet 2. Preparing a Needs Assessment Report, Cont'd.

Summary of major findings for key target groups

- List major conclusions for each group.

- List knowledge/skills needed for current jobs.

- List knowledge/skills needed for future jobs.

- Provide numbers showing extent of gaps in skill and knowledge.

- Provide quotations from managers and employees describing evidence of gaps in skill and knowledge.

Worksheet 2. Preparing a Needs Assessment Report, Cont'd.

Recommendations based on costs/benefits

Describe what you propose to do on the basis of your findings.

1.

2.

3.

4.

Cost/benefit comparison

Justify the cost-effectiveness of your recommendations. (Compare cost/benefit of solving problem by HRD or some other solution versus not solving problem.)

Cost of HRD solution   *Cost of other solution*   *Cost of not solving*

Next steps in implementation

List next steps and tentative due dates in carrying out your recommendations.

1.

2.

3.

4.

Worksheet 3. Creating a Mission Statement.

Purpose (Describe the primary purpose of your department and how it supports the organization's business.)

Target audience (Identify the populations you serve.)

Programs and services (Describe the types of programs and services you offer or plan to offer.)

Strategies (Describe the ways in which you will work with the organization to accomplish your mission. For example, will you provide programs directly or train others to teach programs?)

243

Worksheet 4. Selecting a First Program.

List your two best bets for a first program under Program A and Program B. Use the criteria on the left to help you evaluate each program. Rate each criterion as follows: 4 = excellent, 3 = very good, 2 = satisfactory, 1 = unsatisfactory. You may add other criteria or weight some criteria more heavily than others. Record your rating and any comments in the spaces next to each criterion.

Criteria for selection	*Program A*	*Program B*
Supports critical area of the business Business unit or function addressed is vital to accomplishing business objectives.		
Management sponsorship Senior management clearly supports this program.		
Receptivity of target audience Target audience really wants this program and is unlikely to resist it.		
Real need Program meets a real need, not just a perceived need. HRD is an appropriate solution to the need.		
Value added Program demonstrates how HRD adds value to the business.		
Doable You can meet the deadline with an acceptable level of quality.		
Resources The organization will make appropriate resources available to you.		
Visibility Program allows you some visibility to help build credibility and make contacts.		

Worksheet 5. Selecting a Consultant.

Rate each consultant: 4 = excellent, 3 = good, 2 = average, 1 = poor.

Criteria	Consultant A	Consultant B

Content of written proposal
  Course content (complete / appropriate)
  Design / methods (appropriate, creative)
  Professionalism of written proposal		

Resources (development team)
  Background / related experience
  Industry-relevant expertise
  Flexibility / interpersonal skills
  Ease of access to your organization		

Material production capability
  Capable of producing professional materials
  Capable of producing quality AV materials
  Able to meet production deadlines
  Able to provide timely revisions / updates		

Instructional capabilities
  Experience / credibility of instructors
  Fit with your organization
  Availability of instructors
  Able / willing to train the trainer		

Organization
  Reputation
  Financial strength / solvency
  Potential to meet other needs of your organization
  References		

Cost of deliverables (indicate amounts)
  Program development
  Pilot program
  Instructor training
  Ongoing instruction
  Materials (licensing fees, and so on)		

Presentation of proposal
  Quality of presentation
  Understanding of your organization's needs
  Responsiveness to questions		

Overall strengths: _____

Overall weaknesses: _____

Worksheet 6. Computing Training Program Costs.

Item	Formula	Total

Staff costs
Salaries: Consulting
       Designing
       Conducting
       Evaluating
	Number of people times median salary times number of hours on the project	

Fees: outside designers and consultants	Total fees and expenses paid out	
Travel: tickets other expenses	Total from expense reports Total from expense reports, *or* per diem times number of days	
Overhead	Use standard organization figures; if none exist, use 100 percent of base salary	
Materials Film	Actual costs if purchased; $1,650 to $3,000 per minute to produce; $45 to $120 per 10 minutes for prints	
Videotape	Prorated overhead from own studio, or rental rate plus operator salary, or staff salary median times number of hours	
Videodiscs	From $35,000 to $100,000 per hour	
Audiotapes	$50 to $200 per minute to produce, $2.50 per print to duplicate, $5 to $10 for commercial products	
35-mm slides	$15 to $50 per slide to produce, 45¢ per print to duplicate	
Overhead transparencies	$30 to $100 to produce (includes artwork), 45¢ to $15 per print	
Artwork	Minimum of $1.50 per square inch to create	
Manuals and materials	Local figures; outside or in-house printshop quotations	
Announcements	Local figures needed here	
Special equipment	Total purchase price, normally amortized over 10 years	

Total cost to produce program _____

Source: Laird, 1985, pp. 233–234. © 1985 by Addison-Wesley Publishing Company, Inc. Reprinted with permission of the publisher.

Worksheet 7. Projecting a Training Budget.

Category	Monthly budget	Annual budget
Salaries and benefits of HRD staff (HRD manager and administrative assistant)		
Data processing equipment (computer, printer, software)		
Supplies (office supplies; training materials such as binders, tabs, books, tapes, memento gifts)		
Shipping, messenger, and telephone		
Consultants and professional fees (design and instructor expenses)		
Training facilities (conference rooms, meals, equipment rental)		
Travel and entertainment (airfare, ground transportation, lodging for training manager and staff)		
Training/professional development (attendance expenses of training manager and staff at conferences, workshops; professional society memberships)		
Overhead (corporate charges for space, furniture, and so on)		
Total gross expenses		
Service recoveries (charge-backs to participants for programs)	( )	( )
Net expenses		

Source: Managing a Small HRD Department, by Carol P. McCoy. San Francisco: Jossey-Bass. Copyright © 1993. Permission to reproduce and distribute (with copyright notice visible) is hereby granted. If material is to be used in a compilation to be sold for profit, please contact publisher for permission.

Worksheet 8. Estimating Service Recoveries.

Program	Program fee	Projected number of participants	Number of programs	Total number of participants per program	Total recovery per program

Worksheet 9. Budget Tracking Report.

Budget category	Month			Quarter			Year to date			Year 19___		
	Plan	Act.	Var.	Plan	Act.	Var.	Plan	Act.	Var.	Plan	Fore.	Var.
Salaries and benefits												
Consultants												
Training facilities												
Travel and entertainment												
Training												
Computer												
Materials and supplies												
Other operating expenses												
Total expenses												
(Recoveries)												
Net expenses												

Note: If a monthly forecast is required, you can substitute forecast (Fore.) for actual (Act.) when you submit your forecast. At the end of the month, you may want to look at variance (Var.) from your budget plan, from your monthly forecast, or from both.

Worksheet 10. Service-Recovery Tracking Report.

Program	Cost per participant	Planned number of participants	Actual number of participants	Planned recoveries	Actual recoveries	Variance
Total						

Worksheet 11. Project Planning for Program Development.

Phase	Tasks	Resource requirements	Start-to-finish time estimate
Program design: conduct needs assessment	Review available information on organization Select needs assessment approach Write interview guide Determine list of people to interview Schedule interviews Conduct interviews Write summary needs report		3 weeks
Program design: prepare design specifications	Write program background and target population description Write program goals and objectives Write program design requirements/constraints Review design specifications with task force Modify design specifications on basis of task force's input		1–2 weeks
Program design: prepare design document (leader's guide)	Review design specifications Revise learning objectives Determine program length Determine units and unit objectives Determine learning activities Write block diagram Write overview of program activities Determine prework activity Prepare materials list Prepare design document Review design document Modify design document		3–4 months
Development of materials: create participant materials	Finalize materials list (include participant manual and any other materials used) Order films, games, articles Hire writer to assist Determine format for materials Type draft of participant materials Revise materials with task force's input Edit revised materials Reproduce materials		3 months (overlaps with leader's guide development)

Worksheet 11. Project Planning for Program Development, Cont'd.

Phase	Tasks	Resource requirements	Start-to-finish time estimate
Development of materials: design participant binders	Estimate binder requirements Order binders from purchasing Meet with printer to design, order cover and tabs Review mechanicals for binder cover and tabs Stock binders Insert covers and tabs in binders Collate materials and insert into binders		1 month (overlaps with other tasks)
Instructor selection and preparation	Identify internal experts and/or consultants to teach Use criteria to select consultants Create and sign a contract if using consultants Put together instructor briefing package (leader's guide and participant materials) Meet with instructors to review program requirements Create flip charts, overhead transparencies, or other instructor aids		1 week
Program delivery: pilot program	Schedule pilot program Identify participants to evaluate pilot program Confirm attendees Conduct pilot		(Schedule pilot at least two months prior to actual program.)
Program evaluation	Create evaluation form Attend pilot program and make observations and adjustments Keep running-time log of unit's timing and effectiveness Immediately following program, conduct debriefing session and solicit pilot participants' input for needed changes Collect and tally evaluation forms from participants Write evaluation report		1 week

Phase	Tasks	Resource requirements	Start-to-finish time estimate
Program revision	Review evaluation report and your notes Determine most critical changes that are feasible Revise program materials and leader's guide Offer revised program Evaluate revised program and make refinements as needed		(Plan for two weeks to one month to make changes.)

Worksheet 12. Program Logistics Tracking Sheet.

Logistical tasks	Responsibility	Starting date	End date	Task complete
1. Schedule program				
2. Announce program				
3. Secure booking of training facility				
4. Arrange for equipment				
5. Plan for meals				
6. Collect registration forms				
7. Notify registrants of application status				
8. Create tentative participant list				
9. Create program materials list				
10. Design and order binders and tabs				
11. Create information package for participants				
12. Send confirmation material to participants				
13. Reproduce training materials				
14. Arrange for transport of materials to training center				
15. Finalize participant list				
16. Prepare site for training				
17. Conduct program				
18. Clean training room and return unused materials				
19. Tabulate evaluations				
20. Take care of finances				
21. Send thank-you letters to guest speakers / sponsors				
22. Create and maintain program records				
23. Revise administrative checklist to adjust for timing				

Worksheet 13. Program Evaluation Form.

Program name: _____

Thank you for completing this evaluation. It will help us improve future programs.

Date: _____   Name: (optional) _____

Business division: _____   Years with company _____

Reason for attending: _____

Please circle the number that best represents your evaluation of each of the following program criteria:
5 = excellent   4 = very good   3 = good   2 = needs improvement   1 = poor.

1. Overall quality of the program	5	4	3	2	1
2. Relevance to my job	5	4	3	2	1
3. Personal value to me	5	4	3	2	1
4. Program objectives were met	5	4	3	2	1
5. Training activities	5	4	3	2	1
6. Knowledge of speakers	5	4	3	2	1
7. Quality of written materials	5	4	3	2	1
8. Appropriateness of topics	5	4	3	2	1
9. Logical flow of topics	5	4	3	2	1
10. Preprogram information	5	4	3	2	1
11. Length of program (circle one)	Just right		Too long		Too short

12. Would you recommend this program to other employees?
    Yes _____   No _____   Maybe _____ (please explain)

13. Who is the most appropriate audience for this program? Why?

14. How has this program been helpful to you?

Worksheet 13. Program Evaluation Form, Cont'd.

15. What was of most value to you? Why?

16. What topics would you add or expand upon? Why?

17. What topics would you cut back on or eliminate? Why?

18. What will you do differently on the job as a result of this program?

19. Please list any other suggestions you have on how to improve the program.

Worksheet 14. Evaluation Report on Pilot Program.

To: Management   cc: Relevant managers

Re: Program: _____

Introduction (Provide a brief introductory statement regarding reasons for offering the program. Refer to an attached evaluation summary for details of program content and participant evaluations.)

Target audience (Briefly identify the target audience for the program.)

Participation (Briefly describe how many and what types of people attended the pilot program and the revised program.)

Program quality improvement (Describe the suggestions made during the pilot. Explain the types of improvements you have made and their impact. Identify improvements in perceived overall program quality, degree to which program objectives were met, training activities, appropriateness of topics as well as topic flow, and the like.)

Initial impact (Give examples of how the program has had an impact on the way people perform their jobs.

Next steps (Explain intended future use of the program—how many sessions you plan to offer to which groups of people.)

Source: Managing a Small HRD Department, by Carol P. McCoy. San Francisco: Jossey-Bass. Copyright © 1993. Permission to reproduce and distribute (with copyright notice visible) is hereby granted. If material is to be used in a compilation to be sold for profit, please contact publisher for permission.

Worksheet 15. Program Evaluation Summary.

Program: _____ Date: _____

1. How has the program been helpful to participants? (Provide relevant quotes.)

2. What was of most value to participants?

3. What suggestions did participants have for improvement? (Include topics to add or delete; changes in timing, methodology, and so on.)

Category	Excellent 5	Very good 4	Good 3	Needs improvement 2	Poor 1	Pilot average	First session average
Program quality							
Relevance to participants' job							
Personal value to participant							
Program objectives met							
Speaker knowledge							
Training activities							
Written materials							
Appropriate topics							
Topic flow							
Preprogram information							
Length of program		(Just right)		(Too long)		(Too short)	
Recommend to others?		(Yes)		(Maybe)		(No)	

▲ ▲

References

Abella, K. T. *Building Successful Training Programs: A Step-by-Step Guide.* Reading, Mass.: Addison-Wesley, 1986.

Albrecht, K., and Zemke, R. *Service America: Doing Business in the New Economy.* New York: Warner Books, 1985.

Allen, E. L. (ed.). *ASTD Trainer's Toolkit: Needs Assessment Instruments.* Alexandria, Va.: American Society for Training and Development, 1990.

American Society for Training and Development. *Consortium Study of Corporate Training.* Alexandria, Va.: American Society for Training and Development, 1986.

American Society for Training and Development. *1992 ASTD Buyer's Guide and Consultant Directory.* Alexandria, Va.: American Society for Training and Development, 1992.

Bard, R., Bell, C. R., Stephens, L., and Webster, L. (eds.). *The Trainer's Professional Development Handbook.* San Francisco: Jossey-Bass, 1987.

Bard, R., and Loftin, B. P. "Building a Learning Network." In R. Bard, C. R. Bell, L. Stephens, and L. Webster (eds.), *The Trainer's Professional Development Handbook.* San Francisco: Jossey-Bass, 1987.

Behring, R. "A Caravan of One: Looking Beyond the Desert." *Training and Development Journal,* 1987, *41*(3), 64–70.

Bell, C. R. "HRD: Past, Present, and Future." In R. Bard, C. R. Bell, L. Stephens, and L. Webster (eds.), *The Trainer's Professional Development Handbook.* San Francisco: Jossey-Bass, 1987.

Block, P. *Flawless Consulting: A Guide to Getting Your Expertise Used*. San Diego, Calif.: Learning Concepts, 1981.

Bricker's International Directory, Vol. 1: Long-Term University-Based Executive Programs 1992. (23rd ed.) Princeton, N.J.: Petersons Guides, 1991a.

Bricker's International Directory, Vol. 2: Short-Term University-Based Executive Programs 1992. (4th ed.) Princeton, N.J.: Petersons Guides, 1991b.

Budd, M. L. "Self-Instruction." In R. L. Craig (ed.), *Training and Development Handbook: A Guide to Human Resource Development*. (3rd ed.) New York: McGraw Hill, 1987.

Cohen, S. L. "The Challenges of Training in the Nineties." *Training and Development*, 1991, *45*(7), 30–35.

Craig, R. L. (ed.). *Training and Development Handbook: A Guide to Human Resource Development*. (3rd ed.) New York: McGraw-Hill, 1987.

Fritz, R. *The Path of Least Resistance: Learning to Become the Creative Force in Your Own Life*. New York: Fawcett Columbine, 1989.

Geber, B. "Building a Training Department from Scratch." *Training: The Magazine of Human Resources Development*, 1988, *25*(9), 28–39.

Gilley, J. W., and Eggland, S. "Hook, Line, and Sinker." *Training and Development Journal*, 1987, *41*(9), 22–28.

Gordon, J., Zemke, R., and Jones, P. (eds.). *Designing and Delivering Cost-Effective Training and Measuring the Results*. (2nd ed.) Minneapolis, Minn.: Lakewood Books, 1988.

Graham, J. K., jr, and Mihal, W. "Can Your Management Development Needs Surveys Be Trusted?" In E. L. Allen (ed.), *ASTD Trainer's Toolkit: Needs Assessment Instruments*. Alexandria, Va.: American Society for Training and Development, 1990.

Harless, J. "Performance Technology and Other Popular Myths." *Performance and Instruction Journal*, July 1985, pp. 4–6.

Hart, F. A. "Computer-Based Training." In R. L. Craig (ed.), *Training and Development Handbook: A Guide to Human Resource Development*. (3rd ed.) New York: McGraw-Hill, 1987.

Heinich, R., and Molenda, M. *Instructional Media and the New Technologies of Instruction*. (2nd ed.) New York: Macmillan, 1985.

Johnson, R. B., and O'Mara, J. "Shedding New Light on Diversity Training." *Training and Development*, 1992, *46*(5), 44–52.

Kaman, V. S. "Why Assessment Interviews Are Worth It." In E. L. Allen (ed.), *ASTD Trainer's Toolkit: Needs Assessment Instruments.* Alexandria, Va.: American Society for Training and Development, 1990.

Kearsley, G. *Computer-Based Training: A Guide to Selection and Implementation.* Reading, Mass.: Addison-Wesley, 1983.

Kearsley, G. *Training and Technology: A Handbook for HRD Professionals.* Reading, Mass.: Addison-Wesley, 1984.

Kirkpatrick, D. L. "Evaluation." In R. L. Craig (ed.), *Training and Development Handbook: A Guide to Human Resource Development.* (3rd ed.) New York: McGraw-Hill, 1987.

Laird, D. *Approaches to Training and Development.* (2nd ed.) Reading, Mass.: Addison-Wesley, 1985.

Lakein, A. *How to Get Control of Your Time and Your Life.* New York: David McKay, 1973.

Lee, C. "Who Gets Trained in What: 1991." *Training: The Human Side of Business*, 1991, *28*(10), 47–59.

Lloyd, T. "Winning the Budget Battle." *Training: The Magazine of Human Resource Development*, 1989, *26*(5), 57–62.

London, M. *Managing the Training Enterprise: High-Quality, Cost-Effective Employee Training in Organizations.* San Francisco: Jossey-Bass, 1989.

McCampbell, J. F. "How to Produce Great Job Aids." *ASTD Infoline: Practical Guidelines for Training and Development Professionals*, issue 904. Alexandria, Va.: American Society for Training and Development, Apr. 1989.

McDermott, B. "Collaboration on the Demands of Adult Education." In B. McDermott (ed.), *Managing the Training Function*, Book I: *Trends, Politics and Planning Issues.* Minneapolis, Minn.: Lakewood Books, 1990.

Mager, R. F. *Preparing Instructional Objectives.* Belmont, Calif.: Lear Siegler/Fearon, 1962.

Margolis, F. H., and Bell, C. R. *Instructing for Results.* San Diego, Calif.: University Associates; Minneapolis, Minn.: Lakewood Books, 1986.

Michalak, D. F., and Yager, E. G. *Making the Training Process Work.* New York: Harper & Row, 1979.

Nadler, L., and Nadler, Z. *Developing Human Resources.* (3rd ed.) San Francisco: Jossey-Bass, 1989.

Nasman, P. C. "Job Aids: Improving Performance Without Formal Training." In J. Gordon, R. Zemke, and P. Jones (eds.), *Designing and*

Delivering Cost-Effective Training and Measuring the Results. (2nd ed.) Minneapolis, Minn.: Lakewood Books, 1988.

Nathan A., and Stanleigh, M. "Is Your Department Credible?" *Training and Development*, 1991, *45*(1), 41–45.

Newstrom, J. W., and Lilyquist, J. M. "Selecting Needs Analysis Methods." In E. L. Allen (ed.), *ASTD Trainer's Toolkit: Needs Assessment Instruments*. Alexandria, Va.: American Society for Training and Development, 1990.

Olivetti, L. J. (ed.). *ASTD Trainer's Toolkit: Mission Statements for HRD*. Alexandria, Va.: American Society for Training and Development, 1990.

Petersons Guides. *Bricker's International Directory. Volume One: Long-Term University-Based Executive Programs 1992*. Princeton, N.J.: Petersons Guides, 1991.

Pfeiffer, J. W. (ed.). *The Human Resource Development Annual Set*. San Diego, Calif.: Pfeiffer, 1987–1992.

Pfeiffer, J. W., and Goodstein, L. (eds.). *The Human Resource Development Annual Set*. San Diego, Calif.: Pfeiffer, 1982–1986.

Pfeiffer, J. W., and Jones, J. E. (eds.). *The Human Resource Development Annual Set*. San Diego, Calif.: Pfeiffer, 1972–1981.

Piturro, M. C. "Decentralization: Rebuilding the Corporation." *Management Review*, Aug. 1988, pp. 31–34.

Robinson, A. D. "Tapping Your Inner Resources and Learning from Yourself." In R. Bard, C. R. Bell, L. Stephens, and L. Webster (eds.), *The Trainer's Professional Development Handbook*. San Francisco: Jossey-Bass, 1987.

Robinson, D. C., and Robinson, J. C. *Training for Impact: How to Link Training to Business Needs and Measure the Results*. San Francisco: Jossey-Bass, 1989.

Rosenberg, M. J., and Smitley, W. "Constructing Tests That Work." In B. McDermott (ed.), *Managing the Training Function*, Book II: *The Nuts and Bolts of Personal, People, and Resource Management*. Minneapolis, Minn.: Lakewood Books, 1990.

Schrello, D. M. *Marketing In-House Training Programs*. Long Beach, Calif.: Schrello Direct Marketing, 1984.

Senge, P. M. *The Fifth Discipline: The Art and Practice of the Learning Organization*. New York: Doubleday, 1990.

Sheridan, D. "Off the Road Again: Training Through Teleconferencing." *Training: The Human Side of Business*, 1992, *29*(2), 63–66.

Siemasko, D. "CBT Fantasies: The Ground Beckons." In J. Gordon, R. Zemke, and P. Jones (eds.), *Designing and Delivering Cost-Effective Training and Measuring the Results*. (2nd ed.) Minneapolis, Minn.: Lakewood Books, 1988.

Silberman, M. *Active Training: A Handbook of Techniques, Designs, Case Examples, and Tips*. San Diego, Calif.: Pfeiffer, 1990.

Smith, B., Delahaye, B., and Gates, P. "Some Observations on TNA." In E. L. Allen (ed.), *ASTD Trainer's Toolkit: Needs Assessment Instruments*. Alexandria, Va.: American Society for Training and Development, 1990.

Smith, J. "How to Design Interactive Training Programs." In J. Gordon, R. Zemke, and P. Jones (eds.), *Designing and Delivering Cost-Effective Training and Measuring the Results*. (2nd ed.) Minneapolis, Minn.: Lakewood Books, 1988.

Steadham, S. V. "Learning to Select a Needs Assessment Strategy." *Training and Development Journal*, 1980, *34*, 56–61.

Thompson, C. *ASTD Infoline: Project Management: A Guide*, issue 004. Alexandria, Va.: American Society for Training and Development. Apr. 1990.

Wallington, C. "Audiovisual Methods." In R. L. Craig (ed.), *Training and Development Handbook: A Guide to Human Resource Development*. (3rd ed.) New York: McGraw-Hill, 1987.

Warshauer, S. *Inside Training and Development: Creating Effective Programs*. San Diego, Calif.: University Associates, 1988.

Zemke, R., and Kramlinger, T. *Figuring Things Out: A Trainer's Guide to Needs and Task Analysis*. Reading, Mass.: Addison-Wesley, 1989.

Index

W

Wallington, C., 70
Warshauer, S., 18, 31, 32, 112, 156, 178, 202
Webster, L., 201
Willis Corroon. *See* Corroon and Black
Workshops: as delivery option, 64, 66, 80; for managerial skills, 200

Y

Yager, E. G., 178

Z

Zemke, R., 29, 32, 64, 111, 146